A Theological Assessment of Reconciliation for Missiology in the Korean Context

Evangelical Missiological Society Monograph Series

Anthony Casey, Allen Yeh, Mark Kreitzer, and Edward L. Smither
SERIES EDITORS

———————————

A Project of the Evangelical Missiological Society
www.emsweb.org

A Theological Assessment of Reconciliation for Missiology in the Korean Context

Hyo Seok Lim

☛PICKWICK *Publications* · Eugene, Oregon

A THEOLOGICAL ASSESSMENT OF RECONCILIATION FOR MISSIOLOGY IN THE KOREAN CONTEXT

Evangelical Missiological Society Monograph Series 8

Copyright © 2021 Hyo Seok Lim. All rights reserved. Except for brief quotations in critical publications or reviews, no part of this book may be reproduced in any manner without prior written permission from the publisher. Write: Permissions, Wipf and Stock Publishers, 199 W. 8th Ave., Suite 3, Eugene, OR 97401.

Pickwick Publications
An Imprint of Wipf and Stock Publishers
199 W. 8th Ave., Suite 3
Eugene, OR 97401

www.wipfandstock.com

PAPERBACK ISBN: 978-1-7252-8919-2
HARDCOVER ISBN: 978-1-7252-8920-8
EBOOK ISBN: 978-1-7252-8921-5

Cataloguing-in-Publication data:

Names: Lim, Hyo Seok, author.

Title: A theological assessment of reconciliation for missiology in the Korean context / by Hyo Seok Lim.

Description: Eugene, OR: Pickwick Publications, 2021 | Evangelical Missiological Society Monograph Series 8 | Includes bibliographical references.

Identifiers: ISBN 978-1-7252-8919-2 (paperback) | ISBN 978-1-7252-8920-8 (hardcover) | ISBN 978-1-7252-8921-5 (ebook)

Subjects: LCSH: Missions—Korea | Christianity—Korea | Church and social problems—Korea | Mission of the church—Korea | Reconciliation—Religious aspects—Christianity

Classification: BV2470.K6 L56 2021 (print) | BV2470.K6 (ebook)

Scripture quotations are from The ESV® Bible (The Holy Bible, English Standard Version®), copyright © 2001 by Crossway, a publishing ministry of Good News Publishers. Used by permission. All rights reserved.

To my parents in grateful appreciation for their
love, prayer, and faithfulness

Soli Deo Gloria

Contents

List of Illustrations | ix
Acknowledgments | xi
Abbreviations | xiii

1. **Introduction** | 1
    Research Problem   1
    Purpose of the Study   6
    Research Questions   6
    Definitions of Terms   6
    Methodology   8
    Structure   10
    Significance   11
    Delimitations   12

2. **Framing the Discussion** | 13
    The Emergence of Reconciliation as a Paradigm in Mission Studies   13
    Biblical References to Reconciliation   15
    Theological Discussions on God as the Foundation of Reconciliation   17
    The Dimensions of Reconciliation   18
    A Disagreement on the Issue of the Vertical Dimension of Reconciliation between the Conciliar and Evangelical Groups in Reflection on The Underlying Differences in Missiology   23

3. "Fellow-Humanity": Karl Barth's Contribution to Mission as Reconciliation | 43
   Karl Barth   43
   Understanding God as a Relational God   44
   Fellow-Humanity: Relational Anthropology of Barth   50
   Restoration of Fellow-Humanity by Being Reconciled with God   70
   The Witness of Reconciliation by The Church   85
   Evaluative Summary   88

4. Reconciliation in the Theologies of Miroslav Volf, Son Yang-Won, and Desmond Tutu | 95
   Miroslav Volf   95
   Son Yang-won   132
   Desmond Tutu   153

5. An Evaluation of Robert Schreiter's Theology of Mission as Reconciliation and the Presentation of a Proposal | 181
   A Theological Evaluation of Robert Schreiter's Theology of Reconciliation   181
   A Proposal   197

6. The Divided Contexts of the Korean Peninsula | 215
   A Brief History of National Division in Korea from Liberation to the Korean War   215
   The South–South Conflict: Division in Views toward the North in the South   219
   The Issue of North Korean Refugees in South Korea Today   229
   South Korea Churches' Ministry for North Korean Refugees   231

7. Summary and Conclusion: Reconciliation for Missiology in the Korean Context | 233
   The Issue of Justice and Liberation in the Korean Context   233
   The Ministry of Reconciliation by the South Korean Churches   240
   The Need for Renewed Spirituality in Korean Christianity   247
   Concluding Thoughts   249
   Suggestions for Future Research   250

Bibliography | 251

List of Illustrations

1. The Types of South-South Conflicts (by Son, Ho-Chul) | 221
2. The Categories of Missional Activities to North Korea (by Yoon, Eun-Ju) | 228

Acknowledgments

When I was doing my dissertation research and writing, I read, "make your dissertation an act of worship," from a few former TEDS graduates' reflections of their dissertation journey. I would say my own experience in the dissertation process has been a prayer to God. Throughout my research and writing in the year of 2019, I have prayed that God would shape His church with Christ-like reconciling character; equip the whole church with the spirit of reconciliation; give spiritual renewal to the Korean churches; and have mercy on the Korean peninsula. I have also prayed that God would give me wisdom and strength so that I can finish this task. Despite my own weaknesses, God has been bountifully merciful to me, allowing me to focus on research and writing this dissertation. Throughout the journey, I have learned to trust and obey God as one step further. Thanks be to God.

I am deeply grateful to my dissertation mentor, Dr. Tite Tiénou, who has continuously offered essential lessons and insights in classes as well as in private talks which have profoundly transformed my theological and missiological perspectives. He has always understood my crude research concerns and interests, and guided me to sharpen my conceptualizations in a more refined way.

I also especially thank to my dissertation committee members: Dr. Chung, Sung-Wook, who has graciously become my second reader and shared his invaluable insights, and Dr. Craig Ott, who strengthened me with unforgettable encouraging words at the beginning of my doctoral study, and continuously helped me to navigate this journey successfully.

I am very thankful to TEDS faculty members who have improved my academic qualifications as well as spiritual formation: Dr. Harold Netland, Dr. James Plueddeman, Dr. Alice Ott, Dr. Kevin Vanhoozer, Dr. David Gustafson, Dr. Peter Cha, Dr. Steve Kang (former), Dr. Robert Priest (former), and Dr. Joy Tong (former).

I am also indebted to a number of my TEDS colleagues, with whom I was honored to learn together in classes, and by whose opinions my own thoughts have been sharpened, and especially to Samuel Kang, who has been a friend and brother in Christ, continuously encouraging each other throughout the process.

I am deeply grateful for my parents, and my brother's family as well as my in-laws, who all together have prayed and supported me and my family during this doctoral study.

Special thanks to my wife Eunji Kwon and my son Joshua Juwon Lim, who have patiently endured with me in this strenuous journey and graciously encouraged me with prayer and love at every moment.

Abbreviations

AG	*Ad Gentes*
CD	Church Dogmatics
CWME	Commission on World Mission and Evangelism
DPRK	Democratic People's Republic of Korea (North Korea)
EN	*Evangelii Nuntiandi*
GS	*Gaudium et Spes*
LM	Lausanne Movement
LOP	Lausanne Occasional Paper
MMR	Mission as Ministry of Reconciliation
NCCK	National Council of Churches in Korea
RM	*Redemptoris Missio*
ROK	Republic of Korea (South Korea)
TRC	Truth and Reconciliation Commission
WCC	World Council of Churches

1

Introduction

Research Problem

TODAY, PEOPLE LIVE IN troubled times of widespread conflicts. Christians are called to be agents of reconciliation in the midst of conflicts.[1] In spite of this, however, the idea of mission as reconciliation, though not new, has not received a full treatment.

In mission studies, the emergence of discourse on mission as reconciliation has occurred since the second half of the twentieth century. The theme of reconciliation has garnered remarkable attention in missiological circles due to the urgent needs surfacing from the continuous conflicts and enmity around the world today. The significance and appropriateness of reconciliation in current mission settings have created an understanding of reconciliation as a paradigm of mission.[2]

In the discourse of mission as reconciliation, several theological loci of discussions exist. One concerns the theological foundation of reconciliation. It denotes that the whole idea of mission as reconciliation is based on reconciliation with God—the vertical dimension of reconciliation. Based on this, discussions on the dimensions of reconciliation appear. There are three dimensions of reconciliation being discussed in academic conversations: vertical, horizontal, and cosmic[3] dimensions. Considering the relentless conflicts found within today's world, the main focal point of the discussion highlights the horizontal dimension of reconciliation in the Christian understanding of reconciliation.

---

1. In reference to Matt 5:9 and 2 Cor 5:17–20. Although the latter passage primarily indicates reconciliation with God, this study holds the perspective that in Christian understandings of reconciliation, horizontality is inseparably embedded in the vertical reconciliation with God. The former passage confirms this perspective in a way.

2. Schreiter, "Reconciliation and Healing," 74–83.

3. Although it is necessary for the church to give attention to the growing significance of the cosmic dimension of reconciliation due to the serious and rapid environmental deterioration of the earth, the focus of the study here will remain in the first two dimensions, particularly the relationship between the two dimensions.

In mission studies, there is a consensus that vertical and horizontal dimensions of reconciliation should not to be separated. Many would agree with these statements. It is, however, still necessary to examine deeper theological understandings. For instance, what does the statement that they should not to be separated actually mean—in theory and practice? How does the vertical dimension of reconciliation become the source and foundation of the horizontal dimension? What are the similarities and differences between the nature of the two dimensions? To what extent should the horizontal dimension follow the foundational principles of the vertical dimension to be called a *Christian* understanding of reconciliation? These are the questions of how the vertical and horizontal dimensions are related to each other.

Furthermore, discussions thus far have not sufficiently answered the questions arising from the broken realities of the world in current and historical times. Why and how are these vertical and horizontal dimensions so far from each other in the real world, to the point that they sometimes do not appear related in the church's understanding and practice? Several studies have approached these questions from different perspectives, yet a clearer picture of the Christian understanding of reconciliation is still required.[4] Today, the realities faced by the church necessitate more robust and wholesome theological and missiological reflections on reconciliation.

These questions from our realities lead our attention to some further theological concerns for the church. How should the church maintain its theology of reconciliation, which includes both dimensions? What kinds of theological, social, or historical understanding within the church have promoted or hindered the separation of these dimensions? These questions, which are strongly related to the church's theology, also remain not fully answered. Therefore, in this study, a key theological question related to the aforementioned questions is examined—how the relationship between the vertical and horizontal dimensions of reconciliation is to be theologically understood in Christian mission.

A difference seems to exist among scholars in comprehending and systematizing mission as reconciliation involving the vertical and horizontal dimensions, which generally speaking is between conciliar and evangelical scholars. They agree with each other on many major statements of the discourse; however, differences in theological emphases, usage of terms, and

---

4. To name several studies: *Divided by Faith* by Michael Emerson and Christian Smith; *Reconciliation of Peoples* edited by Gregory Baum and Harold Wells; *Embodying Forgiveness* by L. Gregory Jones; *Reconciliation: Restoring Justice* by John W. De Gruchy; Resources for Reconciliation Series by IVP; and *Oxford Handbook of Religion Conflict and Peacebuilding* edited by Atalia Omer et al.

missiological motivations and rationales in discussing mission as reconciliation can be identified between the two missiological families.

The issue of the debate centers around the extent of attention given to each of the two dimensions. In other words, this means how the two dimensions of reconciliation should be understood (including the relationship between them) and practiced in the church's ministry. No one seems to oppose the vertical dimension being foundational for the remaining dimensions of reconciliation, and the dimensions are inseparably related. Some, however, have expressed concern that the current discussions on reconciliation unduly lean toward the horizontal dimension of reconciliation, overlooking the significance of the vertical dimension.[5]

In documents addressing the issue of reconciliation by the World Council of Churches (WCC) and the Lausanne Movement (LM), theological differences can be observed, which are in some extent parallel to the disagreements among these groups. As an example, although the documents of both groups mention the theological importance of the vertical dimension, Athens 2005 by the Commission of World Mission and Evangelism (CWME), and a WCC document, Mission as Ministry of Reconciliation (MMR), tend not to evidently link reconciliation to verbal proclamation,[6] whereas the LM's documents—the Lausanne Occasional Paper No. 51 (LOP No. 51) and the Cape Town Commitment—explicitly state the needs of evangelism in connection to the ministry of reconciliation.

A few exceptions exist. For example, Jacques Matthey says, "We need to recapture the link between reconciliation and evangelism . . . The search for an ecumenically responsible evangelism was not at the centre of the preparatory process nor of the Athens conference, and this lack of emphasis has been rightly criticized, in particular from European mission circles and by Pentecostals and evangelicals."[7] Also, reflecting these criticisms probably, in the most recent article on reconciliation, Robert Schreiter acknowledges the importance of evangelism and proclamation as the "co-existed" missional theme with reconciliation.[8] However, this acknowledgment still needs to be examined. Further discussion is given in chapter 5. Besides, theological differences still can be observed between conciliar and evangelical groups, even with this reflection from the conciliar group.

---

5. Ott et al., *Encountering Theology of Mission*, 96–97, Engelsviken, "Come Holy Spirit, Heal and Reconcile," 191; Engelsviken, "Reconciliation with God," 86–88.

6. Matthey, *Come Holy Spirit, Heal and Reconcile*, 334.

7. Matthey, *Come Holy Spirit, Heal and Reconcile*, 334.

8. Schreiter, "Emergence of Reconciliation," 21.

Furthermore, the visible differences between conciliar and evangelical scholars reflect their underlying theological differences in understanding mission. For example, many reports on the Athens 2005 of CWME have observed that pneumatological emphasis was featured throughout the conference.[9]

The emphasis on the Spirit has reshaped the conciliar theology of mission, which seems to go beyond the Christ-centered understanding of reconciliation in the perception of evangelicals. Even though evangelicals have welcomed a trinitarian understanding of mission, they have warned of the inseparable connection between the Spirit and the Son, maintaining the centrality of the Cross in their theology. Some may consider this a merely theological difference; however, considering that reconciliation and harmony within the church are significant for its ministry of reconciliation in society, and that developing a more wholesome theology of reconciliation is a timely job, the theological difference must be examined.

Therefore, to develop a more wholesome and robust theology of mission for reconciliation, it is necessary to critically assess the discourse of mission as reconciliation by focusing on the theological understanding of the two dimensions. Robert Schreiter has been a pioneer and leader of academic conversation of mission as reconciliation. In assessing the recent discourse of mission as reconciliation, Schreiter's theology is evaluated in the present research.

It is true that the significance of mission as reconciliation has been continuously highlighted in many mission contexts since "the turn of the twenty-first century."[10] Moreover, it is true that "the theology of mission naturally leads into a discussion of the ethics of reconciliation."[11] However, the discussion of mission as reconciliation has not been an exclusive discourse among mission theologians. This is because the conversation relates to the fundamental doctrine of Christianity—love God and love your neighbors—and Christian theology has a rich heritage that values careful interaction.

Thus, the conversation on mission as reconciliation would be enriched by welcoming and interacting more with theologians from other fields. A vast variety of literature by theologians with various focuses exists and must be explored to further discuss and develop a more wholesome

---

9. Vassiliadis, "Reconciliation as a Pneumatological," 32; Thomas, "Athens 2005," 452; Pachuau, "Athens 2005," 417–18; "Report of the Inter-Orthodox," 193; and Kinnamon, "Report," 390. The theme of the conference was "Come Holy Spirit, Heal and Reconcile."

10. Schreiter, "Emergence of Reconciliation," 10–12.

11. Gunton, *Theology of Reconciliation*, 7.

theology of mission as reconciliation. All areas of theology are not mutually exclusive to each other, but there are multiple ways of doing theology.[12] Every field of theology is expected and welcomed to contribute to how the church develops its theology, involving two of its key themes together—mission and reconciliation.

Regarding the missiological implications of this study, the discussion of mission as reconciliation is highly related to the current situation on the Korean peninsula. The divided contexts of the Korean peninsula include not only the national division between North and South Korea, but also South–South conflicts caused by the issue of North Korea. This situation within the Korean peninsula has not only drawn the attention of Koreans and neighboring states, but has also come to the forefront of international news.

The South Korean church, as a private organization, actively participates in various human rights and unification activities regarding North Korea, while North Korean refugees also resettle in South Korean society. However, the South Korean church now faces the necessity of reexamining its missiology regarding North Korea, particularly from the perspective of reconciliation. With grave conflicts occurring within the church, North Korean refugees have found certain difficulties in settling within the South Korean church.

According to the Ministry of Unification of the Republic of Korea, 33,247 North Korean refugees had entered South Korea by December 2019.[13] Unfortunately, many studies on North Korean refugees have identified multiple difficulties in settling down in their new home. These refugees' experiences in South Korean churches are not much different; for example, based on his research findings from interviewing twenty North Korean refugees, Song Young-Sub asserted that they experience social barriers in South Korean churches, and thus feel distant and detached from South Korean Christians.[14]

South Korean theologians have discussed the issues of reconciliation and unification in the Korean context, while some of them have even engaged the emerging discussions of mission as reconciliation. However, Korean missiology for reconciliation is still far from sufficiently established. Therefore, this dissertation contributes to the theological conversation on mission as reconciliation, as well as South Korean Christians' missiology to North Korea.

12. Tiénou and Hiebert, "Missional Theology," 221.

13. http://www.unikorea.go.kr/unikorea/business/NKDefectorsPolicy/status/lately/.

14. Song, "Socio-Cultural Factors," 163–64.

Purpose of the Study

The purpose of this study is to contribute to a theological assessment of reconciliation in mission studies by focusing on the issue, the relationship between the vertical and horizontal dimensions of reconciliation, in order to contribute to missiology in the Korean context.

Research Questions

This study conducts research to answer the following questions:

RQ 1. What is the relationship between the vertical and horizontal dimensions of reconciliation?

Sub RQ 1.1. How would interacting with the theologies of Karl Barth, Miroslav Volf, Son Yang-Won, and Desmond Tutu contribute to the understanding of the relationship between the vertical and horizontal dimensions of reconciliation?

Sub RQ 1.2. How can Robert Schreiter's writings on mission as reconciliation, in particular regarding the two dimensions, be assessed based on the answers to Sub RQ1.1?

Sub RQ 1.3. What would be a more wholesome and robust theological understanding of the relationship between the two dimensions in discussing mission as reconciliation?

RQ 2. What are the missiological implications of such theology of reconciliation for the church in the Korean context?

Definition of Terms

Evangelical

The term "evangelicalism" proves difficult to define because of its fluidity in crossing denominations as well as the historical and societal connotations that it contains. Because defining the term is not a simple task, it may be acceptable to discuss some characteristics of the term *evangelical* here. This study uses a commonly acknowledged explanation of the term by David Bebbington, which describes evangelicalism's four characteristics, namely conversionism, activism, biblicism, and crucicentrism.[15] Historically and

---

15. Bebbington, *Evangelicalism in Modern Britain*, 2–17.

theologically in mission studies, the evangelicals (represented as the LM in this study) have a counterpart—the conciliar (or ecumenical)—who are often represented as the WCC. These groups, however, are not mutually exclusive nor limited to these two representations.

Conciliar

Conciliar Christians implies a group of Christians who pursue the unity of diverse local churches in their missionary tasks, sacraments, and confession of their faith.[16] This conciliar fellowship is sought through the ecumenical movement in which they promote the connections and fellowships among the representatives and denominations of local churches, and also with Roman Catholics and Eastern Orthodox. As mentioned, the WCC has been a salient representation of today's conciliar Christians.

Reconciliation

This research explores a theological definition of reconciliation. In the words of Kim Seyoon, "the Greek words of reconciliation '*katallassein*' and '*diallassein*' have fundamental meanings of 'exchange'"; they denote "a change from a relationship of conflict and enmity to one of peace and friendship."[17] This study follows Kim's definition of reconciliation. It means the restoration of peaceful and friendly relations. For connotation of the term, it needs to be noted that justice is a core aspect of genuine form of reconciliation. This study rejects a form of reconciliation without justice, so-called "hasty reconciliation,"[18] or "cheap reconciliation."[19]

North Korean Refugees

(Bukhanitaljumin, Talbukja, or *Saeteomin* in Korean)

This "legal term officially employed by the South Korean government [refers] to a person who has escaped from North Korea and is living in any region other than in North Korea."[20] Although the term "North Korean

16. Keshishean, *Conciliar Fellowship*, 54–56, 65–71, 104–5.
17. Kim, "Reconciliation," 219.
18. Schreiter, *Reconciliation*, 19.
19. Kairos Theologians (Group), *Kairos Document*, sec. 3.1; Volf, "Forgiveness, Reconciliation, and Justice," 867.
20. Chung and Seo, "Study on Posttraumatic Stress Disorder," 367.

defectors" has also been widely used, it is repudiated by some because it leads people to hold a negative impression of the people. Some prefer other terms such as North Korean "migrants" or "resettlers." In this dissertation, North Korean refugees, a more prevalent term in academic discussions than migrants or resettlers, and which holds a weak negative frame (or at least less than defector), is used; however, a few cases of direct quotes that contain the word defector remain unchanged.

Methodology

This dissertation uses a literature-based research method. By nature, this dissertation is a theological study with missiological intent. Literature by Karl Barth, Miroslav Volf, Son Yang-Won,[21] and Desmond Tutu, as well as their theologies are reviewed to investigate the relationship between the vertical and horizontal dimensions of reconciliation. Carefully listening to all of their voices is highly worthwhile for understanding reconciliation theologically.

Regarding the reasons for these selections, no one has written on and impacted the theological discussion of reconciliation more than Karl Barth, and reconciliation is one of the central themes in his theological thought. The entire volume IV of his *Church Dogmatics* (*CD*) is titled The Doctrine of Reconciliation. Miroslav Volf, largely owing to his book *Exclusion and Embrace*, has become a significant voice in the discussion of reconciliation today. Son Yang-Won's life and practice of reconciliation remain the symbol of reconciliation in Korean Christianity. The voices and works of reconciliation by Desmond Tutu have been recognized in the church as well as throughout the world. This study expects these four people, who come from different times, places, and backgrounds, to underscore different aspects of reconciliation, yet also hold a certain degree of consistency in Christian theology. Furthermore, their voices are expected to contribute to the focus of this research because they are a fair representation of the existing variety in the world of Christianity. This is particularly the case as Protestant responses to the theology of Robert Schreiter, a Roman Catholic theologian, despite observable similarities among Schreiter, Barth, and Volf in terms

---

21. Korean names are written with the surnames first. All historians and scholars (including Americans) that this study refers to have Korean surnames listed first to avoid possible confusion in reading their names. To be consistent, the names of Korean theologians and scholars are written in the same order. However, if their names contain English names, they are not written following the order.

of trinitarian theology. Engaging the Orthodox theologies is limited in this study, but suggested for future research.

To explain further, in chapter 3, in the theological examination of Karl Barth's theology of reconciliation focused on the concept of fellow-humanity, his monumental writing on reconciliation, *The Church Dogmatics*, volumes III (the parts of creation and humanity) and IV (the entire volume) are primarily reviewed. Barth's other works such as *The Humanity of God*, *Ethics*, *Christian Life*, and *The Theology of John Calvin* are also explored. Moreover, some selected secondary sources on Barth's theology are explored when deemed necessary; for example, literature by John Webster, Paul Molnar, Kenneth Oaks, Eberhard Busch, John Flett, Matt Jenson, Kelly Kapic, Kevin Vanhoozer, Ronald Feenstra, Henri Blocher, and Daniel Price.

In chapter 4, in the theological discussions of the theologies of reconciliation by Volf, Son, and Tutu, Miroslav Volf's books *Exclusion and Embrace*, *After Our Likeness*, *End of Memory*, *Against the Tide*, and *Free of Charge* are first examined. In addition, Volf has consistently published academic journal articles on the topics of embrace and reconciliation, which are also reviewed.

Subsequently, for the research on Son Yang-Won's theology of reconciliation, his sermons, personal diaries, and letters that have been preserved until today and contain much of his theology are investigated. In this study, 221 sermons transcripts and abridgments, forty personal letters, and 1129 personal diaries are reviewed. Almost all of these historical resources were recently collected and published through the historiographic efforts of Korean historians and historical theologians. These historical and theological writings along with scholarly journals on Son's life and theology are explored.

Next, literature by Desmond Tutu himself as well as academic literature on Tutu's ministry and theology are engaged. These include *Hope and Suffering*, *Crying in the Wilderness*, *The Rainbow People of God*, *No Future without Forgiveness*, *God has a Dream*, *God is not a Christian*, *In God's Hands*, several (authorized) bibliographies on Tutu, and analytical books on Tutu's theology by such authors as Michael Battle, Johnny Bernard Hill, and Hendrik Pieterse.

In chapter 5, Robert Schreiter's writings, such as *Reconciliation*, *The Ministry of Reconciliation*, and *Mission as Ministry of Reconciliation* (which he edited with Knud Jørgensen), as well as book sections and journal articles on reconciliation are evaluated in light of the insights provided by the four thinkers and practitioners of reconciliation.

On the basis of these discussions, the researcher proposes a more wholesome and robust theology for the discourse of mission as reconciliation in mission studies, particularly in regard to the relationship between the vertical and horizontal dimensions of reconciliation.

In chapter 6, the divided context of the Korean peninsula is illustrated. The researcher examines both historical and sociopolitical writings for analyzing the national and social-ideological division of Korea (both North–South and South–South). The historical works are written by such scholars as Bruce Cummings, Yi Ki-Baek, Lew Young-Ik, Carter Eckert, Michael Robbinson, Edward Wagner, Kang Man-Gil, Seo Joong-Seok, and Kim Sung-Bo.

Furthermore, the sociopolitical works are written by scholars such as Baek Han-Soo, Choi Wan-Gyu, Chung Soondool (with Seo Ju-Yun), Han Kwansoo, Jang Yoonsoo, Kang In-Chul, Kang Won-Taek, Kim, Gab-Sik, Kim Hyun-Sik, Kwon Sook-do, Andrei Lankov, Lee Woo-Young, Park Isuk, Son Ho-Chul, Yoon Hyun-Gi, and Yoon In-Jin.

Additionally, theological writings are explored that describe South–South divisions within the South Korean church, the South Korean church's mission to North Korea, and the ministry for North Korean refugees. These are by scholars such as Chung Won-bum, Han Jeong-Woo, Jeon Woo-Taek (with Cho Young-A), Kim Eui-Hyuck, Kim In-Soo, Sebastian Kim, Kirsteen Kim, Chris Rice, Sarah Son, Yang Chang-Seok, Yi Man-Yeol, and Yoon Eunju.

In chapter 7, based on the previous theological examinations, a proposal as well as descriptions of the Korean context and several missiological implications are suggested for the church in the Korean context. In analyzing and proposing the missiological implications for the Korean context, the researcher engages with the literature written by Korean (or Korean diaspora) theologians, such as Ahn Kyo-Seong, Cho Yo-Sep, Kim Seyoon, Sebastian Kim, Morse Tan, Song Young-Sub, Ha Chung Yuebe (Youb), Hwang Hong-Eyoul, Ko Jye-Gil, and Chung Sung-Wook.[22] Then, conclusive words and suggestions for the future research will be presented.

Structure

After the chapter of introduction, this study frames the research focus of the study, indicating that in the discourse of mission as reconciliation, a disagreement exists concerning how the vertical and horizontal dimensions of reconciliation are related between the conciliar and evangelical theologians.

---

22. Unless otherwise noted, all translations of Korean into English are done by the researcher.

In engaging the four theologians, considering the significance and volume of Karl Barth's writing on reconciliation, the entire chapter 3 examines his literature on reconciliation in order to discuss the details. The examination focuses on "fellow-humanity," which is one of the most relevant concepts by Barth to the research focus in this study.

The following chapter explores the theologies of Miroslav Volf, Son Yang-Won, and Desmond Tutu in order to offer some theological resources in assessing Robert Schreiter's theology of reconciliation, regarding the relationship between the vertical and horizontal dimensions of reconciliation.

An evaluation of Schreiter's theology is placed in chapter 5 because this study assesses his reflections on reconciliation based on the previous conversations with the four theologians. A proposal is then presented based on the evaluation.

The proposal is relevant to the missiology in the Korean context. After discussing the divided context in the Korean peninsula, the last chapter suggests some missiological implications for the South Korean churches in light of the proposal presented.

Significance

This study seeks to contribute in three main areas. First, it aims to contribute to the ongoing discussion of mission as reconciliation in mission studies. This research engages the theologies of Barth, Volf, Son, and Tutu, four thinkers and practitioners of reconciliation who will enrich the discussion of relationships between the vertical and horizontal dimensions of reconciliation. Even though most of these four people are well-known and their works have been widely read, they have not interacted with the discourse of mission as reconciliation sufficiently enough to discuss the specific issue—the relationship between vertical and horizontal dimensions of reconciliation in mission studies. Therefore, this study attempts to initiate such interactions and perform analysis based on the dialogues.

The second contribution is that, based on the theological examinations of the abovementioned four people, this study assesses the theology of reconciliation of Schreiter, whose voice has been influential in the current discussion, focusing on his view of the dimensions of reconciliation in particular. Furthermore, the second contribution includes the proposal of a more wholesome and robust theology for mission as reconciliation. Some may simply acknowledge the apparent disagreements among scholars as a mere variety of views, but they still continuously require critical evaluations and suggestions to develop the academic discourse itself.

Regarding this point, not much literature in mission studies has tackled the relationship between the two dimensions; therefore, deeper analysis and critical assessment are required. Considering that the church's missionary activities of reconciliation are based on its theological reflections,[23] it may contribute to both the theological understanding of reconciliation and the practical ministry of reconciliation.

The third contribution is a discussion of implications for the missiology of reconciliation in the Korean context. This will contribute to South Korean churches' missiology to North Korea. In the approaching era of national uncertainty, missiology of reconciliation embedded in the Korean context is urgently required in regard to the struggles of North Korean refugees in South Korea and mission for North Korean people.

Delimitations

As mentioned above, interacting with all fields of theology is worthwhile for the discussion of mission as reconciliation; however, engaging every field of theology here is impossible. This study only interacts with the few selected theologians in addition to mission theologians.

Furthermore, in discussing the relationship among the dimensions of reconciliation, the third dimension—reconciliation with creation—is not a focus. This third dimension has increasingly merited attention in mission studies. It is true that the violence and hostility of humans does not limit itself to other humans—it often victimizes the entire creation. It is encouraging that creation care has often emerged as a crucial theological topic on many occasions, including in missiological circles, yet the focus of this dissertation shall remain on examining the relationship between the vertical and horizontal dimensions of reconciliation.

Lastly, in examining the divided contexts within the Korean peninsula, the scope of study largely remains in South Korea, with the inclusion of the national division between North and South Korea. Different types of divisions exist, even in the totalitarian state of North Korea, which are related to social classes and views toward the South; however, they are largely inaccessible because of the highly restricted nature of the nation. Moreover, despite the "official" existence of North Korean Christianity and the presence of "underground" churches, the discussion on the Korean missiology of reconciliation shall mainly focus on South Korean Christianity, except for brief mentions of North Korean Christianity when deemed necessary.

---

23. Bosch, *Witness to the World*, 24.

2

Framing the Discussion

The Emergence of Reconciliation as a Paradigm in Mission Studies

THIS CHAPTER REVIEWS THE scholarly discussion of mission as reconciliation in mission studies. It investigates the following topics: the emergence of reconciliation as a paradigm, the biblical and theological foundations of reconciliation, the dimensions of reconciliation, and the missiological differences in the vertical dimension between conciliar and evangelical scholars represented by the WCC and LM.

Wilbert Shenk indicates that the "theological theme of reconciliation has never played a central role in missionary motivation and the theological rationale for missionary witness."[1] It has been regarded as more of "personal" faith and ethics before God.[2] Similarly, Referring to David Bosch, Robert Schreiter implies that reconciliation was hardly considered a separate paradigm in mission studies in the past.[3] It is true that it was not included for the past missiological paradigms nor the future prospective ones in David Bosch's book, *Transforming Mission*, although he includes several closely relevant themes to reconciliation, such as the quest for justice and liberation.[4] However, since "the turn of the twenty-first century," the topic of reconciliation has increasingly become visible in mission studies.[5]

Tormod Engelsviken notes that the "[Mission as Ministry of Reconciliation] MMR and several other authors claim that reconciliation is an 'emerging paradigm' of mission since the late 1980s and early 1990s."[6] Robert Schreiter and Knud Jørgensen, in a book they edited in 2013,

---

1. Shenk, "Christian Mission," 303.
2. Shenk, "Christian Mission," 303.
3. Schreiter, "Reconciliation and Healing," 75–76.
4. Bosch, *Transforming Mission*, 400, 432.
5. Schreiter, "Emergence of Reconciliation," 10–12.
6. Engelsviken, "Reconciliation with God," 80.

asserted that, "Reconciliation has over the last 7–10 years emerged as a paradigm of mission."[7] Ross Langmead also states that the topic of reconciliation is "increasingly being understood as an 'integrating metaphor'" in theology of mission.[8]

Reconciliation has been discussed as a theme in the following conferences: the British and Irish Association of Mission Studies (2002), the Lutheran World Federation (2004), A Forum for World Evangelization in Pattaya by the LM (2004), the Commission on World Mission and Evangelism by the WCC (2005), and the International Association for Mission Studies (2008), as well as in the Third Lausanne Congress on World Evangelization (2010).[9]

When one considers the conflicts worldwide world, it is not surprising that reconciliation has acquired more attention as a paradigm in mission studies. Several examples can be named: ethnic cleansing in the Balkans, the Rwandan genocide, the legalized apartheid of South Africa, South and North Koreans, Palestinians and Israelis, and all other forms of divisions within society, such as racism and ethnocentrism in the United States, sectarianism in Northern Ireland, the "untouchable" Dalit caste in India, and aboriginal people in Australia.[10]

Two factors can be identified in explaining how reconciliation has emerged as a paradigm. One factor is theological alteration in the theology of mission. As Schreiter explains, there have been profound discussions on "the very nature of mission itself," often led by the Global South after World War II, which have renewed the understanding of "missionary praxis," emphasizing the aspects of social responsibility and "mutuality" in mission.[11]

Another factor is contextual demand arising from the mission contexts. Reconciliation has emerged as a response to ceaseless strife around the world. Schreiter remarks that the collapse of communism in the late twentieth century has resulted in "the demise of a bipolar world," and consequently, civil wars have occurred in numerous places.[12] The conflicts "within countries rather than between countries" have dramatically increased, and

---

7. Schreiter and Jørgensen, "Editorial Introduction," 3.

8. Langmead, "Transformed Relationships," 5–6

9. Schreiter, "Reconciliation and Healing," 75–76; Schreiter, "Emergence of Reconciliation," 12; Engelsviken, "Reconciliation with God," 80; LOP No. 51; Skreslet, *Comprehending Mission*, 72.

10. LOP No. 51 ch. 1; Schreiter "Emergence of Reconciliation," 10–11; Ott et al., *Encountering Theology of Mission*, 95.

11. Schreiter, "Emergence of Reconciliation," 10.

12. Schreiter, "Emergence of Reconciliation," 10.

thus churches have faced them more closely, often from their neighbors.[13] This does not imply that conflicts across countries have ended. For example, from the US location, the 9/11 terror incident in New York City became a watershed in discussing the subsequent violent international terrorism. In the midst of conflicts, church leaders have often felt "unprepared" and helpless, or have even reflected that they have participated—knowingly or unknowingly—in a series of violent and hateful conflicts.[14]

Acknowledging the realities of the world, Shenk proposes that, "Theology of mission thus needs to be recast so as to embrace the human situation comprehensively."[15] For similar reasons, Steve Bevans and Roger Schroeder suggest considering reconciliation as a new model of mission, stating that, "the possibility of reconciliation is one of, if not the most compelling way of expressing the meaning of the gospel today. In the midst of unspeakable violence, unbearable pain and indelible scars on people's memory, the church as God's minister of reconciliation proclaims that in Christ and in his community, healing is possible."[16] Thus, it is necessary to give more attention to reconciliation as a "paradigm" that shapes and defines what Christian mission.[17] The theme of reconciliation has indeed multiple biblical references.

Biblical References to Reconciliation

Reconciliation can be considered as an overarching theme throughout the Old and New Testaments. The reconciliation between Jacob and Esau, as well as between Joseph and his brothers, are good examples in the Old Testament.[18] In addition, referring to Isa 9:6 and Mic 5:5, J. C. Hoekendijk stated, "the Messiah is the prince of shalom" in the Old Testament.[19] Langmead notes, how the Hebrew notion of *shalom* in the Old Testament is pertinent to reconciliation, and can be considered "the goal of reconciliation."[20]

---

13. Schreiter, "Emergence of Reconciliation," 10–11.
14. Schreiter, "Emergence of Reconciliation," 11.
15. Shenk, "Christian Mission," 303.
16. Bevans and Schroeder, *Constants in Context*, 390–91.
17. Schreiter and Jørgensen, "Editorial Introduction," 3.
18. Schreiter, "Emergence of Reconciliation," 12.
19. Hoekendijk, "Call to Evangelism," 168.
20. Langmead, "Transformed Relationships," 8. He further indicates that some differences exist between reconciliation and *shalom*, such as how reconciliation "more often refers to a process," whereas "*shalom* is a state (albeit a dynamic one)." Langmead, "Transformed Relationships," 8.

In addition, a document of the LM on mission as reconciliation, LOP No. 51, finds the Hebrew word *shalom* to be relevant to the theme of reconciliation. The document states that *shalom* is a comprehensive word that "encompasses all dimensions of human life."[21] LOP No. 51 argues that *shalom*[22] includes the "right relationships of human beings with God, within themselves, with one another and with the created world."[23]

In the New Testament, several narratives indicate the theme of reconciliation. Stanley Skreslet claims that he finds "the theme of reconciliation powerfully portrayed in the story of the prodigal son (Luke 15:11–32)."[24] He also writes that, "An ethic of reconciling love, summed up in the command to love one's enemies (Matt 5:44), may be said to lie at the heart of the Beatitudes."[25] In this respect, Skreslet argues that, "Reconciliation as a master-theme within mission theology can be reinforced and broadened by pairing it with related concerns," such as peacemaking and dialogue.[26]

Schreiter suggests that all the stories of Jesus's resurrection can be understood as narratives of reconciliation.[27] He states, "the stories of the post-resurrection appearances of Jesus can be read as stories of reconciliation" in that they provide healing, forgiveness, and consequently reconciliation between Jesus and his disciples, who struggled with the feelings of guilt and loss.[28]

Agne Nordlander asserts that reconciliation is "an overarching concept used to explain the saving significance of the Cross."[29] Schreiter also writes, "The term reconciliation may not figure prominently as a theme in the scriptures, but as a theme it runs like a red thread through all the sacred texts. For is not the story of salvation the story of God's reconciling the world to God's self?"[30] In short, the whole redemptive story of God in the Bible can be understood under the theme of reconciliation.

Nevertheless, explicit references to the term "reconciliation" are found only in the epistles of the Apostle Paul in the New Testament. The Greek

---

21. LOP No. 51 ch. 1.

22. For the examples of *shalom*, LOP No. 51 suggests: "Leviticus 26:4–6; Psalms 34:14; Isaiah 1:16–17, 32, 11:6–9a, 16–17; Jeremiah 29:10–14; Ezekiel 34:25–31; Amos 5:14–15; Micah 4:2–4." LOP No. 51 ch. 1.

23. LOP No. 51 ch. 1.

24. Skreslet, *Comprehending Mission*, 34.

25. Skreslet, *Comprehending Mission*, 34.

26. Skreslet, *Comprehending Mission*, 34.

27. Schreiter, *Ministry of Reconciliation*, 19–22.

28. Schreiter, *Ministry of Reconciliation*, 21–22.

29. As quoted in Engelsviken, "Reconciliation with God," 83.

30. Schreiter, *Reconciliation*, 12.

term for "to reconcile," *katallassein,* appear thirteen times in Pauline letters.[31] They are written in Romans 5, 2 Corinthians 5, Colossians 1, and Ephesians 2. Specifically, "Greek: *katallage,* reconciliation, four times: Rom 5:11; 11:15; 2 Cor 5:18, 19; *katallasso,* reconcile, six times: Rom 5:10, 2 Cor 5:18–20; *apokatallasso,* reconcile, three times: Eph 2:16; Col 1:20, 22."[32] Each passage indicates a different aspect of reconciliation. For instance, Romans 5 is often viewed as a reference to the vertical dimension of reconciliation; 2 Corinthians 5 to the church's entrusted ministry of reconciliation; Ephesians 2 to the horizontal dimension; and Colossians 1 to the cosmic dimension. Based on the biblical references, theological elaboration on reconciliation becomes possible. The first and foremost theological discussion is God as the foundation of reconciliation.

Theological Discussions on God as the Foundation of Reconciliation

Reconciliation finds its origin in God. It begins with God.[33] In mission studies, a consensus seems to exist among scholars that the foundation of mission as reconciliation is in God. Reconciliation is related to the very nature of God. Simultaneously, reconciliation is what God has done. Rose Dowsett writes, "Truly, reconciliation begins in the heart of God."[34] Schreiter claims that "we do not bring about reconciliation, especially in the profound and complex situations described above; it is God who reconciles."[35] Schreiter further argues, "reconciliation is first and foremost the work of God . . . It is based in the very *missio Dei* of God in the world."[36] Tormod Engelsviken similarly claims that, "It has to be emphasized that reconciliation has its source in God. It is the Triune God who is the initiator and author of reconciliation."[37]

Both the LM and WCC have declared that God is the foundation of reconciliation in their gatherings under the topic of reconciliation. LOP No. 51, which was produced by the Issue Group at the 2004 Pattaya meeting, states that, "Reconciliation is God's initiative."[38] Similarly, the MMR

31. Schreiter, *Reconciliation,* 42.
32. Engelsviken, "Reconciliation with God," 83.
33. Rice, "Cape Town 2010," 58.
34. Dowsett, "Reconciliation as Reconstruction," 111.
35. Schreiter, *Reconciliation,* 26.
36. Schreiter, "Emergence of Reconciliation," 15.
37. Engelsviken, "Reconciliation with God," 83.
38. LOP No. 51 ch. 1.

addresses how "reconciliation is the work of the Triune God bringing fulfillment to God's eternal purposes of creation and salvation."[39]

In that respect, referring to Irenaeus, Engelsviken states, "When the Trinity turns towards the world, the Son and the Holy Spirit become the two arms of God by which humanity was made and taken into God's embrace. It is thus through the work of the incarnate God and by the mediation of the Spirit that reconciliation with God is realized."[40]

Chris Rice distinguishes two aspects of reconciliation: indicative (who God is, and what He has done) and imperative (the human response to God), and underlines that "indicative precedes imperative."[41] For the indicative, he asserts that, "Reconciliation begins with God, with God's love, with God's work, achievement, and ultimate reconciliation. The risen Christ is the centre of this story, and this indicative shapes the kind of 'radical' and 'cross-centred' Christian life and mission called for later."[42] He then states that any imperative of reconciliation becomes possible "only by getting the story and reality of God's reconciling love deep into our bones."[43] In short, God is the foundation of reconciliation.

The Dimensions of Reconciliation

Another significant theological discussion is about the dimensions of reconciliation. Engelsviken introduces the dimensions of reconciliation as follows: "Reconciliation is commonly seen as existing in three major dimensions: the vertical dimension (reconciliation with God), the horizontal dimension (reconciliation between humans), and the circular dimension (reconciliation with the physical and spiritual cosmos or the universe)."[44] Schreiter and Jørgensen also describe reconciliation as needing "to heal three overlapping realms of brokenness: reconciliation between God and human beings; reconciliation of different groups of human beings; and reconciliation of the cosmos."[45]

Although there are differences in the extent of emphasis and ways of describing how the horizontal dimension of reconciliation is sought, none of participants in the dialogue seems to deny that the vertical dimension is

39. Matthey, "*You are the Light*," 96.
40. Engelsviken, "Reconciliation with God," 83.
41. Rice, "Cape Town 2010," 58.
42. Rice, "Cape Town 2010," 58.
43. Rice, "Cape Town 2010," 58.
44. Engelsviken, "Reconciliation with God," 79.
45. Schreiter and Jørgensen, "Editorial Introduction," 4.

the basis for the rest, and that the vertical and horizontal dimensions are inseparable. Their inseparableness is a visible agreement among them in the dialogue of mission as reconciliation.

Acknowledging that "the first fruit of mission is reconciliation with God," Ott, Strauss, and Tennent state that, "On the basis of vertical reconciliation, horizontal reconciliation becomes possible in the most profound way. The vertical and horizontal dimensions of Christ's work of reconciliation are inseparably related."[46]

Schreiter and Jørgensen similarly observe that, "Reconciliation to God cannot be separated from reconciliation to one another. And a radical cross-centred reconciliation cannot be separated from the call to radical obedient discipleship. In a new paradigm of mission these two, reconciliation and discipleship, walk hand in hand."[47]

Likewise, Engelsviken maintains that being forgiven by God—"the vertical reconciliation"—and forgiving others—"the horizontal reconciliation"—have an intrinsic relationship.[48] Engelsviken refers to Ephesians 2, in which Paul says the "dividing wall of hostility" between Jews and Gentiles are destroyed in Christ (Eph 2:14–18); furthermore, he states reconciliation is "achieved both in relation to God and each other."[49] Then, he argues that it is "the common basis of the salvation of both Jews and Gentiles," and it is the grace of God that has enabled the horizontal dimension of reconciliation: they all become a new creation (Eph 2:18; 2 Cor 5:17).[50] He highlights the Lord's prayer (Matt 6:12) and the parable of the unmerciful servant (Matt 18:21–35) to show how intrinsically the vertical and horizontal dimensions of reconciliation are related. Engelsviken claims that, "It should be impossible to be reconciled with God, and at the same time be enemies."[51]

Kyrika Atzvi considers that Christian reconciliation, which is "a gift from God," is a "two-fold process," and "the two aspects of reconciliation are deeply interrelated and cannot stand separately."[52] Referring to Matt 5:24, which says "First be reconciled to your brother or sister, and then come and offer your gift," Atzvi states that the vertical dimension of reconciliation

---

46. Ott et al., *Encountering Theology of Mission*, 96–97.
47. Schreiter and Jørgensen, "Editorial Introduction," 4.
48. Engelsviken, "Reconciliation with God," 88.
49. Engelsviken, "Reconciliation with God," 87.
50. Engelsviken, "Reconciliation with God," 87.
51. Engelsviken, "Reconciliation with God," 87–88.
52. Atzvi, "Ecumenism as Reconciliation," 30.

is foundational to the others, and it "goes through our already reconciled relationships with our brothers and sisters."[53]

Haddon Willmer's argument, which is based on his examination of the Epistle to the Romans, is particularly noteworthy. He asserts that Christians "should refuse to be one-dimensional" because the works of God, which "may be seen by us as distinguishable vertical and horizontal elements," still "*are* in God, simultaneous and in harmony."[54]

Willmer, providing a warning over the "dichotomic" use of "language" between "vertical and horizontal" reconciliation, even suggests that if our language is not sufficient to contain the "all-around comprehensive" work of God, we must find other words to reflect "the wholeness of God's loving action" because our words are "merely analytical or rhetorical tools."[55] According to Willmer, the "dichotomic" language and "superficial" interpretation of Romans have caused the divorce between the two dimensions.[56]

As he divides the entire letter of Romans intro three, 1–8, 9–11, and 12–16, Willmer addresses how reconciliation in all three parts is apparently integrative of all dimensions, and none of these exclusively relates to a single dimension.[57] In his words, "The word Paul shares is God's; God's word is not a word that comes vertically down from heaven, but is spoken in a history, works itself out through being incarnated horizontally, without losing its verticality."[58]

In this sense, Willmer thinks that Paul's understanding of reconciliation has taken "the same principle" of 1 John, which says, "we cannot talk about the love of God if we do not love our neighbour (I John 4.20, 21)."[59] Willmer argues that, "The love of God is not only incomprehensible but also incredible if it is confined to verticality."[60]

However, Willmer recognizes that the church consistently hesitates to participate in social justice and resisting oppressive structures, especially among some evangelicals and Catholics who understand the work of God in Christ as mainly vertical.[61] He asserts that the church must "live and think the vertical in its horizontality and the horizontal in its verticality, in the

---

53. Atzvi, "Ecumenism as Reconciliation," 30.
54. Willmer, "'Vertical' and 'Horizontal,'" 151.
55. Willmer, "'Vertical' and 'Horizontal,'" 151.
56. Willmer, "'Vertical' and 'Horizontal,'" 154–56.
57. Willmer, "'Vertical' and 'Horizontal,'" 152.
58. Willmer, "'Vertical' and 'Horizontal,'" 154.
59. Willmer, "'Vertical' and 'Horizontal,'" 154.
60. Willmer, "'Vertical' and 'Horizontal,'" 154.
61. Willmer, "'Vertical' and 'Horizontal,'" 153, 155, 158.

wholeness of the gospel, where God and humanity are inseparably together in one history."[62] Willmer hopes that this type of integrative theology would dissolve the unhelpful dichotomy and separation of the vertical and horizontal dimensions of reconciliation. Willmer states, "Paul's historical action and hope—the horizontal he was engaged in—are nothing apart from the relation with God, the vertical; but God is one who not only made history in the past but is making it here and now."[63]

Willmer's main argument is that one dimension should not be divorced from the other. The separation between (theological) vertical and (ethical) horizontal aspects of reconciliation is unbiblical and does not accord to the reconciliatory intent of Paul in Romans.[64] Therefore, he proposes that, "in response to the vertical grace of peace with God, the church responds in an ethically guided horizontality."[65] Emphasizing the holistic unity of the two dimensions in God, Willmer concludes the following:

> We do not read Paul to escape into a pious verticality, but we live with the living God in the gift of vertical-horizontality God gives us today—which includes the risk of participating in history, where things often do not turn out as we expect or hope even when we venture in faith.[66]

Similarly, Ross Langmead argues for the inseparable connectedness of the dimensions of reconciliation. Langmead mentions that when we participate in the mission of God, "we find ourselves talking about transformed relationships in several dimensions—between humans and God, between humans and between humans and creation."[67] He states that reconciliation is essentially a restoration of relationships and the restoration of the relationship between humans and God, which "involves a reordering of relationships with others."[68]

Langmead further asserts that, "It is clear that a renewed relationship between humanity and God is determinative in the biblical account, but that many other relationships are integrally bound up in this renewal."[69] Promoting the integrative understanding of reconciliation, Langmead

---

62. Willmer, "'Vertical' and 'Horizontal,'" 158.
63. Willmer, "'Vertical' and 'Horizontal,'" 158.
64. Willmer, "'Vertical' and 'Horizontal,'" 156.
65. Willmer, "'Vertical' and 'Horizontal,'" 157.
66. Willmer, "'Vertical' and 'Horizontal,'" 160.
67. Langmead, "Transformed Relationships," 5–6.
68. Langmead, "Transformed Relationships," 10.
69. Langmead, "Transformed Relationships," 10.

regards reconciliation as a holistic concept that covers "a wide range of ideas," such as "cosmic reconciliation, the Hebrew notion of *shalom*, the meaning of the Cross, the psychological effects of conversion, the work of the Holy Spirit, the overcoming of barriers between Christians, the work of the church in the world, peacemaking, movements towards ethnic reconciliation, and the renewal of ecological balances between humanity and its natural environment."[70]

In this discussion, Langmead pays attention to the notion of *shalom*, noting that it has been used as "a very strong motif in the Bible . . . meaning well-being, harmony or wholeness, typically in a social context."[71] He argues that *shalom* illustrates that "God's mission is centrally one of the reordering and renewing of relationships so that humanity may live fully in relationship to God, each other and creation."[72]

Moreover, in discussing the dimensions of reconciliation, Langmead notably subdivides the three dimensions into the following five, providing a closer look at reconciliation in our living realities: conversion as reconciliation, international peacemaking, reconciliation between indigenous and nonindigenous peoples, reconciliation between Christians and reconciliation with creation.[73]

In addition, Chris Rice endorses the inseparable connectedness of the dimensions of reconciliation, referring to it as "triple reconciliation."[74] He notes that, "the scope of God's reconciliation stretches beyond the dichotomy of personal salvation (evangelicals) or social salvation (ecumenicals [sic])" and it is "to embrace . . . God's 'triple reconciliation'"—namely individuals, society, and creation.[75] Moreover, he asserts that "All three are placed on a level field of interwoven divine redemption."[76]

Exploring the arguments thus far, one may observe the following: the dimensions of reconciliation are inseparably related. One would also realize that based on such inseparable connectedness, Christians' understanding of mission has begun to involve the pursuit of horizontal reconciliation in an attempt to not repeat the previous mistake of focusing solely on vertical reconciliation. However, as the change has been taken place and become more visible, several voices of concern have expressed that the current trend of this

---

70. Langmead, "Transformed Relationships," 6.
71. Langmead, "Transformed Relationships," 8.
72. Langmead, "Transformed Relationships," 10.
73. Langmead, "Transformed Relationships," 10–17.
74. Rice, "Cape Town 2010," 58.
75. Rice, "Cape Town 2010," 58.
76. Rice, "Cape Town 2010," 58.

change has already exhibited a risk of overlooking the significance of vertical reconciliation in its pursuit of horizontal reconciliation. This particular disagreement is focused on in the following section.

Regarding the statements of the two dimensions inseparable connectedness, however, they do not sufficiently answer the questions that arise from our broken realities and history. Why and how are the dimensions far from each other in the real world, as if they are totally unrelated? Furthermore, what kinds of understanding (theological, social, or historical) in the church have promoted or hindered the separation of the dimensions? These questions are highly related to the question of *how*; that is, how horizontal reconciliation can happen based on vertical reconciliation. These remain legitimate questions, and this dissertation provides answers and offer some helpful resources to do so.

A Disagreement on the Issue of the Vertical Dimension of Reconciliation between the Conciliar and Evangelical Groups in Reflection on The Underlying Differences in Missiology

As discussed previously, a disagreement within the discussion of mission as reconciliation concerns the understanding of the vertical dimension of reconciliation, and the extent and how it is emphasized in the church's ministry of the horizontal dimension of reconciliation. Some evangelical voices such as Engelsviken and Ott, Strauss, and Tennent have warned of weakening the significance of the vertical dimension in the church's mission theology, referring to the recent voices of the conciliar theologians.[77]

However, before examining their concerns, for an enhanced understanding, one must recognize how this visible disagreement reflects the underlying debate between the evangelical and conciliar theologians. The underlying debate is about theological features in shaping the understanding of mission, which each group has developed interactively but differently over the years.

Why do their attitudes on the vertical dimension differ? What are the theological and missiological backgrounds and features that have each group's notion of reconciliation? Are there weak emphases on the vertical dimension among ecumenical theologians' discussions as far as evangelicals are concerned?

To answer these questions, a survey is presented in a somewhat diachronic manner, *focusing* on several salient missiological themes and

---

77. Engelsviken, "Reconciliation with God," 191; Ott et al., *Encountering Theology of Mission*, 97.

paradigms that have shaped and laid foundations for each group's understanding of mission as reconciliation today. Along with the relevant literature on theology of mission, the MMR and other reports on Athens 2005 of the WCC, as well as LOP No. 51 and The Cape Town Commitment of the LM, are reviewed with a focus on the two dimensions of reconciliation. This should contribute to explaining the different attitudes toward the vertical dimension of reconciliation exhibited by the conciliar and evangelical scholars in mission studies.

In the case of the WCC, reconciliation was officially chosen as a main theme for the first time in CWME in Athens in 2005. According to the official report of the conference, the theme was "Come Holy Spirit, Heal and Reconcile," and it was "chosen back in August 2001."[78]

As Norman Thomas comments in reference to Jacques Matthey, "this trilogy of Holy Spirit, healing, and reconciliation had never before been at the core of mission conferences."[79] One should recognize how the term "Holy Spirit" was in the theme alongside healing and reconciliation. In recent decades, pneumatology has received attention in discourse on mission within the circle of the WCC. The development of pneumatological emphasis in the WCC's mission theology demonstrates the development of the group's theology of mission in a certain way.

The pneumatological emphasis in the WCC's theology of mission became visible from the late twentieth century onward. Lalsangkima Pachuau asserts, "During the last two decades, the Holy Spirit, as an ecumenical theme, has been surfacing in the WCC."[80] In the seventh assembly of the WCC in Canberra in 1991, the official theme had a pneumatological nuance for the first time: "Come Holy Spirit, renew the whole creation," which is a form of prayer, calling the Holy Spirit as that of Athens 2005 did.[81] However, the assembly in Canberra was not remembered positively by many. It was marred by "tremendous controversy" during and after the assembly caused by a Korean theologian, Chung Hyun Kyung.[82] Michael Kinnamon comments, "The Athens conference affirmed the pneumatological focus of the earlier assembly, but insisted on linking the Spirit with the Son" probably owing to the critical reflections on Canberra controversy.[83]

78. Matthey, *Come Holy Spirit, Heal and Reconcile*, 9.
79. Thomas, "Athens 2005," 451.
80. Pachuau, "Athens 2005," 420.
81. Before Canberra, the term, "Holy Spirit," was never mentioned in a theme of any of previous assembly, but only "Jesus Christ" was mentioned four times out of six times of assemblies.
82. Kinnamon, "Report," 390.
83. Kinnamon, "Report," 390.

After Canberra, Athens 2005 was the second conference of the WCC with a pneumatological emphasis. Many reports on Athens 2005 indicate that pneumatology was featured throughout the meeting.[84]

After Athens 2005, even though not employed in main themes, pneumatology still remains at the core of the WCC's dialogue on mission. For example, a plenary speech by Stephen Bevans in the most recent WCC Assembly in Busan in 2013 demonstrated this is still the case. During his speech, Bevans repeatedly underscored the role of the Holy Spirit in Christian mission as a main frame of understanding mission.[85] One key sentence was as follows: "Mission is finding out where the Spirit is at work and joining in," which he cited from the former Archbishop of Canterbury, Rowan Williams.[86]

Why is this noteworthy? Highlighting the pneumatological dimension reflects several characteristics and exposes some directions featured in the conciliar theology of mission. First, it is related to broader missiological paradigms, such as the trinitarian understanding of mission and *missio Dei*. These terms and their connotations among conciliar scholars have made them revisit and rethink the Christocentric understanding of Christian mission.

For example, in their book *Constants in Context*, Stephen Bevans and Roger Schroeder discuss how the pneumatological emphasis (in trinitarian theology) shapes the Christological view of mission as:

> A *Christology* rooted in a trinitarian understanding of God could certainly avoid the temptation of a focus on Christ that is too narrow, on what some theologians have called a "Christomonism" . . . On the other hand, a *Spirit Christology* would emphasize both the central role of the Spirit in Jesus' mission . . . and the Spirit's presence before Jesus' coming and in places beyond the boundaries of the church (see AG 4, GS 22, RM 29[87]). Jesus is, at it were, the "face" of the Spirit, who is "God inside out" in the world. He is the agent par excellence of the Spirit's work of stirring up prophecy; re-creating; restoring life; and bringing healing, reconciliation and forgiveness. As the "face" of

---

84. Vassiliadis, "Reconciliation as a Pneumatological," 32; Thomas, "Athens 2005," 452; Pachuau, "Athens 2005," 417–18; "Report of the Inter-Orthodox," 193; and Kinnamon, "Report," 390.

85. The researcher of this dissertation himself listened to the plenary speech by Stephen Bevans in 2013.

86. Bevans, "Mission of the Spirit," 30.

87. They are abbreviations of *Ad Gentes*, *Gaudium et Spes*, and *Redemptoris Missio*, respectively, the Roman Catholic documents in the field of theology of mission.

the Spirit, Jesus can be confessed as the unique bearer of God's salvation; at the same time, Jesus does not exhaust God's saving presence and saving activity.[88]

It is not necessarily the case that giving an attention to the Holy Spirit is always associated with pneumatological emphasis as it is in the conciliar theology of mission. The Holy Spirit has continuously received an attention in understanding the church's missionary activities in a different way than that of the conciliar group today. For instance, in his book, *Pentecost and Missions*, Harry Boer, an evangelical theologian, argues as follows:

> If the Holy Spirit given at Pentecost is so centrally the origin and the undergirding, informing and empowering principle of the missionary witness of the Church, it would seem reasonable to expect that He should also have the greatest significance for the *concrete manner* in which the actual missionary work of the Church is performed. It is indeed not possible sincerely to acknowledge the dominant place which the New Testament gives to the Spirit in the missionary proclamation of the early Church without also acknowledging His radical significance for the missionary task of the contemporary Church.[89]

More recently, the WCC recaptured the attention to the Holy Spirit and began to shape their theology of mission based on it. Today, the trinitarian understanding of mission is certainly not exclusively of conciliar Protestant, Roman Catholic, or even Orthodox, which has a legacy of developing trinitarian theology. The recent renaissance of trinitarian theology can be discovered in evangelical or Pentecostal theologians of mission as well.

However, evangelical scholars have not built their theologies upon underlining pneumatology, rather on maintaining a Christocentric view. Furthermore, while placing the significance on the work of the Holy Spirit is in their denominational foundation, many Pentecostal theologians tend not to alleviate the church's concentration on Christ either. As Bevans and Schroeder note, the "evangelical documents" along with "RM [*Redemptoris Missio*]" in Roman Catholic, and that of "Pentecostal," "while often trinitarian and kingdom-oriented, nevertheless maintain a very strong Christocentric focus."[90] That is, how all these groups have developed their theologies of mission accepting the trinitarian view can be distinguished from each other.

---

88. Bevans and Schroeder, *Constants in Context*, 297.
89. Boer, *Pentecost and Missions*, 205.
90. Bevans and Schroeder, *Constants in Context*, 330.

Reflecting these theological differences, Bevans and Schroeder outline three main strains of contemporary mission theology: "1) Mission as Participation in the Mission of the Triune God; 2) Mission as Liberating Service of the Reign of God; and 3) Mission as Proclamation of Jesus Christ as Universal Savior."[91] Again, although the first strain has the word "triune" in its title, this does not denote trinitarian theology belonging to the first group alone—all three strains can be related and enriched by the understanding.

Comparable patterns are observed related to *missio Dei*.[92] Similar to the case of trinitarian theology, Ott, Strauss, and Tennent explain that *missio Dei* has been understood with different missiological emphases and nuances, and furthermore, it has gone in three different directions: (1) the "eschatological, salvation-historical approach," (2) the "fulfillment of kingdom promises," and (3) "personal and social transformation" in participating in the work of "the triune God," rather than "saving souls" in the traditional sense.[93]

Generally, the categories suggested by Bevans and Schroeder as well as by Ott, Strauss, and Tennent overlap. Based on their classifications, three main directions can be said to exist in theology of mission. Each direction reflects a different understanding of the very nature of Christian mission. The disagreement on the vertical dimension of reconciliation reflects, at least partially, these different understandings of mission. Thus, it seems that advocates of each group (although not exclusively to each other) have established at least slightly different definitions of vertical reconciliation (its core and aspects), and of what modes of the church's missionary activities sufficiently reflect the essential elements of mission in the vertical dimension. For many, this may lead to the questions of what salvation is and what the Gospel is.

In reviewing the concepts of salvation, Gospel, and mission, although the diversity in forms and methods of Christianity and its mission that have emerged in various contexts is to be treated with mutual respect and attitude of learning, one still can "recognize an essential continuity in Christianity."[94] Andrew Walls in his book, *The Missionary Movement in Christian History*, identifies that the continuity is in, for example, "the final significance of

---

91. Bevans and Schroeder, *Constants in Context*, 286–346.

92. The concept of *missio Dei* was introduced in the Willingen conference in 1952 despite the absence of mentioning the term explicitly. In Athens 2005, it also underlined *missio ecclesiae* along with *missio Dei* as it is shown in the sub theme, "Called in Christ to be reconciling and healing communities."

93. Ott et al., *Encountering Theology of Mission*, 63–64.

94. Walls, *Missionary Movement*, 7.

Jesus," "of a certain consciousness about history," "of the usage of the Scripture," "of bread and wine," and "of water."[95]

Similarly, in his book, *Comprehending Mission*, Stanley Skreslet writes the following:

> Some notion of salvation lies at the base of every theology of mission. In fact, it could be said that this aspect of theology is more likely to determine the character of one's mission practice than any other doctrinal consideration. Biblical thinking about soteriology presupposes the active participation of God in the salvation process, since it assumes that human beings cannot save themselves. Within the smaller circle of the New Testament canon, a similar consensus has formed around the idea of Jesus Christ as God's indispensable mediator of saving grace. Beyond these two basic convictions, the Christian scripture offer support for multiple understandings of salvation as a theological construct.[96]

In mission studies, regarding the disagreement on the vertical dimension of reconciliation, the voices of concern coming from the evangelical camp mirror the points made by Walls and Skreslet. Such uneasy attention is because of observed attenuation of the Gospel message of Jesus Christ that the church intrinsically delivers to the world. As previously stated, many evangelical scholars have accepted the concepts of *missio Dei* and trinitarian theology, as conciliar scholars have. They define mission as being God's initiative and "rooted in the sending activity of the Triune God—Father, Son, and Holy Spirit."[97] However, they react with apprehension to a gesture that seemingly undermines the message of salvation through Son Jesus Christ, as trinitarian theology, *missio Dei*, or pneumatological emphasis in conciliar theology has reshaped the core ideas of Christian mission.

In the words of Ott, Strauss, and Tennent, "When we survey the book of Acts, it is apparent that nearly every time believers are filled with the Spirit, some form of proclamation occurs."[98] In the same vein, Engelsviken asserts that *missio Dei* in ecumenical terms tends to "separate the work of the Spirit and the Son . . . to give room for an economy of the Spirit outside the church."[99] He continues, "The unity of the Trinity in God's mission has to be maintained. This also means that mission always must have a

---

95. Walls, *Missionary Movement*, 7.
96. Skreslet, *Comprehending Mission*, 70.
97. Ott et al., *Encountering Theology of Mission*, 62.
98. Ott et al., *Encountering Theology of Mission*, 72.
99. Engelsviken, "Mission Dei," 493.

Christological core, and that neither the Father nor the Spirit can be known apart from the Son."[100]

It should be considered here, however, whether the vertical dimension of reconciliation merely implies verbal witness of the Gospel. What is the vertical dimension of reconciliation? Without doubt, it includes declaring the knowledge of Christ as an indispensable beginning stage; however, many evangelicals also think that it does not end there. In the New Testament, several passages urge believers to *grow* in their faith and knowledge of Jesus Christ (or God through Christ; i.e., Eph 4:13; Heb 6:1–2; 2 Pet 3:18; and Col 1:10) as well as in their Christ-like character (i.e., Rom 12:9–21; 13:8–10; Gal 5:13–14; Eph 4:25–32; and Col 3:12–17). This certainly invites the issue of sanctification (with all the other expressions such as spirituality, communion with God, being filled with the Holy Spirit, and discipleship) into the discussion.

When discussing mission as reconciliation, taking this perspective can be helpful for navigating a way to comprehend the relationship between vertical and horizontal reconciliation. This is because much of the fulfillment in horizontal reconciliation depends on the quality of vertical reconciliation, not simply on whether one has heard and accepted the Gospel. In evangelical terms, the Christocentric view of vertical reconciliation connotes all of these aspects. However, again, the entire discussion of quality cannot occur unless one's conversion happens based on the preached Gospel (justification). In this sense, a focal point of the present study is sanctification, not separated from justification in vertical reconciliation.

To resume the first point here, the emergence of pneumatological emphasis in conciliar mission theology is rooted in the trinitarian view of mission. In his report on Athens 2005, Petros Vassiliadis, a Greek Orthodox theologian, indicated that "the pneumatological dimension" is "a new perspective of theology of mission in the third millennium," which has been probably stimulated by "the amazing expansion worldwide of the Pentecostal movement" and "the consolidation of trinitarian theology."[101] Vassiliadis further states,

> The trinitarian revolution in contemporary Christian theology, which was strongly felt across denominational boundaries—from post Vatican II Catholicism to evangelicalism—was a rediscovery of the theology of the Holy Spirit of the undivided Christian church, and in fact a radical overcoming of the old medieval (but also later) Christocentric universalism that in

---

100. Engelsviken, "Mission Dei," 493.
101. Vassiliadis, "Reconciliation as a Pneumatological," 31.

some cases developed in a christomonistic imperialism and oppressive expansionism.[102]

Furthermore, this trinitarian theology is closely related to *missio Dei*. Vassiliadis continually comments that it was based on *missio Dei* that the WCC started the "trinitarian extension" in its third assembly in New Delhi in 1961.[103] This has profoundly reshaped the traditional Christocentric theology of mission in the church for many, particularly for conciliar theologians.

Although assessing this direction theologically is not the research focus nor possible in this dissertation, it may be still done indirectly. The theology of Robert Schreiter, who would be categorized in this group[104] (although with a strong association with the second liberation model) is reviewed later in chapter 5 according to the research focus—the relationship between the vertical and horizontal dimensions of reconciliation.

Second, pneumatological emphasis in theology of mission is also related to the theme of liberation, which highlights "humanization" in the church's missionary activities.[105] The theme of liberation in mission theology is comprehended under the kingdom of God-motif or the reign of God, which requires a total, sometimes subversive, transformation in human society. This point is linked to the second category suggested by Bevans and Schroeder as well as Ott, Strauss, and Tennent. Through the perspective of liberation, salvation and mission have been thoroughly reconsidered. Skreslet explains the emergence of this view as follows:

> Salvation, seen from this perspective [focusing on human ethical response to God's activity], is more about the attainment of well-being in the here-and-now than it is a future state, and human beings are given substantial responsibility for the realization of God's promise. Liberationist proposals developed from the 1960s represent one form of this aspiration, with justice made the standard by which the achievement of salvation could be measured.[106]

David Bosch indicates that the church has been "in need of an interpretation of salvation which operates within a *comprehensive* Christological

---

102. Vassiliadis, "Reconciliation as a Pneumatological," 31.

103. Vassiliadis, "Reconciliation as a Pneumatological," 33.

104. Bevans and Schroeder categorize their colleague Schreiter in the first strain in their book. Bevans and Schroeder, *Constants in Context*, 292–93, 296.

105. Glasser, "Evolution of Evangelical," 11–12; Thomas, "Salvation and Humanization," 27–28, 38; and Beyerhaus, "Mission and Humanization," 19–21.

106. Skreslet, *Comprehending Mission*, 71.

framework" becoming "integral," and "overcoming the inherent dualism in the traditional and more recent models."[107] The liberation model was a "multifaceted phenomenon" and a form of response to the need of the poor and oppressed by churches in various contexts.[108]

According to Bosch, there existed "concern for liberation in missionary circles prior to the 1960s"; however, it was "without challenging societal and political macrostructures."[109] Since the 1950s, starting from Latin America, the church began to realize that "poverty would not be uprooted by pouring technological know-how . . . but by removing the root causes of injustices."[110] In conciliar mission theology, Bosch briefly recalls the diachronic developments when the CWME meeting in Mexico City (1963) "began to notice" this change, "after the Geneva Conference of 1966, the climate changed," and "at Melbourne (1980) the poor were put in the very center of missiological reflection."[111] Furthermore, regarding evangelical mission theology, Bosch states that, "the Lausanne Committee for World Evangelization and the World Evangelical Fellowship (1980)" also started to acknowledge "God's preferential option for the poor" around this moment.[112] For example, in 1985, an evangelical scholar, Arthur Glasser argues for holistic gospel and kingdom of God-motif in evangelical theology of mission.[113] Glasser welcomes Pentecostals' pneumatological perspective since "not only is the role of the Holy Spirit within a trinitarian view of mission clarified, but the essentiality of the kingdom of God to mission theology is wonderfully established."[114]

The key biblical passages that framed Christ mission thinking also reflected this change: from "the Great Commission in Matthew 28:19–20" to "Luke 4:14–19."[115] This change placed "the proclamation of the kingdom or reign of God" at the central thesis of the church.[116] Schreiter explains that, "the proclamation of the reign of God, and the liberation from poverty and oppression, which was another product of Latin American

---

107. Bosch, *Transforming Mission*, 399.
108. Bosch, *Transforming Mission*, 432.
109. Bosch, *Transforming Mission*, 433.
110. Bosch, *Transforming Mission*, 434.
111. Bosch, *Transforming Mission*, 435.
112. Bosch, *Transforming Mission*, 438.
113. Glasser, "Evolution of Evangelical," 11–12.
114. Glasser, "Evolution of Evangelical," 11.
115. Schreiter, "Reconciliation and Healing," 77.
116. Bevans and Schroeder, *Constants in Context*, 305. See their explanations on *Evangelii Nuntiandi* (EN) 8.

thinking that quickly swept throughout the poor of the world, completed this new approach."[117]

Bevans and Schroeder similarly discuss how in the frame of liberation, "salvation is for the whole person."[118] Reflecting the prevalent influence of liberation theology, they comment that the WCC's documents "in the last quarter of the twentieth century" had a "particular focus" "on the church's mission of liberation and its commitment to justice, peace, and the integrity of creation," while maintaining the "trinitarian" theology and "centrality" of Christ.[119]

It seems that the influence of the theme of liberation has remained intact in discussions of mission as reconciliation. This is because reconciliation itself deals with the relationship between victims and perpetrators, although many cases in today's conflicts involve the predicament of ambiguity in specifying who are victims, as noted by Volf.[120]

Liberation is often highlighted in the conciliar discussion of mission as reconciliation. Michael Kinnamon witnessed the Athens 2005 conference as follows: "The plenary speakers and worship leaders in Athens generally affirmed the importance of liberation but coupled it with reconciliation, which implies involvement with perpetrators as well as victims and reconstruction of societies on the other side of the struggle against oppression."[121] Kinnamon observes that, "Much theology of mission, articulated in recent years under the auspices of the WCC, has been liberation-oriented, advocating active engagement in the promotion of justice and solidarity with history's victims."[122]

Furthermore, another report on Athens 2005 by the Greek Orthodox Theological Review views the pneumatological emphasis as being associated with liberation:

> A Spirit-centric theme also provides us with a mission agenda of integral liberation, as the Holy Spirit is portrayed throughout the Bible as the divine force of liberation. This is of crucial import in today's world, which is governed and ruled by several forces of injustice and oppression. The distinct focus on the Holy Spirit

---

117. Schreiter, "Reconciliation and Healing," 77.
118. Bevans and Schroeder, *Constants in Context*, 305.
119. Bevans and Schroeder, *Constants in Context*, 307.
120. Volf, *Exclusion and Embrace*, 103.
121. Kinnamon, "Report," 391.
122. Kinnamon, "Report," 391.

will certainly help us in developing a Trinitarian framework for a mission of identity affirmation.[123]

In this respect, Schreiter's insistence on the liberation of victims and the pursuit of justice in many of his writings on reconciliation can be understood. As it is the case for the first strain of mission theology (trinitarian), Schreiter's theology of reconciliation also seems to be relevant to this trend. He remarks that

> As a result, there came an emphasis on the close relationship between the missionary and those receiving God's word, and how that word liberated them from all kinds of oppression. These twentieth-century impulses toward accompaniment, dialogue, contextualization and liberation are far from spent. They continue to guide and shape missionary activity, and will likely continue to do so for quite some time. The situations that they try to address—mutuality, approaching the other, capacity for local expression, and a variety of forms of oppression—are all still very much with us. Yet alongside all of these have been emerging new voices of reconciliation and healing. How are we to account for this?"[124]

Therefore, the issue of liberation and justice in relation to vertical and horizontal dimensions of reconciliation must be reviewed. Even though Volf slightly engages with this issue, it is mainly attempted in an evaluation of Schreiter's theology of reconciliation in chapter 5.

Lastly, unlike the previous points, pneumatological emphasis in conciliar mission theology does not seem to be fully harmonized with the Christocentric view of mission. Here lies a significant background of the disagreement on the vertical dimension between conciliar and evangelical theologians. Among the three strains of Christian mission that the scholars categorized above, the Christocentric approach, which has traditionally been adopted by the historical church, is now advocated by mostly evangelical and Pentecostal theologians in mission studies.

As Bevans and Schroeder identify when discussing *Redemptoris Missio* (RM), one may recognize a certain degree of tension between previous missiological themes, such as trinitarian or liberation and the finality of Christocentric salvation.[125] However, even though advocates of this position (RM) sometimes "seem to fall into" "exclusivism," as Bevans and Schroeder

---

123. "Report of the Inter-Orthodox," 193.
124. Schreiter, "Reconciliation and Healing," 76.
125. Bevans and Schroeder, *Constants in Context*, 323–24

claim, "this position is not in *opposition* to a fuller trinitarian perspective or a more justice-oriented perspective afforded by focus on the reign of God, but it has been articulated in a way that attempts to avoid the real dangers inherent in both perspectives."[126]

With fellow theologians across the various Christian traditions supporting this position, evangelicals have lifted a representative voice. Bevans and Schroeder[127] explain the view of position in the matter of salvation and mission as follows:

> What is the *salvation*, that is found, in this perspective, only in the name and person of Jesus Christ? While Catholics, Evangelicals, and Pentecostals admit that salvation includes dimensions of economic and social justice and of political, social and individual liberation (the "horizontal dimension), their emphasis is on the reconciliation with God through Christ (the "vertical" dimension). "The content of the message of salvation is Jesus Christ himself, the way to reconciliation with the Father" (EPCW[128] 23). For Evangelicals and Pentecostals, this reconciliation has been achieved through Jesus' "atoning death"; the implication is that the reconciliation is of persons in their individuality. Catholics in RM and Evangelicals and Pentecostals articulate their position very much in contrast to interpretations of salvation that seem to exaggerate the "horizontal" dimension of salvation. RM points out that, while there are understandings of salvation and mission in circulation that are "'anthropocentric' in the reductive sense of the word, inasmuch as they are focused on man's earthly need," such understandings are not consonant with the teaching of the church . . . Salvation "is not of this world . . . is not from the world" (John 18:36) (see RM 17).[129]

In this sense, although theologians of this position welcome trinitarian theology, *missio Dei*, and liberation in their missiological reflections, they are still concerned when pneumatological emphasis seemingly goes beyond the boundary of consistency in Christianity and is not accompanied by a Christocentric view.[130] Engelsviken notes, even though it is often not spelled out, that pneumatological emphasis "relates to the question

---

126. Bevans and Schroeder, *Constants in Context*, 331.

127. Bevans and Schroeder, *Constants in Context*, 344.

128. "Evangelization, Proselytism and Common Witness" (Pentecostal/Roman Catholic Dialogue, 1997).

129. Bevans and Schroeder, *Constants in Context*, 344.

130. Engelsviken, "Mission Dei," 491.

of salvation outside the church through other religions."[131] Pachuau also states that, "The freedom as well as the elusiveness of the Spirit has come to serve as a means of crossing over from Christianity to non-Christian religions and cultures."[132]

Is the attempt to avoid exclusivity of the church's witness through alleviating the significance of Jesus Christ legitimate and possible? The core message of the world of Christianity, which Walls and Skreslet identified previously, can be recalled here. Bevans and Schroeder also remarked that, "any renewal in understanding mission today needs to drink deeply from these more Christocentric sources."[133] Moreover, separating the Son from the Spirit is not faithful to trinitarian theology nor the Bible.[134]

The MMR document seems to be related to this pneumatologically reshaped understanding of mission. In number 8 of the MMR, it states that

> Since Pentecost the Holy Spirit has inspired the church to proclaim Jesus Christ as the Lord and Saviour and we continue to be obedient to the command to preach the gospel in all the world. The Holy Spirit anointed the Son of God to "preach good news to the poor, heal the brokenhearted, proclaim liberty to captives, recovery of sight to the blind and set at liberty those who are oppressed" (Luke 4:18). We seek to continue his liberating and healing mission. This involves bold proclamation of the liberating gospel to people bound by sin, a healing ministry to the sick and suffering, and the struggle for justice on the side of the oppressed and marginalized. Recognizing that the Spirit of God has been present in creation since the beginning and goes before us in our mission and evangelism, we have also affirmed the Spirit's creativity expressed in diverse cultures and we have entered into dialogue with people of other faiths. Now, confronted with the world situation we have described, we are rediscovering the ministry of the Spirit to reconcile and to heal."[135]

In number 19,[136] it also states that

131. Engelsviken, "Mission Dei," 491.
132. Pachuau, "Athens 2005," 420.
133. Bevans and Schroeder, *Constants in Context*, 346–47. Though they follow up, admitting that there is "danger" of this position such as "neglecting" "trinitarian dimension of Christian mission," "'spiritualizing' of conversion," and overlooking the problem of injustice and oppression in our realities. Bevans and Schroeder, *Constants in Context*, 347.
134. Engelsviken, "Mission Dei," 493.
135. Matthey, *Come Holy Spirit, Heal and Reconcile*, 70.
136. No. 19 in the published book is No. 20 in online preparatory paper.

> To share in this ministry of reconciliation—that is to participate in the Holy Spirit's work of reconciliation and communicate God's reconciling activity to all of humanity—is the Christian calling today as much as in Paul's day.[137]

In the discourse of mission as reconciliation, the question needs to be raised of how the current conciliar pneumatological emphasis can fully be in harmony with the Christocentric view of mission. MMR does contain somewhat Christocentric view of the Gospel, and mentions that "God has already achieved reconciliation" with humanity "in Christ" "through the death of Jesus on the cross," and "the church invites all people to be reconciled with God."[138] However, holding pneumatological emphasis and the trinitarian perspective, the MMR concentrates on other subjects than the vertical reconciliation in Christ that enables horizontal reconciliation. Moreover, as Matthey confessed previously, in Athens 2005, the discussions of how to pursue horizontal reconciliation through promoting vertical reconciliation, including verbal proclamation of the Gospel, were not presented.[139]

In this context, after Engelsviken participated in Athens 2005 as an evangelical representative, he expresses "a certain disappointment" toward a plenary speech by Robert Schreiter.[140] He argues that "no significant attention was devoted to 'vertical reconciliation,'" and the "ministry of reconciliation with God was simply assumed."[141] Engelsviken mentions "a group of British missiologists representing the Churches' Commission on Mission" who appealed to the moderator as follows: "The mentions of evangelism in the plenaries seemed primarily cautionary—in the sense that while they (rightly) draw attention to abuses of the Word and the problem of proselytism, no positive picture was offered of the possibilities of healing and reconciling evangelistic practices."[142]

Likewise, being aware of the recent shift in emphasizing horizontality, Ott, Strauss, and Tennent remind us that, "Contemporary discussions of reconciliation that emphasize the horizontal while overlooking the primacy of the vertical focus on the fruit apart from the root."[143] They further assert that, "The ultimate solution to the human conflict will also be found in the solution to the human-divine conflict by reconciliation with God

---

137. Matthey, *Come Holy Spirit, Heal and Reconcile*, 73.
138. Matthey, *Come Holy Spirit, Heal and Reconcile*, 72, 74.
139. Matthey, *Come Holy Spirit, Heal and Reconcile*, 334.
140. Engelsviken, "Come Holy Spirit," 191.
141. Engelsviken, "Come Holy Spirit," 191.
142. Engelsviken, "Come Holy Spirit," 191.
143. Ott et al., *Encountering Theology of Mission*, 97.

FRAMING THE DISCUSSION 37

through Christ."[144] In his most recent book, Craig Ott states, "The deepest reconciliation between hostile parties comes when they have been reconciled with God and become part of the same spiritual family."[145]

In the same vein, Engelsviken comments that the "message of reconciliation" and "its result, the full salvation in the kingdom of the triune God" are "the very content of mission" (Rom 5:10).[146] He continually argues the following:

> A mission that speaks and acts with regard to reconciliation between humans, but fails to proclaim reconciliation with God is a truncated mission that will never accomplish God's ultimate purpose: the salvation of all into his present and coming kingdom.[147]

> Neither should the church in mission omit or neglect the invitation to reconciliation with God and only emphasize the horizontal reconciliation between humans, important as that is.[148]

Nevertheless, as noted in MMR, several WCC documents and speeches of reconciliation still contain a somewhat Christocentric perspective. Engelsviken views that in spite of its pneumatological emphasis, one can still find "the classical Christian view of reconciliation with God through the death and resurrection of Jesus Christ, as well as the need for proclamation of this reconciliation"[149] in the MMR.[150]

144. Ott et al., *Encountering Theology of Mission*, 96.
145. Ott, *Church on Mission*, 89.
146. Engelsviken, "Reconciliation with God," 86.
147. Engelsviken, "Reconciliation with God," 86.
148. Engelsviken, "Reconciliation with God," 88.
149. Engelsviken, "Come Holy Spirit, Heal and Reconcile," 192.

150. There are discussions on vertical dimension of reconciliation in the MMR as follows:
Mission as ministry of reconciliation involves the obligation to share the gospel of Jesus Christ in all its fullness, the good news of him who through his incarnation, death and resurrection has once for all provided the basics for reconciliation with God, forgiveness of sins and new life in the power of the Holy Spirit. This ministry invites people to accept God's offer of reconciliation in Christ, and to become his disciples in the communion of his church. It promises the hope of fullness of life in God, both in this age and in God's future, eternal kingdom. Matthey, *Come Holy Spirit, Heal and Reconcile*, 76.
The primary broken relationship is between *God* and humanity. The gospel of reconciliation is a call to turn to God, to be converted to God and to renew our faith in the One who constantly invites us to be in communion with Godself, with one another and with the whole creation. We rejoice that through our Savior Jesus Christ, this reconciliation has been made possible. Matthey, *Come Holy Spirit, Heal and Reconcile*, 82.

In addition, a plenary speaker at Athens 2005, Kirsteen Kim, underscored Christocentric pneumatology by saying that "for Christians, discerning the Spirit is essentially seeing Jesus Christ . . . the Christian contribution to this debate [spiritual discernment] will always be Christ-centered."[151] This can be viewed as a critical response to the radical proposal by Hyun Kyung Chung at Canberra. She also argues that the first sign of the Spirit coming is "ecclesial: the confession of Jesus as Lord (1 Cor. 12:3; 1 John 4:2)."[152]

Similarly, in his plenary speech at Athens 2005, Robert Schreiter said that the vertical dimension of reconciliation is between God and "a sinful humanity" "through the death of the Son, Jesus Christ."[153] Furthermore, he clarifies that it "is vertical reconciliation that makes the horizontal and cosmic dimensions possible."[154]

However, as Engelsviken criticizes, the vertical dimension was not given attention when describing mission as reconciliation as an emerging theme in Schreiter's plenary speech as well as in the conference in general. After brief discussions on reconciliation with God, Schreiter moved on to horizontal reconciliation, saying

> I will focus here on the horizontal or social dimension of reconciliation. The church participates in the vertical dimension through its sacraments and in the cosmic dimension as well, both in its liturgy and its concern for all of creation. These too constitute part of reconciliation as a model of mission. But because the thinking on the horizontal dimension is more recent and new to many, I will devote more time to it here.[155]

This can still be understandable for some reasons such as time limit and focus of the speech. However, when one reviews the process of reconciliation that Schreiter outlines in his writings, which does not seek to achieve horizontal reconciliation through promoting vertical reconciliation, it seems that Engelsviken's criticism that vertical reconciliation "was simply assumed" is a tenable response to Schreiter's speech and the Athens 2005 conference.[156] Rather than contemplating how vertical reconciliation leads to horizontal reconciliation, his process often primarily underlines steps in horizontal reconciliation, which are inferred from the biblical reflections on the reconciliation with God. Interpretations of this issue can vary.

151. Matthey, *Come Holy Spirit, Heal and Reconcile*, 155.
152. Matthey, *Come Holy Spirit, Heal and Reconcile*, 155.
153. Matthey, *Come Holy Spirit, Heal and Reconcile*, 214.
154. Matthey, *Come Holy Spirit, Heal and Reconcile*, 215.
155. Matthey, *Come Holy Spirit, Heal and Reconcile*, 216.
156. Engelsviken, "Come Holy Spirit, Heal and Reconcile," 191.

Nevertheless, one can notice that the documents produced by the LM on the issue of mission as reconciliation exhibit several differences to those of the WCC. As previously mentioned, in Pattaya 2004, Issue Group 22, one of 31 Issue Groups of the Forum for World Evangelization of the LM, focused on reconciliation and produced LOP No. 51.[157] It was not a main theme, but it was one of many topics that the issue groups dealt with. A few years later in Cape Town (2010), reconciliation was included in the main document titled the Cape Town Commitment.

The documents of the LM contain a trinitarian perspective, but have no pneumatological emphasis to the extent that dilutes their Christocentric frame. Thus, reconciliation remains Christ-centered even for the horizontal dimension. In this sense, evangelism and discipleship are called for as important steps in the process of mission as reconciliation.

LOP No. 51 shares many arguments in common with the WCC. As discussed previously, they both acknowledge the urgency and legitimacy of the ministry of reconciliation in our world today. They both believe that God has initiated and achieved vertical reconciliation with sinful humanity, which has enabled horizontal and cosmic reconciliation. However, the Christocentric understanding of reconciliation can be more easily identified in the LOP No. 51. In discussing the hope of reconciliation, LOP No. 51 states that the "fullness of reconciliation is friendship with God in Jesus Christ, witnessed to in Christ's two-fold command to love God and neighbour."[158]

In that respect, it emphasizes evangelism as a critical step in the process of reconciliation. The introduction of LOP No. 51 states the following: "The argument of this paper is that in a deeply broken world, faithful Christian evangelism can only be envisioned and embodied in direct relationship with the vision and practice of biblical Christian peacemaking."[159] The view on reconciliation presented in LOP No. 51 is that "reconciliation . . . is integral to evangelism and justice," emphasizing the close connection between the two.[160] In conclusion of part 1, it again claims that biblically holistic reconciliation is "integral to evangelism and justice" and "radical discipleship with Christ" is "normative of Christian faith" along with "costly peacemaking" in our world.[161]

157. The document is "the outcome of intense work over 2003–2005 by 47 Christian leaders from six continents and 21 countries" and their early work was "profoundly shaped" by a visit to Rwanda in July 2004, "ten years after the genocide." LOP No. 51, Introduction.

158. LOP No. 51, pt. 1.

159. LOP No. 51, Introduction.

160. LOP No. 51, pt. Pattaya Covenant.

161. LOP No. 51, pt. 1.

In the Cape Town Commitment, a significant part is devoted to the issue of reconciliation. This document, which evidently takes a trinitarian perspective on understanding mission, holds yet a different nuance in discussing reconciliation from the MMR. As in LOP No. 51, the Cape Town Commitment takes a Christocentric view in addressing reconciliation. The term "reconciliation" appears with the term "Christ" rather than "Holy Spirit." Furthermore, such expressions as "Building the peace of Christ in our divided and broken world" and "the peace that Christ made" imply that the LM argues that the complete form of reconciliation remains in Christ.[162]

In a section of the IIB, reconciliation in the name of Christ or the gospel of Christ is emphasized in discussing the horizontal dimension as follows:

> We long to see the worldwide Church of Christ, those who have been reconciled to God, living out our reconciliation with one another and committed to the task and struggle of biblical peace-making in the name of Christ.[163]
>
> *Embrace the fullness of the reconciling power of the gospel and teach it accordingly.* This includes a full biblical understanding of the atonement: that Jesus not only bore our sin on the cross to reconcile us to God, but destroyed our enmity, to reconcile us to one another.[164]

The Cape Town Commitment deeply concerns with the broken nature of our society, as is the MMR, for example, with ethnic conflict, the poor and oppressed, people with disabilities, people living with HIV, and for suffering creation. In addition, regarding Christians' relationship with people of other faiths, the Cape Town Commitment recognizes the people as "human beings created in God's image" and claims that Christians should love and be friends with their neighbors of other religions.[165] It rejects all forms of violence, denouncing hatred and fear against them. Rather than trying to acknowledge the pre-existence or presence of the work of the Holy Spirit among the people of other faiths, as the conciliar document states, it says that "empowered by the Holy Spirit" we must build the peace of Christ.[166] Moreover, evangelism remains at the core of Christian living of love with others:

162. The Cape Town Commitment, sec. IIB.
163. The Cape Town Commitment, sec. IIB.
164. The Cape Town Commitment, sec. IIB.
165. The Cape Town Commitment, sec. IIC.
166. The Cape Town Commitment, sec. 1.5C.

> We are called to share good news in evangelism, but not to engage in unworthy proselytizing. *Evangelism*, which includes persuasive rational argument following the example of the Apostle Paul, is 'to make an honest and open statement of the gospel which leaves the hearers entirely free to make up their own minds about it. We wish to be sensitive to those of other faiths, and we reject any approach that seeks to force conversion on them.' *Proselytizing,* by contrast, is the attempt to compel others to become 'one of us', to 'accept our religion', or indeed to 'join our denomination.[167]

Compared to those of the WCC, one can observe that the documents of the LM address the ways of seeking the horizontal dimension of reconciliation through promoting the vertical dimension of reconciliation in Christ, holding evangelism and discipleship as the central ways of doing it.

In sum, the differences in nuances and subsequent disagreement regarding the vertical dimension of reconciliation between conciliar and evangelical scholars reflect the underlying differences in their theology of mission. The pneumatological emphasis by the WCC is a key feature that indicates theological differences between them in relation to the three major streams of mission theology in today's church. The pneumatological emphasis in conciliar mission theology has often appeared to be expanding its theological elaborations, alleviating the significance of Jesus in salvation. In response, evangelical theologians have continually asserted the significance of the vertical dimension as a way of reminding people of the centrality of Christ in understanding Christian salvation and the church's witness.

As the reviewed statements not only from the evangelical circle but also within the WCC have shown, the discrepancy separating the Son and the Spirit ingrained within some of thoughts in mission theology is unbiblical. If the newly emerging pneumatological emphasis of conciliar mission theology seems to promote the separation, the new paradigm should be reconsidered. This is because the Bible says there is perfect correspondence and harmony between the teachings and the ministry of the Son and the Spirit, and fundamentally within the Trinity (John 14:26; 15:26; 1 Cor 12:3). A further question needs to be explored is rather how the vertical and horizontal dimensions of reconciliation are inseparably related.

Reconciliation is an urgent issue regarding broken realities worldwide today. It requires the holistic involvement: sympathetic lamentation, earnest prayers, rigorous study, and active engagement from the whole church. As mentioned in the previous chapter, the existing disagreement among

---

167. The Cape Town Commitment, sec. IIC.

scholars implies that there is still room for development and it is necessary to establish a more wholesome and robust theology of reconciliation to equip the church as peacemaker in the world.

To do this, the theologies of the four noteworthy theologians of reconciliation are examined—starting with Karl Barth, who is often considered to have opened the "renaissance" of trinitarian theology—centering on the relationship between the vertical and horizontal dimensions of reconciliation.[168]

---

168. Feenstra, "Trinity," 11.

3

"Fellow-Humanity": Karl Barth's Contribution to Mission as Reconciliation

Karl Barth

OUT OF MUCH DISCUSSION covering a wide array of subjects in Karl Barth's writings, several topics worth exploring here concern the research focus—the relationship between the vertical and horizontal dimensions of reconciliation; for example, Barth's doctrine of reconciliation, the doctrine of the Trinity, theological anthropology, and ethics. Barth addresses the topics mainly in *The Church Dogmatics* as well as in *The Humanity of God*, *Ethics*, *Christian Life*, and *The Theology of John Calvin*. Barth's theological thoughts on these topics in the literature may serve as resources from which his view on the relationship between the two dimensions can be inferred. This study also explores some of the secondary literature on Barth's theology because such works may help interpret his theological view.

The theological idea of Barth that is most relevant for this study is the notion of "fellow-humanity" (or co-humanity; *Mitmenschlichkeit* in German). The term "fellow-humanity" represents Barth's theological anthropology which understands a human as a relational being. Christology offers a significant perspective in Barth's anthropology. At the same time, Barth bases relational anthropology on the doctrine of the Trinity in which he explores the understanding of a relational God. Regarding an innovative approach of Barth, Kelly Kapic comments that Barth has influenced many theologians to connect "anthropology to the doctrine of the Trinity."[1] The "renaissance" of discussing the Trinity in the early twentieth century was mainly a response to the theology of Friedrich Schleiermacher

---

1. Kapic, "Anthropology," 142.

in the nineteenth century, which was "initiated by Karl Barth" and then "joined" by many others.²

The doctrine of reconciliation expounds God's being with humans, which is actualized in Christ through whom humans immersed in inhumanity are enabled to regain their fellow-humanity. Barth developed his anthropology upon Christology: Jesus is the only "real man" and elected alone by God through whom all sinful humans can realize and restore their God-given humanity as they participate in Christ. It is Barth's unique and innovative idea that has attracted both praise and critique.³

Barth's ethics are his theological account of human agency in the history of salvation. For ethics, he underlines Christians' act of love for their fellow humans, imitating God's love, which itself becomes a witness to God's love along with the declaration of the Gospel by the church community.

Thus, when engaging Barth's works related to the research focus, the core questions to raise are as follows: (1) What is fellow-humanity? (2) How can it be restored? Barth's answers to these questions can be examined by reviewing the following subjects in his literature. The former question is primarily related to Barth's doctrine of the Trinity, hamartiology (relational aspect and inhumanity), and theological anthropology. The latter question can be answered by exploring the doctrine of reconciliation, ethics, the church's witness, and the Christian understanding of love. Most of Barth's discussions, however, often interchangeably shift from one question to the other, and thus the classifications are not exclusive to each other.

Understanding God as a Relational God

Relationship-Oriented God: The Immanent Trinity and the Economic Trinity

Barth understands God as a relational God. His doctrine of the Trinity identifies this. God eternally exists as Father, Son, and Holy Spirit in the fullness of self-knowledge and love, which are self-sufficient. This is the immanent Trinity and the primary objectivity of God: "God is objective to himself" "within the immanent Trinity" but not known to humanity.⁴

---

2. Feenstra, "Trinity," 11.

3. Kapic, "Anthropology," 138–40; Blocher, "Karl Barth's Anthropology," 101–11.

4. Molnar, *Divine Freedom*, 143. As Paul Molnar discusses, there is a debate on how to understand the nature and relationship of immanent and economic Trinity. See ch. 4 of Molnar's book, *Divine Freedom and the Doctrine of Immanent Trinity* (2nd ed.) for more discussion.

It describes *perichoresis* among the triune God:[5] the mutual knowing and indwelling relationship within God himself. God exists in relationship in "His inner divine being."[6] Barth writes

> To be sure, God is One in Himself. But He is not alone. There is in Him a co-existence, co-inherence and reciprocity. God in Himself is not just simple, but in the simplicity of His essence He is threefold—the Father, the Son and the Holy Ghost. He posits Himself, is posited by Himself, and confirms Himself in both respects, as His own origin and also as His own goal. He is in Himself the One who loves eternally, the One who is eternally loved, and eternal love; and in this triunity He is the original and source of every I and Thou, of the I which is eternally from and to the Thou and therefore supremely I.[7]

On the other hand, the triune God makes himself known in his divine freedom, "making himself objective to us" through Son, the Incarnate Word.[8] This is the economic Trinity and the second objectivity of God. While God knows himself directly in the immanent Trinity, we can only know God in the economic Trinity, indirectly through the history of Israel and in particular through the mediator, Christ.[9] In the economic Trinity, the proclamation of God, which was the central message revealed to and testified by the prophets in the Old Testament, became "concrete" and "clear" in the history of Jesus.[10] Barth explains that

> God gives Himself to be known, and is known, in the substance of secondary objectivity, in the sign of all signs, in the work of God which all the other works of God serve to prepare, accompany and continue, in the manhood which He takes to Himself, to which He humbles Himself and which He raises through Himself. "We saw His glory" now means: we saw this One in His humanity, the humanity of the Son of God, on His way to death, which was the way to His resurrection.[11]

---

5. Barth prefers to triunity than trinity since it emphasizes "unity" and "unity of being one." Barth, *CD* I/1:369.
6. Barth, *CD* III/2:218.
7. Barth, *CD* III/2:218.
8. Molnar, *Divine Freedom*, 142.
9. Barth, *CD* II/1:19–20.
10. Barth, *CD* II/1:19–20.
11. Barth, *CD* II/1:19–20.

Because there is a relationship within God himself (*ad intra*), God has also established a relationship with humans (*ad extra*), which is "God's eternal covenant" with humans.[12] The covenantal relationship has "repeated and reflected" the relationship within God himself.[13] Kevin Vanhoozer explains that, "the economic actualizes the immanent Trinity" in Barth's thought.[14]

In Barth's expression, the economic Trinity *corresponds* to the immanent Trinity.[15] Barth clarifies that they are not *analogia entis* (analogy of being), but *analogia relationis* (analogy of relation).[16] Barth explicates the relationships as follows:

> The correspondence and similarity of the two relationships consists in the fact that the eternal love in which God as the Father loves the Son, and as the Son loves the Father, and in which God as the Father is loved by the Son and as the Son by the Father, is also the love which is addressed by God to man. The humanity of Jesus, His fellow-humanity, His being for man as the direct correlative of His being for God, indicates, attests and reveals this correspondence and similarity . . . It is this inner being which takes this form *ad extra* in the humanity of Jesus, and in this form, for all the disparity of sphere and object, remains true to itself and therefore reflects itself.[17]

The correspondent relationship that Barth indicates between *ad intra* and *ad extra* is salient. In Barth's thinking, the self-giving love of God in Jesus for humanity follows and corresponds to the perichoretic love within God himself. It is thus reasonable to consider how God's missionary activity toward humans finds its fundamental ground in the immanent Trinity. As John Flett correctly argues in his book *The Witness of God*, the concept of *missio Dei* should be placed in the central part of the church's talk of the doctrine of Trinity as well as its ministry to the world, not as a secondary activity. Flett states, "That human relationship with God takes this missionary form is precisely a consequence of the doctrine of the Trinity."[18]

Therefore, based on who He is (the immanent Trinity), God has disclosed Himself to us (the economic Trinity) in the salvific life and work of Christ in whom God seeks and chooses to be for us. In Barth's idea,

12. Barth, *CD* III/2:218.
13. Barth, *CD* III/2:218–19.
14. Vanhoozer, "Atonement," 194.
15. Barth, *CD* III/2:220.
16. Barth, *CD* III/2:220.
17. Barth, *CD* III/2:220.
18. Flett, *Witness of God*, loc. 390.

"Everything that Jesus is, does, and suffers enacts . . . God's very being."[19] Vanhoozer thus comments, Barth understands "the incarnation and atonement accomplish in time God's eternal self-determining decision to be 'for us.'"[20] This is how God's essence and His work through Christ are correspondent and similar—they are distinguished but not to be separated. Barth argues that

> To the unity of Father, Son and Spirit among themselves corresponds their unity *ad extra* [outside of God]. God's essence and work are not twofold but one . . . The work of God is the essence of God as the essence of Him who (N.B. in a free decision grounded in His essence but not constrained by His essence) is revealer, revelation and being revealed, or Creator, Reconciler and Redeemer. In this work of His, God is revealed to us. All we can know of God according to the witness of Scripture are His acts . . . Though the work of God is the essence of God, it is necessary and important to distinguish His essence as such from His work, remembering that this work is grace, a free divine decision, and also remembering that we can know about God only because and to the extent that He gives Himself to us to be known. God's work is, of course, the work of the whole essence of God.[21]

Another concept that Barth develops and uses to illustrate God's very being "for us" and his "turning toward" humans is the humanity of God.[22]

The Humanity of God

In Barth's idea, humanity denotes being (oriented to be) together with humans. In this sense, God has deity *and* humanity. In *The Humanity of God*, Barth says

> The humanity of God! Rightly understood that is bound to mean God's relation to and turning toward man. It signifies the God who speaks with man in promise and command. It represents God's existence, intercession, and activity for man, the intercourse God holds with him, and the free grace in which He wills to be and is nothing other than the God of man.[23]

19. Vanhoozer, "Atonement," 195.
20. Vanhoozer, "Atonement," 194.
21. Barth, *CD* I/1:371.
22. Barth, *Humanity of God*, 37.
23. Barth, *Humanity of God*, 37.

As discussed previously, God is self-sufficient in His own being and does not stand "in need of" humans "in order to be truly God."[24] God exists "in all the fulness of His Godhead," the Trinity, "in which He might well have been satisfied with Himself."[25] Therefore, God "would in truth be no lonesome, no egotistical God even without man, yes, even without the whole created universe."[26] However, God in His humanity, "wills Himself together with us" and "will[s] Himself in fellowship with us"[27] Stated differently, God "exists, speaks, and acts as the *partner* of [hu]man[28]" and has chosen humans to be partners of Him based on His free choice of love.[29]

Barth, therefore, discusses how it is "precisely God's *deity* which, rightly understood, includes his *humanity*."[30] It was God's free choice based on his deity. Barth elaborates, "that is mystery in which He meets us in the existence of Jesus Christ. He wants in His freedom actually not to be without man but *with* him and in the same freedom not against him but *for* him, and that apart from or even counter to what man deserves. He wants in fact to be man's partner, his almighty and compassionate Saviour."[31]

Barth unfolds the humanity of God from a Christological perspective. God's deity, which includes humanity, has been revealed and actualized in Christ.[32] Barth thus notes that in order to understand the humanity of God, "the question must be, who and what is God in Jesus Christ."[33] "The consideration of the Christ as Person and Event" seems to be "the only source of theological anthropology[34]" of Barth, as Henri Blocher identifies. In the Immanuel God (God with us), the genuine form of the

---

24. Barth, *Humanity of God*, 50.

25. Barth, *CD* IV/2:777.

26. Barth, *Humanity of God*, 50.

27. Barth, *CD* IV/2:777.

28. Barth says, "though of course as the absolutely superior partner." Barth, *Humanity of God*, 45.

29. Barth, *Humanity of God*, 45.

30. Barth, *Humanity of God*, 46.

31. Barth, *Humanity of God*, 50.

32. Barth, *Humanity of God*, 46.

33. Barth, *Humanity of God*, 47.

34. Citing Daniel J. Price, Blocher mentions that Barth in later years opened his mind to the worth of scientific claims in discussing anthropology and "granted" "there may be "material parallelism" "between theology and psychology." Blocher, "Karl Barth's Anthropology," 103. Besides, Blocher notes several scholars such as Henri Bouillard, Gerrit Berkouwer, and Wolfhard Pannenberg "doubt the strict Christological origin of Barth's propositions." Blocher, "Karl Barth's Anthropology," 106–7.

humanity of God can be found.³⁵ It is God's will to be with humans that Jesus demonstrates. Barth argues

> To put it in the simplest way, what unites God and us men is that He does not will to be God without us, that He creates us rather to share with us and therefore with our being and life and act His own incomparable being and life and act, that He does not allow His history to be His and ours ours, but causes them to take place as a common history. That is the special truth which the Christian message has to proclaim at its very heart.³⁶

In other words, God "does not will anything for Himself" and God "does not will Himself without us."³⁷ It is based on who God is. In Barth's thoughts, God does not exist or choose not to exist otherwise. Barth argues, "He wills Himself, not as the object of our wishes and desires, of our imagination and aspiration, of our willing and running, but as His gift freely imparted to us. It is in this way that God loves, that He is eternal love. It is in this way that He loves us—[hu]man."³⁸

The love of God shown in Christ speaks of God's denial of Himself to be God in order to love and embrace *a totally other person or wholly other* to us. In Barth theology, particularly in the earlier period usually symbolized in his famous work, *The Epistles to the Romans*, it is known that Barth argues that God is *the total (wholly) other or the very other* to humans (Gott: der ganz Anderer).³⁹ It means that God has "infinite qualitative distinction" from humans.⁴⁰ He later admits that he was "partially" right so that modifies his position as he develops the concept of humanity of God.⁴¹ Henri Blocher explains Barth's "Elijah's style" theological theme of God's deity or God's quality of "*Totaliter aliter*" (totally otherwise) from humans in his earlier years had become "the Humanity of God" in his later years, influenced by Leonhard Ragaz.⁴²

According to Barth, there is "noetically and logically and absolute paradox" "between His being and essence in Himself and His activity and work as the Reconciler of the world created by Him"; furthermore this happened in God's "way into the far country"—to the fallen humanity as "the Incarnation

---

35. Blocher, "Karl Barth's Anthropology," 102–3.
36. Barth, *CD* IV/1:7.
37. Barth, *CD* IV/2:777.
38. Barth, *CD* IV/2:777.
39. Barth, *Epistle of Romans*, 107, 240; Barth, *Humanity of God*, 42.
40. Barth, *Humanity of God*, 42.
41. Barth, *Humanity of God*, 42.
42. Blocher, "Karl Barth's Anthropology," 96.

of the Word."[43] In the paradox, God is "pleased" to choose to be with us as the Reconciler.[44] This is because God is the "One who loves" in "the freedom of His divine being."[45] Then, Barth claims that "The statements "God is" and "God loves" are synonymous; that is, they explain and confirm one another. This is how God's identity has been disclosed to us—in love.[46]

Therefore, the humanity of humans ought to correspond to the humanity of God. As an analogy, God's relationship toward humans is correspondent and similar to the relationship within the triune God.[47] Similarly, the relationship between a human and another human should be correspondent and similar to that within the triune God and between God and humans.[48] Barth calls this "fellow-humanity," which is based on the covenantal relationship with God in Christ (the economic Trinity, and the humanity of God), and thus which has its fundamental beginning from God Himself (the immanent Trinity). To Barth, considering humans as *imago Dei*, it is fellow-humanity that "makes humans human."[49]

Fellow-Humanity: The Relational Anthropology of Barth

As previously stated, fellow-humanity is the concept in Barth's theology most relevant to the relationship of the vertical and horizontal dimensions of reconciliation. It shows how Barth thinks the two dimensions are related. The concept of fellow-humanity represents Barth's theological anthropology, which can be described as relational anthropology.

In Barth's relational anthropology, the status of humans is discerned by their relationship: to what extent their humanity has been restored as the humanity of God. Inhumanity, which is the opposite status of fellow-humanity, is an outcome of humans' sinfulness and being separated from God, who is relationship-oriented. Sin affects all those dimensions together. Barth refers to sin as "enmity against God, as fratricide and as self-destruction."[50]

The only way that Barth suggests acknowledging and resolving the problem of inhumanity is being connected to God, who discloses the

43. Barth, *CD* IV/1:184.
44. Barth, *CD* IV/1:184.
45. Barth, *CD* IV/2:755.
46. Barth, *CD* IV/2:755.
47. Barth, *CD* III/2:220.
48. Barth, *Humanity of God*, 52.
49. Blocher, "Karl Barth's Anthropology," 105.
50. Barth, *CD* IV/1:410.

reality of inhumanity and enables the restoration of fellow-humanity. Fellow-humanity is thus related to *agape*—love for one's neighbor—which God has shown to humans.

Barth claims that unless one encounters the humanity of *agape* actualized in Christ, it is impossible to restore one's fellow-humanity.[51] Reconciliation with God initiates, enables, and achieves reconciliation with fellow humans.

A Brief Survey of Barth's Methodology of Theological Anthropology

Barth's anthropology is theological. Unlike other approaches driven by "scientific discoveries regarding human origins" in his time, Barth maintained the development of his anthropology in the theological domain.[52] Barth seems adamant that sound (at least Christian) anthropological pursuit should start from theological consideration of the concrete history of Christ's personality and works, instead of paying instant heed to humans themselves or beginning from any other approach such as naturalistic, ethical or idealistic philosophical thought.[53]

It was not because Barth had "doubts" or did not respect other disciplines, but because he "did not consider them theologically significant."[54] As Daniel Price argues, Barth seems to "respect the boundaries" between theology and "the natural sciences."[55] Furthermore, Barth's relational anthropology seems to have similarities, particularly with object relations psychology.[56]

However, Barth considers those approaches to presuppose that humans' "self-contained" and "self-existent reality" is incomplete.[57] As John Webster comments, "Barth is profoundly perturbed by one of modernity's primary images of the human person: that of the self as a centre of judgment, creating value by its acts of allegiance or choice, organising the moral world around its consciousness of itself as the ethical *fundamentum*."[58]

---

51. Barth, *CD* III/2:226.
52. Kapic, "Anthropology," 138.
53. Barth, *CD* III/2:109.
54. Kapic, "Anthropology," 138.
55. Price, *Karl Barth's Anthropology*, 116.
56. Price, *Karl Barth's Anthropology*, 9, 102–7, 231–44.
57. Barth, *CD* III/2:109.
58. Webster, *Barth's Ethics of Reconciliation*, 18.

It seems clear that Barth "argues forcefully that theological anthropology must begin with dogmatics, not with an a priori philosophy, cosmology, or speculative world view."[59] Price identifies several factors in Barth's opinions, thereby forming his own opinion on this:

> First, Barth was influenced by existential philosophy with its suspicion of abstract modes of thought and its preference for action. Second, Barth's dynamic anthropology reflects certain elements of Calvin's anthropology that describe the human as a creature in immediate and momentary dependence on God. But most of all, Barth's dynamic [emphasizing "interpersonal action"] anthropology issues from his interpretation of the *imago Dei* in light of his relational under standing of the Trinity.[60]

In this respect, Barth's anthropology begins from the doctrines of the Trinity and Christology. A well-known characteristic of Barth's theology is that it is Christocentric or Christologically shaped. His Christology shapes his every theological reflection, including theological anthropology. As Matt Jenson notes, Barth "consistently seeks to think from the triune God's self-revelation in Christ."[61] The significance of God's revelation in Christ can hardly be overestimated in Barth's theological anthropology. This is because Barth believes "only the Word of God reveals the reality of human sin and corruption," and thus, humans are "unable to understand 'real man' because of both the ontic and noetic effects of sin."[62]

In his relational anthropology, Barth believes that what makes a human genuinely human is his or her humanity in relations. As several scholars have observed, Martin Buber, a philosopher who has been recognized for establishing an anthropological understanding of the basis of the concept of I and Thou personalism, has probably influenced Barth.[63] In his book *I and Thou*, Buber contends the life of self can find its meaningfulness in an I-Thou relationship, rather than an I-It relationship. With his Jewish religious background, Buber extends this I-Thou relationship to the eternal Thou, God.[64] He even comments how the Gospel of John, which addresses the "mystical" relationship between the Father and the Son, is "really the Gospel of pure relation."[65]

---

59. Price, *Karl Barth's Anthropology*, 116.
60. Price, *Karl Barth's Anthropology*, 9–10.
61. Jenson, *Gravity of Sin*, 135.
62. Price, *Karl Barth's Anthropology*, 116–17.
63. Schults, *Reforming theological Anthropology*, 118; Jenson *Gravity of Sin*, 153.
64. Buber, *I and Thou*, loc. 1099.
65. Buber, *I and Thou*, loc. 1115.

Similar to Buber, Barth defines humans as beings who exist in I and Thou relationships. It seems that Barth accepts and deepens Buber's idea based on his doctrine of the Trinity and Christology. Barth argues that Christ is the only human who is truly human in that he alone has perfectly lived and existed as the being of an I and Thou relationship—with God and with other humans. By contrast, all human beings except Christ are broken in their relations. Obtaining the knowledge of God in God's self-revelation in Christ is therefore crucial in understanding what human and becoming a true human is.[66]

Barth suggests that all humans should correspond to the relational humanity (fellow-humanity) that Christ has shown. This has become possible for humans because of what Christ has already achieved and given to humanity. If anyone seeks to exist in any other ways than this—being in relations (restored by Christ), one would end up being a "relationless [hu]man" who "withdraws into himself [or herself]" and falls into "self-isolation," "self-destruction," and "self-containment"—"*incurvatus in se.*"[67]

Thus, sin can be defined through one's relations. Jenson remarks that to Barth, "sin is the refusal to conform to our determination in Christ to be relationally constituted and relationally directed."[68] Christology is salient for it becomes the exemplar. In this sense, Kelly Kapic asserts that, "Put simply, Barth argues that we should begin our anthropological discussion with the second Adam, Jesus the Christ, rather than the first Adam, because only Jesus Christ reveals 'real man' (his term) and therefore the contradiction of sin that plagues him and his world."[69] Humans can truly understand themselves in the light of God's self-revelation "by looking at Jesus." Jenson would agree with Kapic, saying that "The method of theological anthropology [of Karl Barth] is indirect. Nevertheless, this is the only approach to true (that is, theological) knowledge of humanity."[70]

The Humanity of Humans in the Creation of God

In his doctrine of creation, Barth explains that God created human beings as the beings who hold "the inviolable correspondence" with Himself in that they are beings "in encounter between I and Thou."[71] This is the

66. Price, *Karl Barth's Anthropology*, 116–17.
67. Barth, *CD* IV/1:421; IV/2:442–43; and Jenson, *Gravity of Sin*, 151.
68. Jenson, *Gravity of Sin*, 152.
69. Kapic, "Anthropology," 138.
70. Jenson, *Gravity of Sin*, 135.
71. Barth, *CD* III/2:203.

humanity of humans as "God's covenant-partners" and as the "likeness" of their Creator.[72] These statements demonstrate the core idea of his theological anthropology. Barth's discussion can be divided into two sections according to the types of relationship that humans have, namely those with God and with fellow humans.

Humans as God's Covenant-Partner

Barth defines real humans as God's covenant-partners.[73] It is how they are "determined by God for life with God" that is "the distinctive feature" of their beings "in the cosmos."[74] Barth denies the possibility of being a real human apart from God's determination in the covenant. Barth states that, "real man does not live a godless life—without God. A godless explanation of man, which overlooks the fact that he belongs to God, is from the very outset one which cannot explain real man, man himself. Indeed, it cannot even speak of him."[75]

Thus, every human basically stands in "connection and correspondence" with their "divinely given determination" as God's covenant-partner.[76] The devastating power of sin has been so forceful that humans have betrayed and obscured God. However, Barth claims that "the power of sin" is not "illimitable," and "cannot, therefore, annul the covenant."[77] A human being still holds "something constant and persistent, an inviolable particularity" "which cannot be effaced or lost or changed or made unrecognizable even in sinful man."[78] This "does not mean" that Barth claims that humans are "the covenant-partner of God by nature."[79] It is God's gracious determination operated in His creation and salvation.[80] Barth thus identifies that it is "the task of theological anthropology" to recognize these "inviolable and constant" factors in humans, enabling them to be God's covenant-partners.[81]

Because Barth defines reconciliation as "the fulfillment of the covenant between God and man," he views human beings through the lens of the

---

72. Barth, *CD* III/2:203–4.
73. Barth, *CD* III/2:203.
74. Barth, *CD* III/2:203–4
75. Barth, *CD* III/2:203.
76. Barth, *CD* III/2:205.
77. Barth, *CD* III/2:206.
78. Barth, *CD* III/2:206.
79. Barth, *CD* III/2:320.
80. Barth, *CD* III/2:320.
81. Barth, *CD* III/2:206.

covenant of God.⁸² It is the distinctiveness of human beings as creatures that they have a covenantal relationship with God. In this sense, again, Christology shapes Barth's anthropology. Christ who has fulfilled the covenant serves the key role in Barth's understanding of humans. Barth thus suggests to behold Jesus Christ, who has shown the perfect humanity as well as his divinity, to investigate the "general" issues of human beings.⁸³ Barth argues that "in theological anthropology what man is, is decided by the primary text . . . by the humanity of the man Jesus."⁸⁴ In their relationship with God, humans should be for God as God is for them. Jesus, the perfect model, Barth comments, is the man "for God."⁸⁵

Fellow-Humanity: The Basic Form of Humanity

Jesus is not only for God but also "for his fellow-humans."⁸⁶ Barth argues that, "When we think of the humanity of Jesus, humanity is to be described unequivocally as fellow-humanity. In the light of the man Jesus, man is the cosmic being which exists absolutely for its fellows."⁸⁷ According to Barth, all other forms of humanity that are not fellow-humanity should be "ruled out."⁸⁸ The basic form of humanity is, therefore, fellow-humanity.⁸⁹

Similar to the discussion on the humanity of God, Barth asserts that the fellow-humanity of Jesus "mirrors and reflects" His divinity with "the closest correspondence."⁹⁰ The freedom in which God has executed the covenant with humans is divine. Furthermore, the salvific works of Jesus toward humans in which He "disposes Himself" are divine.⁹¹ The humanity of Jesus—directed toward the wholly other Thou (sinful humans)—is based on the divinity of the triune God. Barth comments that "this whole mystery of the man Jesus is rooted in the mystery of God Himself."⁹² Moreover, he continually asserts that

---

82. Barth, *CD* IV/1:22.
83. Barth, *CD* III/2:207.
84. Barth, *CD* III/2:226.
85. Barth, *CD* III/2:201, 207–8, 216–17.
86. Barth, *CD* III/2:208.
87. Barth, *CD* III/2:208.
88. Barth, *CD* III/2:229.
89. Barth, *CD* III/2:223, 225–26, 228.
90. Barth, *CD* III/2:216.
91. Barth, *CD* III/2:215.
92. Barth, *CD* III/2:218.

> If "God for man" is the eternal covenant revealed and effective in time in the humanity of Jesus, in this decision of the Creator for the creature there arises a relationship which is not alien to the Creator, to God as God, but we might almost say appropriate and natural to Him. God repeats in this relationship *ad extra* a relationship proper to Himself in His inner divine essence.[93]

As discussed in the section of Barth's understanding of the triune God, it must be recalled that "God exists in relationship and fellowship" in I and Thou encounters, "confronting Himself," yet being always in "one and the same" God.[94] Corresponding to "His own being and essence," "God created" humans "in His own image, as male and female,"[95] which Barth considers "the original and proper form of this fellow-humanity."[96] This is humans' "divine likeness" to God.[97]

Therefore, the humanity of humans should "model" itself on Jesus' humanity.[98] The humanity of Jesus is fellow-humanity; whoever holds it "has indeed a part in the divine likeness of the man Jesus, the man for the fellow-man."[99] In other words, humans participate "in the image of God actualised in the humanity of Jesus."[100]

In the fellow-humanity, every human, as I, encounters Thou, his or her fellow humans.[101] Barth argues that "humanity is the determination of our being as a being in encounter with the other" humans.[102] In that respect, Barth claims that "I am as Thou art."[103] The word *as* "does not imply" the cause.[104] Rather, Barth explains that,

> It tells us that every "I am" is qualified, marked and determined by the "Thou art." Owing it to God the Creator that I am, I am only as Thou art; as, created by the same God, Thou art with me. Neither the I am nor the Thou art loses its own meaning and

---

93. Barth, *CD* III/2:218.
94. Barth, *CD* III/2:324.
95. Barth refers to Gen 2:18, saying that "It is not good for man to be alone" (Barth, *CD* III/2:324).
96. Barth, *CD* III/2:292, 324.
97. Barth, *CD* III/2:324.
98. Barth, *CD* III/2:324.
99. Barth, *CD* III/2:324.
100. Barth, *CD* III/2:226.
101. Barth, *CD* III/2:247–48.
102. Barth, *CD* III/2:248.
103. Barth, *CD* III/2:248.
104. Barth, *CD* III/2:248.

force. I do not become Thou, nor Thou I, in this co-existence. On the contrary, as I and Thou are together, their being acquires the character, the human style, of always being I for the self and Thou for the other. As we are in this encounter we are thus distinguished. On both sides—we shall return to this—the being has its own validity, dignity and self-certainty.[105]

Barth outlines the four characters of being in encounter. According to Barth, the encounter with Thou involves: (1) a being in which one man looks the other in the eye;[106] (2) mutual speech and hearing;[107] (3) mutual assistance in the act of being;[108] and (4) act all these in gladness.[109] Humanity is truly about "the realization of this 'with.'"[110]

This fellow-humanity has an inseparable relationship with Christian love, or *agape*. Although humanity is not Christian love, fellow-humanity moves "in the direction of Christian *agape*."[111] Barth expounds the relationship between fellow-humanity and agape as follows:

> And if I am without love I am nothing. For love alone—the love in which there is an awakening and positive fulfilment of humanity, and the Christian is displayed and revealed as real man—is the fulfilment of the Law, because this human and therefore Christian love, the love which includes humanity, is the life of man in the power of the new and saving divine Yes to the creature. This is the connexion between humanity and Christian love.[112]

Barth's further discussions on the restoration of fellow-humanity and *agape* are presented in the following sections.

The Freedom of Humans

To Barth, freedom is a prerequisite of an act of true love, or expressed differently, fellow-humanity. Genuine freedom belongs to God. To Barth, freedom is a word that describes the whole concept of humans' salvation. The

---

105. Barth, *CD* III/2:248.
106. Barth, *CD* III/2:250.
107. Barth, *CD* III/2:252.
108. Barth, *CD* III/2:260.
109. Barth, *CD* III/2:265.
110. Barth, *CD* III/2:268.
111. Barth, *CD* III/2:280.
112. Barth, *CD* III/2:282.

freedom of humans is derived from the freedom of God, as demonstrated in His being and salvific activity toward humanity. God loves us "in His freedom."[113] It is God's "free grace" that saves fallen humanity.[114] In *The Humanity of God*, Barth discusses God's freedom as follows:

> God's freedom is the freedom of the Father, and the Son in the unity of the Spirit. Again, man's freedom is a far cry from the self-assertion of one of many solitary individuals. It has nothing to do with division and disorder. God's own freedom is trinitarian, embracing grace, thankfulness, and peace. It is the freedom of the living God. Only in this relational freedom is God sovereign, almighty, the Lord of all.[115]

God's freedom is relational within Trinity as well as with humans. Barth claims that "God's freedom is essentially not freedom *from*, but freedom *to* and *for*."[116] It is for humans. God is "free to coexist with" humans and "to participate in his [human's] *history*" "as the Lord of the covenant."[117] Then, "God in His own freedom bestows human freedom."[118]

Thus, Barth says that, "Man becomes free and is free by choosing, deciding, and determining himself in accordance with the freedom of God."[119] When one "gives oneself to" God ("love God"), one's "freedom for love becomes and is his [or her] freedom for obedience."[120] Human's freedom, therefore, follows one's "obedience to God."[121] Barth states:

> Man can only stand as God's witness on the basis of the work which He Himself has done. He can only hold by His decision and judgment and therefore by His knowledge revealed there. He lives in virtue of the fact that God knows and does what is necessary, that God is the great crisis without which heaven and earth cannot be even for a single second. He is a free man—free in his thinking and deciding and acting—only as he is willing to accept this . . . He is a free man when he thinks and decides

---

113. Barth, *CD* IV/2:755.
114. Barth, *CD* IV/1:101; IV/2:503, 505; IV/3.2:604; and IV/4:37.
115. Barth, *Humanity of God*, 71–72.
116. Barth, *Humanity of God*, 72.
117. Barth, *Humanity of God*, 72.
118. Barth, *Humanity of God*, 75.
119. Barth, *Humanity of God*, 76–77.
120. Barth, *CD* IV/2:798–99.
121. Barth, *CD* IV/2:798.

and acts at peace with God, when his decision is simply and exclusively a repetition of the divine decision.[122]

Sinful humans who deny God's free act of love cannot be free. A person's freedom is identified with one's humanity and the act of love. To exercise true humanity, one must be genuinely free. Human's freedom is relational as God's and "not realized in the solitary detachment of an individual in isolation from his fellow men."[123] Moreover, human's freedom is primarily "freedom *for*" fellow humans as God's, and it is "only secondarily freedom *from* limitations and threats."[124] True love is therefore "a free action."[125]

This understanding of freedom provides a foundation for Barth's theological reflections on ethics. In Barth's words, "ethics is reflection upon what man is required to do in and with the gift of freedom."[126] Therefore, "ethical reflection . . . has to begin with the recognition that the free God is the free man's Lord, Creator, Reconciler, and Redeemer, and that free man is God's creature, partner, and child."[127] To Barth, freedom is a necessary premise for any Christian ethical discussion. He seems to reject ethical efforts that are not built on the premise of God-given freedom. Barth argues that,

> It [the apostolic admonition given in the New Testament to Christians] is obviously given on the assumption that they are free, and that they can make use of the freedom in which they have been made free in Christ (Gal. 5:1). Without this assumption there would be no such thing as Christian ethics even for us. All the things that we have to develop in ethics in relation to the command of the God who reconciles the world with Himself can only be concretions of the lifting up of themselves, the looking to Jesus, of which Christians are capable because they have been given the freedom for them.[128]

The understanding of freedom presented by Barth offers a clue to what he thinks about the relationship between the vertical and horizontal dimensions of reconciliation. His view on freedom suggests that his theology considers that without vertical reconciliation, there will be no horizontal

---

122. Barth, *CD* IV/1:449.
123. Barth, *Humanity of God*, 77.
124. Barth, *Humanity of God*, 78.
125. Barth, *CD* IV/2:752.
126. Barth, *Humanity of God*, 87.
127. Barth, *Humanity of God*, 87.
128. Barth, *CD* IV/2:532.

reconciliation. Barth repeatedly makes this argument in discussions of other relevant subjects as well, and further examinations shall be introduced.

Barth's Understanding of Sin

It is neither possible nor necessary to cover Barth's hamartiology in this section comprehensively, yet Barth's understanding of sin needs to be briefly addressed because it offers a basis for his relational understanding of sin and the issue of inhumanity.[129]

To begin with, it seems that Barth shares the oft-cited understandings of sin in the Christian tradition. Based on Genesis 3, the first biblical story of sin, Barth indicates that "the root and origin" of sin is "the arrogance in which man wants to be his own and his neighbor's judge."[130] Becoming sinners, humans wanted to be "as God"—"a judge," who would illegitimately exert "the pseudo-sovereign[ity]" looking for their own "pride and dignity" and "knowledge of good and evil" by themselves.[131] In that respect, sin is humans turning away from God.[132] Stated differently, Barth says that sin is "unbelief—man's most inward apostasy from that which is most inward and proper to the being and existence and all the works of God. It is apostasy from God's free grace."[133]

The Three Forms of Sin

The three forms of sin that Barth outlines are pride, sloth, and falsehood. First, pride opposes "God's self-humiliation" in descending Christ, the Word became flesh.[134] It is a rejection of God's justifying activity toward humans. Pride is "unbelief" and "disobedience" to God and rejects God's reconciliation coming down to humans.[135] Pride is a root of sin because sin "in its unity and totality" is "always pride" of man.[136]

---

129. As Henri Blocher comments, it is "quite traditional" to delve into the doctrine of sin when one discusses theological anthropology as it is the case for Karl Hase or Augustus Strong and others because of "the actual sinfulness of present humankind." Blocher, "Karl Barth's Anthropology," 100. See his article for further reading.

130. Barth, *CD* IV/1:231.
131. Barth, *CD* IV/1:231.
132. Barth, *CD* IV/2:733; IV 3.2:620.
133. Barth, *CD* IV/1:414.
134. Barth, *CD* IV/1:145.
135. Barth, *CD* IV/1:414, 418.
136. Barth, *CD* IV/1:413.

Second, sloth opposes the exaltation or ascension of Christ.[137] Sloth denies God's sanctifying works to humans. Barth claims that "reconciling grace is not merely justifying, but also wholly and utterly sanctifying and awakening and establishing grace."[138] Not only pride, which is "the heroic form of sin" but also sloth, which is "the unheroic and trivial form" of sin, is thus a "complete antithesis" against God.[139]

Barth elucidates that, "not only of evil action, but also of evil inaction; not only of the rash arrogance which is forbidden and reprehensible, but also of the tardiness and failure which are equally forbidden and reprehensible" are "also the counter-movement to the elevation which has come to man from God Himself in Jesus Christ."[140] "The divine direction and summons and claim" offered in Christ are rejected by the slothfulness of humans.[141] Sloth is significant to the present study and shall receive further attention, because Barth asserts that it leads to inhumanity.

Lastly, falsehood is in opposition to "the divine promise declared in the prophetic work of Jesus Christ."[142] Falsehood assails the truth of God in Jesus Christ. Barth says, "To be sure, its [the Word] light is resisted by darkness in the many forms of many sinister powers, all of which are connected with the sin of man, all empowered and unleashed by his falsehood, all to be taken seriously as opponents of the one Word of God."[143] Barth also asserts that if "pride and sloth are the works, falsehood is the word of the man of sin."[144]

All these forms of sin are "unmasked" in the light of Christ.[145] As Eberhard Busch attests, Barth is concerned with "the disappearance of a sense of sin, which goes hand in hand with the excesses of humanity's evil," which "was the main theme in his doctrine of sin."[146] The worst tragedy of sinners—"the sin in all sins" to use Barth's expression—is that they would "refuse the name of sinner."[147] In that respect, Busch summarizes Barth's

---

137. Barth, *CD* IV/2:405.
138. Barth, *CD* IV/2:403.
139. Barth, *CD* IV/2:403.
140. Barth, *CD* IV/2:403.
141. Barth, *CD* IV/2:406.
142. Barth, *CD* IV/3.1:434.
143. Barth, *CD* IV/3.1:100.
144. Barth, *CD* IV/3.1:373.
145. Barth, *CD* IV/3.1:371, 389.
146. Busch, *Great Passion*, 200.
147. Barth, *CD* II/2:751.

view as follows: "the decline in the knowledge of sin goes along with the decline in the knowledge of God."[148]

Barth's point here is that sinners of inhumanity would not sense their inhumanity and reject the fact that they are inhuman (the horizontal dimension) unless they acknowledge their realities in the light of Christ (the vertical dimension).

Nothingness

One innovative feature of Barth's doctrine of sin is the concept of nothingness. Barth explains that sin comes from nothingness. He describes nothingness as the "reality" that God utterly "separates Himself" and "does not will."[149] Barth considers Gen 1:2 as "the first and most impressive mention of nothingness in the Bible."[150] Nothingness "owes its existence to God," in that God "has not elected and willed, but ignored, rejected, excluded and judged, or as Schleiermacher would say, 'negated' it."[151]

God, the Creator, is "indeed eternally holy, pure, distinct and separated from the evil which is nothingness.[152]" Intrinsically, nothingness "opposes and resists" God, "himself and his work."[153] It is also to "disturb and destroy man and world," being the threat and cause of corruption to "world-occurrence," and that which makes humans become its "bearer and doer."[154]

Barth argues that the knowledge and reality of nothingness can only be recognized by the "light" of God revealed in Jesus Christ "at the heart of the Gospel."[155] It cannot be known "except as the object of God's activity as always a holy activity."[156] It is also by the "victory of Jesus Christ" at the Cross that the opposition and threat of nothingness against God's "lordship" and the created world were "overthrown" and "extirpated" "once for all."[157] Although nothingness has become "disarm[ed] and impotent" by "the truth of God," it "may still have standing and assume significance to the extent

---

148. Busch, *Great Passion*, 201.
149. Barth, *CD* III/3:351–52.
150. Barth, *CD* III/3:352.
151. Barth, *CD* III/3:327.
152. Barth, *CD* III/3:361.
153. Barth, *CD* III/3:327, 303.
154. Barth, *CD* III/3:327, 296, 307.
155. Barth, *CD* III/3:307, 311.
156. Barth, *CD* III/3:351.
157. Barth, *CD* III/3:295, 305, 363, 530.

that the final revelation of its destruction has not yet taken place and all creation must still await and expect it."[158]

In many Christian traditions, this explanation may sound as it indicates Satan. It seems that Barth's understanding of nothingness can be perceived as something similar to the depersonalized being of Satan. Barth says demons are "of nothingness" and "they derive from it."[159] Barth further describes demons as "always nothingness"—"they are nothingness in its dynamic, to the extent that it has form and power and movement and activity."[160] Sin is a concrete form of nothingness in that "in sin nothingness becomes man's own act, achievement and guilt."[161] Moreover, "sin itself is only man's irrational and inexplicable affirmation of the nothingness which God as Creator has negated."[162]

The Relational Aspect of Sin

Barth's understanding of sin underscores its relational aspect. Not only does the relationship with God receive Barth's attention but also the relationship with other humans does too. All three forms of sin, particularly sloth, illustrate this aspect. As Matt Jenson argues in his book *The Gravity of Sin*, Barth has "broadened" "the range of the metaphor," *homo incurvatus in se* (humanity curved in on itself), which is arguably one of the most influential concepts in describing sin, especially in his discussions of sloth.[163] Jensen asserts that Barth's "relational anthropology, which takes its cue from Christology, leads him to suggest that sin is characterized first and foremost by broken relationships in which people live for themselves rather than for God and others."[164]

Sin impairs the relations of humans because it leads to "enmity against God, fratricide, and self-destruction."[165] In Barth's words,

> In this role and function he is in every respect opposed to the will of God. He denies God, because Jesus Christ against whom he offends is God meeting him in the flesh in eternal love and

---

158. Barth, *CD* III/3:367, 529.
159. Barth, *CD* III/3:523.
160. Barth, *CD* III/3:523.
161. Barth, *CD* III/3:310.
162. Barth, *CD* III/2:143.
163. Jenson, *Gravity of Sin*, 131, 148–49, 173–75.
164. Jenson, *Gravity of Sin*, 131.
165. Barth, *CD* IV/1:400, 410.

for his salvation. He murders his brother because Jesus Christ is the fellowman in whose image God has made every man, in whom as the Head of the human race every man is either honoured or despised, and is now actually despised and denied and rejected and put to death. He destroys himself because Jesus Christ is the eternal Word of God by whom all things are made, and by the suppression of this Word man causes himself to fall and delivers himself up to judgment—as we see from the example of Judas.[166]

Sin is an ugly and improper form of self-love, and this self-love tends toward self-glorification. This sinful attempt will necessarily cause all relationships to collapse. Barth argues that a sinful human who is "wanting to be lord,"—self-glorifying—will find "himself [or herself] . . . in the process of a most serious self-alienation and self-destruction."[167] Barth uses the term "inhumanity" to describe this tragic status of humans' relationships.

The Problem of Inhumanity

WHAT IS INHUMANITY?

Inhumanity means being "without one's fellow-men" "in all our acts and attitudes."[168] It is "the denial of our humanity," asserting that "we can and should exercise" our humanity "apart from our fellow" humans.[169] By contrast, humanity is being with other humans, "orientated on them . . . thinking and willing and speaking and acting as men [and women]."[170] The genuine fellow-humanity is achieved when "one sees and understands the other as a man, or that he accepts him as his ordained companion and helper, and himself as his."[171]

To Barth, this is the way of being and living of Jesus. Because sloth is a denial of sanctification by Christ, inhumanity as a form of sloth is to reject following the "direction" and "movement" that Christ has shown and commanded.[172] Barth claims that, "Our sanctification consists in our

---

166. Barth, *CD* IV/1:399.
167. Barth, *CD* IV/1:421, 435.
168. Barth, *CD* IV/2:434.
169. Barth, *CD* IV/2:437.
170. Barth, *CD* IV/2:434.
171. Barth, *CD* IV/2:420.
172. Barth, *CD* IV/2:434.

participation in His sanctification as grounded in the efficacy and revelation of the grace of Jesus Christ."[173]

It means that inhumanity contradicts Christ, who has shown what it means to be the real man, the man of genuine humanity. As Barth argues in his relational anthropology, a person can be a real human only when he or she lives "as a fellow-[hu]man."[174]

The Cause of Inhumanity is Separation from God

The issue of inhumanity is related to one's relationship with God, for it contradicts who God is in nature—relationship-oriented God within Himself and to humans. It is a form of separation from God and the expression of one's sinfulness.

God has reconciled His relationship with humans in Christ. Regarding the notion of reconciliation, Barth asserts that, "In its literal and original sense the word ἀποκαταλλάσσειν ('to reconcile') means 'to exchange.'"[175] Such exchange indicates "the *exinanitio*, the abasement of God, and the *exaltatio*, the exaltation of man."[176] Barth further explains that,

> It was God who went into the far country, and it is man who returns home. Both took place in the one Jesus Christ. It is not, therefore, a matter of two different and successive actions, but of a single action in which each of the two elements is related to the other and can be known and understood only in this relationship: the going out of God only as it aims at the coming in of man; the coming in of man only as the reach and outworking of the going out of God; and the whole in its original and proper form only as the being and history of the one Jesus Christ.[177]

In Barth's thoughts, the first problem of the doctrine of reconciliation is the descension of Christ. It concerns the justification of humans. It is pride that rejects this activity of God. On the other hand, the second problem of the doctrine of reconciliation is the ascension of Christ, which relates to the sanctification of humans,[178] and again, it is sloth that denies this action of God. It is slothfulness that continuously hinders a person from

---

173. Barth, *CD* IV/2:517.
174. Barth, *CD* IV/2:434.
175. Barth, *CD* IV/2:21.
176. Barth, *CD* IV/2, 21.
177. Barth, *CD* IV/2:21.
178. Barth, *CD* IV/2:21.

resembling Christ and makes him or her become "withdrawn into himself [or herself]" and "self-interest[ed]."[179] This sloth takes different forms—"stupidity, inhumanity, and dissipation," which all take sloth as their "basis and cause."[180] In this respect, inhumanity emerges when one rejects the reconciling activity of God, particularly that related to the restoration of Christ's character and true humanity in us.

Nevertheless, to Barth, any attempt to eliminate inhumanity and restore fellow-humanity without knowing God will end in vain.[181] He refers to this as "fundamental stupidity."[182] In Barth's understanding, it is the relationship with God "which gives to his [or her] existence the character of humanity—his [her] relationship to his [her] fellow-men [and women]."[183] He further asserts that,

> It is God who guarantees this relationship. Its order has its basis in that of his relationship to God. Without this it cannot be maintained. The knowledge of the divine Other by whom he is confronted, and therefore the knowledge that this Other is the triune and not a lonely God, is the indispensable pre-supposition of the necessity, dignity, promise and claim of the other who also confronts him in the form of man. But the fool lacks this knowledge. He tries to evade it. It is foolishness to him. He thinks that he can replace it by his own better wisdom.[184]

In this sense, Barth warns that if one "tries to keep God at a distance, he [or she] will do so all the more emphatically in the case of his [her] equals."[185] Barth doubts that humans are capable of having "fellowship and partnership of I and Thou" and seeking their "brother" on their own without having "God to be . . . Father."[186] Barth's clear conclusion is as follows: "The necessary consequence of vertical self-withdrawal is horizontal self-withdrawal and isolation."[187] Barth's further thoughts are as follows:

> It is possible, and it will indeed take place, that he may need another man, and claim him, and try to exercise a far-reaching

---

179. Barth, *CD* IV/2:435.
180. Barth, *CD* IV/2:468, 495.
181. Barth, *CD* IV/2:420.
182. Barth, *CD* IV/2:420.
183. Barth, *CD* IV/2:420.
184. Barth, *CD* IV/2:420.
185. Barth, *CD* IV/2:420.
186. Barth, *CD* IV/2:420.
187. Barth, *CD* IV/2:420.

control over him. But this does not involve a genuine fellow-humanity. It does not mean that the one sees and understands the other as a man, or that he accepts him as his ordained companion and helper, and himself as his. On the contrary, it means a radical superiority over him, an emancipation from him which because it has the character of a needing, claiming and controlling in which the other may not readily acquiesce, necessarily has, and will sooner or later reveal, the character of opposition to and conflict with him. The solitary man is the potential, and in a more refined or blatant form the actual, enemy of all others. The outbreak of war between him and them is only a matter of time and occasion, and often enough it will be caused by a ludicrous accident. The stupidity of man, the false estimation of his own (in other respects very worthy and excellent) wisdom, wills that this should be the case, and inevitably calls for it. Without the knowledge of God, which the stupid man despises, there is no meaningful companionship between man and man, no genuine co-operation, no genuine sharing either of joy or sorrow, no true society. But work which is not co-operation is busy indolence. Joy which is not shared is empty amusement. Sorrow which is not shared is oppressive pain. The man who is not the fellow of others is no real man at all. And a society composed of men like this breaks up as soon as it is formed and even as the most zealous attempts are made to build and maintain it. But the stupidity of man calls for this. Even in its noblest forms humanity without the knowledge of God has in it always the seed of discord and inhumanity, and sooner or later this will emerge. From the vacuum where there is no "Glory to God in the highest" even the sincerest longing and loudest shouting for peace on earth will never lead to anything but new divisions. This is the first thing which all the concealment of human folly can never alter.[188]

Barth's argument here sounds quite unyielding. Acknowledging Barth's political advocacy of (religious or ethical) socialism, which he believed was more likely to correspond to fellow-humanity, one may wonder to what extent Barth did attach value to the effort of rebuilding humanity in a society without explicit knowledge of God. It is true that Barth had interest in and passion for the socialist movement, which he considered a social system corresponding to, or as an analogy of, the Gospel, yet he "distanced himself from secular socialists" for his idea was rooted in his theology.[189]

188. Barth, *CD* IV/2:420–21.
189. Chung, *Karl Barth*, 56.

To investigate this matter, one needs to be reminded that Barth's understanding of humanity is derived from his doctrine of God. The doctrine of the Trinity and God have shaped and offered a foundation for his theological anthropology, as explored above. Furthermore, Barth consistently identified the works in the realm of one's relationship with God such as knowledge of God, participation in Christ's humanity, or having *agape* love for God as the only sources that initiate and enable the restoration of one's fellow-humanity. Moreover, in Barth's mind, the service of the church is primarily witnessing Christ and His Gospel to the world no matter what forms it takes, because separation from God is the root of evil and suffering of sinful humans. With these points in mind, a comprehensive and accurate representation of Barth's theology on this issue is that without vertical reconciliation, there can be no true horizontal reconciliation.

Some Features of Inhumanity

Barth identifies three features of inhumanity that emerge as outcomes: uncontrollable power, contagiousness, and the concealment of inhumanity.

First, the influence of inhumanity becomes stronger when permitted. Inhumanity has "its outward aspect," which includes "the character of power."[190] This power, or force, of inhumanity is uncontrollable when "once unleashed, as in the activity or inactivity of our refusal, escapes our control, follows its own law and has its own dynamic."[191] Barth states,

> By renouncing our true humanity we do, of course, achieve a kind of liberation, an independence, a superior capacity to act, in the exercise of which we gain a peculiar advantage over others and seem to be the stronger. But even as we enjoy and assert it this power is strange and alien in relation to ourselves. It is stronger than we are. Our inhumanity sets us under a rule according to which every man's hand is necessarily against his brother's, and we are all subjects.[192]

In the beginning stage, the power of inhumanity begins with (1) "the omissions and actions of an indifferent association with one's neighbor to which there can be no juridical and hardly any moral objection," and then (2) it "becomes the secret or blatant oppression and exploitation of one's fellow" in which his fellow's "dignity, honour and right are actively or passively

---

190. Barth, *CD* IV/2:436.
191. Barth, *CD* IV/2:436.
192. Barth, *CD* IV/2:436.

violated."[193] Eventually, inhumanity brings us to the place of (3) "actual transgression" against our fellow humans—"stealing and robbery; murder in the legal sense; and finally war, which allows and commands almost everything that God has forbidden."[194] All of these are under the influence of the force of inhumanity, and they are "the same in essence."[195]

Second, inhumanity is "so supremely infectious."[196] Inhumanity "has such great powers of reproduction" and is easily spread among people if inhumanity is "lived by one [person]" because it challenges "others to live it."[197] Barth elaborates,

> One man imposes on another by the power won and exercised through great or little inhumanities because by its he raises the question why the other is so simple as not to exercise it himself. Is he not just as capable of doing so as anyone else? Indeed, when he is the accidental or intentional victim of someone else, he is given a legitimate reason to exercise it. Why should he be the fool? Why not repay like for like: indifference for indifference; threat for threat; pressure for pressure? Why not find a place for inhumanity in answer to inhumanity? Even the most pious man cannot live at peace if a bad neighbour will not let him. Why, then, should he remain a pious man, or the most pious? And in this way an endless series of aggressions and reprisals is initiated, as happens no less in the small sphere of personal relationships than in the greater of world-politics.[198]

Third, inhumanity conceals itself. It is "the concealment in which [hu]man is inhuman."[199] The concealment of inhumanity is evidence that inhumanity is a form of slothfulness because sloth makes it difficult to admit.[200]

Slothful humans conceal their inhumanity to be "justified" or to escape a sense of guilt and shame.[201] Inhumanity sometimes even disguises itself with philanthropy "as though it were genuinely human."[202] To Barth, it is one's hypocrisy: "The aim of hypocrisy is to conceal the inhumanity which

---

193. Barth, *CD* IV/2:436.
194. Barth, *CD* IV/2:436.
195. Barth, *CD* IV/2:436.
196. Barth, *CD* IV/2:436.
197. Barth, *CD* IV/2:436.
198. Barth, *CD* IV/2:436–37.
199. Barth, *CD* IV/2:437.
200. Barth, *CD* IV/2:437.
201. Barth, *CD* IV/2:437.
202. Barth, *CD* IV/2:439.

we will not confess."²⁰³ As one conceals one's inhumanity, however, the situation only worsens, because concealment strengthens inhumanity.²⁰⁴ Concealment is, therefore, "an element of sin itself."²⁰⁵

The only way that Barth suggests acknowledging the reality of inhumanity in us is coming to the light of Christ. The acknowledgment of sin is consequent upon the acknowledgement of Christ.²⁰⁶ As previously mentioned in the discussion of sin, Barth focuses on the issue of losing "a sense of sin" and "refusing the name of sinner" by sinners in his reflection on sin.²⁰⁷ Barth believes it is impossible to realize the reality of our sin, and inhumanity in particular, because they conceal themselves. To Barth, every aspect of inhumanity—identification, causes, effects, and even solutions—can all be unveiled by the knowledge of God. Barth's own solution to inhumanity is thus theological rather than "sociological," "psychological," or "pedagogical."²⁰⁸

Restoration of Fellow-Humanity by Being Reconciled with God

The entire theological discussion of Barth on the restoration of fellow-humanity is established upon his conclusion from the previous section: the inhumanity of humans is derived from separation from God who exists in relations of love within Himself and to us. Stated differently, Barth would agree that vertical reconciliation initiates, enables, and achieves horizontal reconciliation. This argument is made based on several premises; for example, the two dimensions of reconciliation are indivisible, as Barth claimed. Furthermore, one will not have true horizontal reconciliation with fellow humans unless vertically reconciled with God. When one is reconciled with God, the fruit of being reconciled with one's fellow humans is supposed to be there.

In this section, which discusses Barth's theology on the issue of resolving inhumanity, the following subjects are examined. First, the premise of inseparable dimensions of reconciliation is briefly explored. Then, a further theological and ethical discussion is presented on how there can be no horizontal reconciliation without vertical reconciliation. Lastly, Barth's

203. Barth, *CD* IV/2:437–38.
204. Barth, *CD* IV/2:437.
205. Barth, *CD* IV/1:436.
206. Barth, *CD* IV/3.1:369
207. Barth, *CD* II/2:751; Busch, *Great Passion*, 200.
208. Barth, *CD* IV/2:435.

reflections on how being reconciled with God enables horizontal reconciliation are examined.

The Dimensions of Reconciliation are Indivisible

As most scholars acknowledge when they discuss the dimensions of reconciliation, Barth similarly suggests a picture of reconciliation as follows: "the vertical line is atoning work of God in Jesus Christ," "the horizontal is the object of that work; man and humanity" or "of the Church," and "the Christology is like a vertical line meeting a horizontal."[209]

In Barth's thought, these two lines of reconciliation are indivisible, as demonstrated by his discussions on the doctrine of the Trinity, inhumanity, and Christians' love. It can also be inferred from his discussion on justification and sanctification. As previously discussed, to Barth, justification is an issue of the first problem of the doctrine of reconciliation, the descension of Christ, and sanctification is related to the second problem, the ascension of Christ. Although both are the divine activity of God toward humans, which unmask the sinfulness of humans, pride and sloth respectively, Barth includes inhumanity as a central topic in his discussion of sanctification. This is because sanctification involves one's response to God as well as one's relationship with other humans.

Barth's primary argument on the relationship between justification and sanctification is that they are distinguished but not to be separated. Barth discusses how the two are distinguishable "different moments" and "two different aspects of the one event of salvation," accomplished together at "the one redemptive occurrence," "wholly and immediately with the other."[210] They "are not identical, nor are the concepts interchangeable."[211] Simultaneously, however, they "are only two moments and aspects of one and the same action, they do belong inseparably together."[212] Both are found in Christ without separation. Barth asserts that the "self-humiliating Son of God" and "the exalted Son of Man" are in "one actuality of Jesus Christ and the Holy Spirit."[213]

Barth contends that if we "ignore the mutual relationship" between the two, we will face "false statements" and "corresponding errors in practice."[214]

209. Barth, *CD* IV/1:643.
210. Barth, *CD* IV/2:501–3.
211. Barth, *CD* IV/2:503.
212. Barth, *CD* IV/2:505.
213. Barth, *CD* IV/2:505.
214. Barth, *CD* IV/2:505.

For instance, justification without sanctification is "the idea of a God who works in isolation, and His 'cheap grace' (D. Bonhoeffer) and therefore an indolent quietism"; on the other hand, sanctification without justification is related to "a favoured man who works in isolation, and therefore to an illusory activism."[215] Barth questions the validity of a divided understanding of justification and sanctification as follows:

> We have only to ask ourselves: What is the forgiveness of sins (however we understand it) if it is not directly accompanied by an actual liberation from the committal of sin? What is divine sonship if we are not set in the service of God and the brethren? What is the hope of the universal and definitive revelation of the eternal God without striving for provisional and concrete lesser ends? What is faith without obedience? And conversely: What is a liberation for new action which does not rest from the very outset and continually on the forgiveness of sins? Who can and will serve God but the child of God who lives by the promise of His unmerited adoption? How can there be a confident expectation and movement in time without the basis of eternal hope? How can there be any serious obedience which is not the obedience of faith?[216]

Examining Barth's claim on justification and sanctification helps one comprehend a significant premise of his view on the relationship between vertical and horizontal reconciliation. Justification and sanctification are "in the *simul* of the one divine will and action": "justification is first as basis and second as presupposition, sanctification first as aim and second as consequence."[217] They are "the two moments and aspects" of one loving and saving act of Jesus Christ, which "is justifying and sanctifying grace."[218]

Barth's doctrine of reconciliation seems to unfold based on this premise of the indivisibility of justification and sanctification. As *analogia relationis* (analogy of relation) implies, as previously mentioned, human agents should stand in continuity with what God has done to humanity (the economic Trinity) and participate in and imitate it—Barth's understanding of ethics.[219] This correspondence is based on the premise of indivisibility. Horizontal reconciliation, which is inseparable from its basis, vertical reconciliation, cannot maintain itself apart from the basis. As discussed

215. Barth, *CD* IV/2:505.
216. Barth, *CD* IV/2:505.
217. Barth, *CD* IV/2:508.
218. Barth, *CD* IV/2:508–9.
219. Barth, *CD* III/2:220.

in chapter 2, no scholar who participates in the dialogue of reconciliation would disagree with Barth that the two dimensions are not to be separated. However, not everyone seems to be as resolute as Barth, who asserts that there will be no true horizontal reconciliation without vertical reconciliation. This is discussed in the following section.

No Horizontal Reconciliation Without Vertical Reconciliation: Shaping Ethics as Dogmatics

The importance of knowledge of God cannot be overestimated in Barth's discussion of restoring fellow-humanity, nor in the entire theological anthropology and ethics. This is probably because Barth finds God to be the source of humanity—being oriented to others—and considers inhumanity to be the sinfulness (slothfulness) of humans being separated from God. The influence of inhumanity in humans will not, therefore, cease to exist unless they accept and participate in God's redemptive work, which has defeated the problem of sin.

According to this point of view, Barth warns that no matter how many "noble forms" the humanity "without the knowledge of God" has, inhumanity will eventually "emerge" in the humanity.[220] Barth asserts that "the dissolution of our relationship with our fellows" is "the necessary consequence of the dissolution of our relationship with God."[221]

It seems that Barth's whole reflection of ethics is established upon this view. In *Ethics*, Barth says that ethics is "an auxiliary discipline" related to theology, asking "the question of the goodness of human conduct."[222] Barth advocates dogmatic ethics, which considers human action as a proper response to God's redemption. Barth persistently denies the complete validity of human's moral consciousness apart from the command of God.[223] Ethics itself is not self-evident apart from God's command. Barth regards such approaches that underscore humans' own inwardness, moral consciousness, or conscience as anthropologically deficient because they "envisage" humans' "interior moral life as existing in at least relative isolation from the determining presence of God."[224]

---

220. Barth, *CD* IV/2:421.
221. Barth, *CD* IV/2:441.
222. Barth, *Ethics*, 3, 18.
223. Webster, *Barth's Moral Theology*, 42.
224. Webster, *Barth's Moral Theology*, 59.

However, it is not true that Barth has denied the entire validity of non-Christian ethics.[225] As Busch comments, Barth "did not promote a specifically 'Christian' ethics detached from" secular ethics.[226] Barth thinks Christian ethics can be opened in its discussion with non-Christian ethics, and it can still "learn" from it.[227] Nevertheless, it is indisputable that Barth is skeptical that ethical questions can be answered solely by humans' moral-consciousness. Barth argues that "the grace of God protests against all man-made ethics as such," albeit "positively."[228] Thus, Busch sums up Barth's attitude as "a critical openness."[229]

In Barth's mind, the very attempt of humans to answer ethical questions of what is good and evil *ironically* "confirms" they are sinful and "trying to escape the grace of God."[230] He states that, "Strange as it may seem, that general conception of ethics coincides exactly with the conception of sin."[231] "To go behind" God's "divine ethics," which is attested in Christ "is quite impossible."[232] As true humanity is revealed and actualized in its full extent in Christ, ethics—which is humans responses to God's will and command—is also answered entirely in Jesus Christ: Jesus "does not *give* the answer . . . He *is* the answer."[233]

As Busch indicates, Barth keeps problematizing that ethics has been "emancipated" "from theology"—it is "the law divorced from the Gospel."[234] Barth believes ethics is supposed to be shaped by dogmatics as a dogmatic concern. In light of dogmatics, "good" human conduct can be discussed.

In another of his books, *The Theology of John Calvin*, Barth agrees with Calvin about the anthropological efforts apart from the dogmatic foundation being in vain; he contends that it is only in light of the knowledge of God that we can obtain "full and sufficient" knowledge of humanity, and "everything else . . . is simply a development, expansion, and elucidation of this original knowledge."[235] If one considers ethics as self-evident based on humans' own moral consciousness or conscience, there will be confusion

---

225. Barth, CD II/2:517.
226. Busch, *Great Passion*, 154.
227. Barth, CD II/2:518; Busch, *Great Passion*, 155.
228. Barth, CD II/2:517.
229. Busch, *Great Passion*, 155.
230. Barth, CD II/2:518.
231. Barth, CD II/2:518.
232. Barth, CD II/2:517–18.
233. Barth, CD II/2:517.
234. Busch, *Great Passion*, 155–56.
235. Barth, *Theology of John Calvin*, 162–63.

and caprice because they are not "non-reflective voice of our own" nor "less caught up in the immediacy of desire and action."[236] Barth warns of this as follows: "In conscience, our own voice is undoubtedly *God's voice*."[237] Webster supports Barth's point, stating that, "For most of the moral traditions of modernity, philosophical and theological, conscience has been an authoritarian and autonomous faculty of self-governance, increasingly detached from rational consideration of moral order."[238]

Instead, Barth asserts that ethics has its place fundamentally in the notion of the divine judgment of God, which is executed in correspondence with the command of God. Barth says that "the ethical reflection" can be understood "in awareness of the absolute *givenness* of the command," which is "itself the truth of the good" from God.[239] Moreover, "*Good* means *sanctified by God*."[240] This is a primary rationale of ethics in Barth's thought. Barth's reflection on human conduct is shaped by his theological understanding of the divine judgment. As Webster comments, "the significance of the notion of divine judgment in the *Ethics* can hardly be overestimated."[241] Webster names Barth's anthropology as "the-anthropology."[242] In his anthropology, Barth recognizes and reshapes ethics into a theological and dogmatic topic. Webster explains that

> Barth's ethics tends to assume that moral problems are resolvable by correct theological description of moral space. And such description involves much more than describing the moral consciousnesses of agents. A Christianly successful moral ontology must be a depiction of the world of human action as it is enclosed and governed by the creative, redemptive, and sanctifying work of God in Christ, present in the power of the Holy Spirit.[243]

---

236. Webster, *Barth's Moral Theology*, 59.
237. Barth, *Ethics*, 480.
238. Webster, *Barth's Moral Theology*, 58.
239. Barth, *Ethics*, 76.
240. Barth, *Ethics*, 16.
241. Webster, *Barth's Moral Theology*, 45.
242. Webster, *Barth's Ethics of Reconciliation*, 3; Webster, *Barth's Moral Theology*, 3–4. Unlike common perceptions that Barth has not engaged ethics in a serious manner, but only emphasized dogmatics in his theology, John Webster asserts ethics has consistently been an important "theological theme" in Barth's theology not only in his mature works, but in his early writings "as early as 1923." Webster, *Barth's Moral Theology*, 6, 11. If one wants to explore the development of Barth's theological reflections on human agency, see *Barth's Moral Theology* by John Webster.
243. Webster, *Barth's Ethics of Reconciliation*, 2.

In this respect, the issue of inhumanity is a theological concern, and so too is the restoration of humanity. The problem of inhumanity based on humans' "slothful and sinful being" will not be resolved by "any admonition" or "counter-measures," or "any psychology or individual or social pedagogics," or "any social revolution or individual conversion however radical."[244] In other words, horizontal reconciliation cannot be achieved without vertical reconciliation. Barth suggests that inhumanity is "necessarily and indissolubly connected with its godlessness."[245]

As discussed previously, in Barth's understanding of sin, the realization of sin "derives subsequently and retrospectively from a knowledge of the existence and work of Jesus Christ."[246] Sin can be "known in its nature, reality, implications, and consequences as it is opposed, vanquished and done away by Him [Christ]."[247] This is why Barth argues that the "doctrine of sin cannot be established, expounded or developed independently of or prior to the doctrine of reconciliation. It forms an integral part of the latter."[248] Therefore, efforts to investigate and remove the nature of inhumanity without holding the Gospel of Christ are "incomplete" and impossible.[249] Again, in Barth's view, there can be no true horizontal reconciliation among humans without vertical reconciliation with God.

In sum, Barth has consistently claimed that achieving genuine horizontal reconciliation with others through restoring fellow-humanity is entirely conditioned by knowing God and being reconciled with Him through Christ. This knowledge enables one to perform a free act of true love to neighbors through one's restored fellow-humanity. Once more, Barth's summarizing remarks are as follows: "it is God who guarantees" our "relationship" with "fellow" humans and "without this [relationship with God] it cannot be maintained."[250]

Vertical Reconciliation Necessarily Leads to Horizontal Reconciliation

Having discussed Barth's first point on the relationship between vertical and horizontal reconciliation (there is no true horizontal reconciliation without

---

244. Barth, *CD* IV/2:435.
245. Barth, *CD* IV/2:435–36.
246. Barth, *CD* IV/3.1:369.
247. Barth, *CD* IV/3.1:369.
248. Barth, *CD* IV/3.1:369.
249. Barth, *CD* IV/1:106.
250. Barth, *CD* IV/2:420.

vertical reconciliation), this study must now explore his second point. This is that true vertical reconciliation must bear the fruit of horizontal reconciliation, which is a necessary consequence of genuine vertical reconciliation with relationship-oriented God. Putting the two points together, Barth's essential idea can be addressed as the two dimensions of reconciliation having their genuineness and completeness verified by each other's existence. This inference corresponds to Barth's own idea of theological ethics: "dogmatics itself is ethics; and ethics is also dogmatics."[251] Barth's first point applies to "ethics is dogmatics" and the second point applies to "dogmatics is ethics."[252]

According to John Webster, Barth's dogmatics is "intrinsically an ethical dogmatics," which advocates that "true man is characterized by . . . good action."[253] Webster admits some critiques of Barth exist that he has reduced humans to "the utterly passive recipient of divine disclosure" and "God is sole agent."[254] However, Webster maintains that when one explores Barth's anthropology, theological epistemology, and moral ontology, humans are not merely recipients but active agents.[255] Although Barth rejects the idea of humans as self-initiated moral agents, he still considers them to be corresponding moral agents to God.

Webster quotes Barth by saying that God's grace is "in action" that "applies to us, affects us," and furthermore, "His action does not revolve within Himself, but is aimed at *our* action, at getting our action into conformity with His."[256] In this sense, Webster regards Barth's claim as saying that "divine grace is not simply information, but action-eliciting divine activity."[257] In Christian love, Barth contends that loving neighbor "on the horizontal level" is not "merely conscious, but ready and indeed voluntary" and not "mere feelings," "mere outlook," or "mere words," but "an active being"; thus, it becomes "a perfect counterpart to the vertical coming together of man with God."[258]

Correspondingly, in his book *The Christian Life*, Barth construes the gracious God as the commanding God.[259] Ethics concerns a person's response when he or she encounters the commanding God; the response

---

251. Barth, CD I/2:793.
252. Barth, CD I/2:793.
253. Webster, *Barth's Ethics of Reconciliation*, 4.
254. Webster, *Barth's Ethics of Reconciliation*, 6.
255. Webster, *Barth's Ethics of Reconciliation*, 4–7.
256. Webster, *Barth's Ethics of Reconciliation*, 7; Barth, *God, Grace, and Gospel*, 8–9.
257. Webster, *Barth's Ethics of Reconciliation*, 7.
258. Barth, *CD* IV/1:106–7.
259. Barth, *Christian Life*, 34; Webster, *Barth's Ethics of Reconciliation*, 174.

can only be two options—obey or disobey.²⁶⁰ In this sense, ethics points to "the event of the encounter between God and man" and "to the mystery of the specific divine ordering, directing, and commanding and of the specific human obeying or disobeying."²⁶¹

Barth understands that the fellowship between God and humans is between commanding God and obeying humans.²⁶² Dogmatics, therefore, always includes ethics, which should be "coherent with" God's divine action.²⁶³ As Webster explains, it is because Barth believes that "the narration of God's mighty deeds" should always proceed with "the narration of the corresponding deeds of God's fellow-workers, for grace evokes correspondences."²⁶⁴

God's grace *evokes* humans' correspondences, leading them to participate in, imitate, and repeat what God has done to them in the vertical dimension. Barth identifies two types of God's activity that evoke humans' correspondence. Barth discusses the first type through Christology: there is the power of the resurrection of Jesus Christ. The power of Jesus Christ is the peacemaking power,²⁶⁵ and Barth suggests that the power of (the resurrection of) Christ renews our fellow-humanity. In Christ, one has one's (motivation for) inhumanity healed.

> When this power [of reconciliation in Christ] at work, peace is established in all these dimensions. A fine skin begins to grow over all these wounds, open and painful though they still are. They are not yet healed. But it is the sign and beginning of their healing. The evil conflict will not be interminable. It can no longer be waged with a final seriousness, whether it is against God, our fellow-men, or ourselves.²⁶⁶

As previously stated, Barth regards inhumanity as the sinfulness (slothfulness) of humans, meaning that slothful humans are not free to practice humanity. The power of Christ will cease the power and contagiousness of inhumanity, heal the wounds caused by each other's inhumanity, and restore fellow-humanity in oneself.

---

260. Barth, *Christian Life*, 34.
261. Barth, *Christian Life*, 34.
262. Barth, *Christian Life*, 30.
263. Webster, *Barth's Ethics of Reconciliation*, 9.
264. Webster, *Barth's Ethics of Reconciliation*, 8.
265. Barth, *CD* IV/2:315.
266. Barth, *CD* IV/2:314.

Barth explains that the power of the resurrection of Jesus Christ "impels us to peace with God and our fellows and ourselves."[267] Because God's activity of justification is inseparably related to sanctification, a human justified by God in Christ is necessarily led into participating sanctification by Christ overcoming one's slothful inhumanity.[268]

Thus, one's fellow-humanity is fully restored and actualized in Christ. In this "actualization" of humanity that is "found" in Christ, "humanity means to be bound and committed to other" humans.[269] Barth discusses this as follows:

> In Him, therefore, man is turned not merely to God but to other men. In Him he is quite open and willing and ready and active for them. In Him he gives glory to God alone, but in so doing sees and affirms and exalts the dignity and right and claim of the other man. In Him he does not live only in fellowship with God, but in so doing he also lives in fellowship with other men. In Him, in this man, God Himself is for all other men. This cannot be said of any other. In the fact that as He is with us He is also for us He remains exalted above all. In this exaltation above all He is also a direction for all; a summons to participate, as thankful recipients of His grace, in the humanity actualised in Him, to share this humanity with a concrete orientation on the fellow-man, the neighbour, the brother. To receive His Holy Spirit is to receive this direction and accept this summons. It is to see oneself in Him as one who is elected and created and determined for existence in this humanity.[270]

The second type of God's activity that evokes humans' correspondence that Barth identifies is pneumatological. Barth asserts it is "the quickening power of the Holy Spirit" that enables oneself to practice true love in correspondence of God's *agape* love, which is not self-interested (as *eros* love is), but self-giving.[271] Barth states that

> The primary and decisive difference—and here we must anticipate—is that it is in the quickening power of the Holy Spirit, and therefore in a new act of God who is man's Creator and Lord, that in his life-act and individual actions a man can actually love in the Christian sense and thus be a true man

---

267. Barth, *CD* IV/2:315.
268. Barth, *CD* IV/2:517.
269. Barth, *CD* IV/2:432.
270. Barth, *CD* IV/2:432–33.
271. Barth, *CD* IV/2:752.

in this positive way; whereas the new thing about *eros*-love can consist only in the inconceivable and absurd and materially impossible fact that man arbitrarily entangles himself in a contradiction of his own creaturely nature, of himself, and therefore of God and his neighbour.[272]

Later in the same volume, Barth similarly claims that Christian communities should perform "new and supremely astonishing" acts "to the world" "because they rest on an endowment with extraordinary capacities."[273] The astonishing acts denote acts of *agape* love, which Barth considers impossible for humans without the knowledge of God. Then, "the extraordinary capacities" mean the "quickening power of the Holy Spirit."[274] Barth indicates that "this distinctive reality"—*agape* love—can be obtained through "the work of the Holy Spirit," or in other words, when "awakened by the Holy Spirit."[275]

In this respect, Barth argues that if there were no evoking works of God through the power of Christ and the Holy Spirit, which should necessarily be given with reconciliation with God, one ought to examine the genuineness of one's vertical reconciliation. Barth seems to regard one's horizontal reconciliation as a significant sign of authentic vertical reconciliation.

Referring to 1 John 4:20, Barth argues that without the horizontal dimension of reconciliation with fellow humans, vertical reconciliation "would not be vertical," which "inexorably includes" the horizontal dimension.[276] Barth expounds his argument in the following manner:

> If I choose myself in my isolation from other men, *eo ipso* [by that itself] I enter the sphere of the even more terrible isolation in which God can no longer be my God. If they are indifferent to me, I am involved wittingly or unwittingly in indifference to Him. If I can despise men, the praise which I may bring ever so willingly and joyfully to God will stick in my throat. If I merely exploit my neighbour according to my own needs, I will certainly think that I can do the same with God . . . In short, if I am inhuman, I am also stupid and foolish and godless. The great crisis in which all worship and piety and adoration and prayer and theology constantly finds itself derives of course from the question whether and how far in these things we really have to do with

272. Barth, *CD* IV/2:747.
273. Barth, *CD* IV/2:828.
274. Barth, *CD* IV/2:828.
275. Barth, *CD* IV/2:826.
276. Barth, *CD* IV/2:441–42.

the true and living God who reveals Himself in His Word, and not with an idol. But this question is decided concretely in practice by another one which is inseparable from it—whether and how far in these things we come before God together and not apart from and against one another. True Christianity cannot be a private Christianity, i.e., a rapacious Christianity. Inhumanity at once makes it a counterfeit Christianity. It is not merely a superficial blemish. It cuts at the very root of . . . witness which Christianity owes to the world.[277]

To Barth, no horizontal reconciliation stands without vertical reconciliation, yet at the same time, the converse is also true—one has not been truly reconciled with God if one remains inhuman. This is based on his understanding that a sinful and inhuman human does not know God, who is relationship-oriented. Barth discusses further:

If man wills and chooses inhumanity, he can only imagine that he can believe and attain to a knowledge of God . . . At the point where it is a matter of God and His words and acts, where there can and should and must be the *intellectus fidei* [understanding of faith], he is dealing with pure illusions and myths. Without one's fellow-man, God is an illusion, a myth. He may be the God of Holy Scripture, and we may call upon Him as the Yahweh of Israel and the Father of Jesus Christ, but He is an idol in whom we certainly cannot believe.[278]

Because God exists in relation within Himself and with us in His free grace, every human being exists in relation with God as well as with fellow people—the I and Thou relationship.[279] If an individual truly knows God, who is relational by nature, then he or she would not withdraw into him or herself but be oriented toward fellow humans.[280]

---

277. Barth, *CD* IV/2:441–42.

278. Barth, *CD* IV/2:442–43.

279. Barth, *CD* IV/2:443. This could possibly be influenced by Martin Buber's I-Thou personalism as Wolfhart Pannenberg and others point out. Schults, *Reforming theological Anthropology*, 118; Jenson *Gravity of Sin*, 153. Nevertheless, Barth claims that he understands I-Thou relationship based on the doctrine of the Trinity. Barth, *CD* III/2:218; Barth, *CD* III/1:185.

280. Barth, *CD* IV/2:443.

Summary: Twofold Love of Christianity

Having discussed the two previous sections, it can be concluded that Christians' love is twofold: love to God and love to neighbors. The two dimensions of reconciliation are truly indivisible, as was presented previously. Barth has been clear that Christian love always includes these two dimensions.

Barth maintains that "Christian love" for neighbors "will not take place without love to God." Christian love "can only follow, and must follow, this prior love [love to God]" and "love to God . . . evokes love to the neighbour and the brother."[281] Then, Christian love "would fail altogether . . . if it did not take this twofold form, the one having priority as the great commandment of Mk. 12:29f."[282] The two "stand side by side" as the "love for God" does "entail" "love for the neighbor."[283]

Barth understands that the history of salvation is not exclusively vertical as based on "the acts of God's love," but it includes "the corresponding act of humans"—love for God and mutual love to each other "on the horizontal plane" as well.[284] On mutual love, Barth expounds as follows:

> It takes place unavoidably that there is a definite connexion of these men among themselves posited in and with their twofold passive and active relationship to God. This connexion is their mutual love; the love of each for his neighbour. It is their love for one another because they are those who together are loved by God and love Him in return. Since it is a matter of love on the vertical plane, how can it be anything else on the horizontal? The two planes are distinct and must not be confused. But they are also inseparable. Liberation for God is one thing, and liberation for our fellow-men another.[285]

The love for God necessarily leads to love for neighbors—they walk "side by side."[286] The former initiates, thereby enabling and achieving the latter. In sum, in Barth's words, "Christian love for God necessarily means Christian love for the neighbor."[287]

---

281. Barth, *CD* IV/1:106.
282. Barth, *CD* IV/1:106.
283. Barth, *CD* IV/2:809.
284. Barth, *CD* IV/2:809.
285. Barth, *CD* IV/2:809–10.
286. Barth, *CD* IV/2:810.
287. Barth, *CD* IV/2:811.

The Significance of Knowing the Personality of the Reconciler: Rejecting the Abstract Notion of Reconciliation

Barth has underlined the significance of knowing the concrete historical event of Jesus Christ in grasping reconciliation. Barth rejects both the legitimacy and possibility of seeking reconciliation as an abstract notion and understanding reconciliation as an attainable goal apart from the Reconciler, Christ. He asserts that reconciliation can be obtained through knowing the Reconciler. This claim can be understood in the context of Barth's denial of natural theology. During his lifetime, he consistently refuted natural theology. This offers a foundational premise and shapes the methodology of Barth's theology—the theology of revelation.

In *The Epistle to the Romans*, Barth accentuates that God is the "wholly other" from humans in His divinity, as well as unreachable from the human side.[288] Thus, God's self-revelation becomes essential. His emphasis on the divinity of God was modified in his later years, as he confesses in *The Humanity of God*.[289] However, referring to his mature theology in *The Church Dogmatics*, Barth had not changed his position that knowing the Reconciler is essential for understanding the message of reconciliation.

Barth, therefore, disputes the understanding of "The peace between God and man" in a "general" sense.[290] Rather, he highlights that it is "the specific thing itself" and "concrete thing which is indicated by the name of Jesus Christ and not by any other name."[291] "The eternal Word of God" cannot be discussed "*in abstracto.*"[292] This is because the attempt goes against "the [free] decision of God" and this decision "was also made bindingly, inescapably and irrevocably," and "We cannot, therefore, go back on it."[293] Barth continues:

> We must not ignore it [Jesus is the free decision of God] and imagine a "Logos in itself" which does not have this content and form, which is the eternal Word of God without this form and content. We could only imagine such a Logos. Like Godhead abstracted from its revelation and acts, it would necessarily be an empty concept which we would then, of course, feel obliged to fill with all kinds of contents of our own arbitrary invention.

---

288. Barth, *Epistle of Romans*, 107, 240.
289. Barth, *Humanity of God*, 42.
290. Barth, *CD* IV/1:21.
291. Barth, *CD* IV/1:21.
292. Barth, *CD* IV/1:52.
293. Barth, *CD* IV/1:52.

Under the title of a λόγος ἄσαρκος [discarnate Word] we pay homage to a *Deus absconditus* [hidden God] and therefore to some image of God which we have made for ourselves.[294]

Because reconciliation between God and humans is "actualized in a history," if an individual attempts "to grasp it as supra-historical or non-historical truth," he or she will fail.[295] The truth of reconciliation does not evade the true Witness, Jesus Christ; instead, it is attested by Him.[296] However, confronting the Reconciler can be painful and even offensive to the sinner. Barth explains why humans tend to evade the Reconciler as follows:

> The truth which He attests is the reconciliation of the world to God, but this reconciliation as effected in Him. It is the covenant between God and man, but this covenant as fulfilled in Him . . . He attests this *truth* as He attests Himself. But He attests it as He attests *Himself* . . . The painful and scandalising thing which man wishes to avoid is the identity between this man and this truth, between this truth and this man. For in its identity with this man the truth makes an attack on him which it would not make if it were the mere notion of intercourse between God and man. And in His identity with the truth this man claims and indeed already possesses and exercises a power over him which He could not have, and which could thus be evaded, if He were merely its supreme manifestation or most impressive symbol. Since this man is identical with the truth and the truth with Him, the encounter with the truth and therefore with Him—we refer to the encounter with Jesus Christ—becomes an absolutely vital, binding, decisive and even revolutionary affair. That is why the man of sin would like to escape it. He cannot accept this identity, and since he cannot alter the fact of it he tries to reinterpret it, to transform it into non-identity. The truth may be accepted on the or side, the man who attests it on the other, and thus separated they cannot violate or offend him, nor cause him any discomfort, nor demand any decision . . . This is the work of falsehood. It is by cleaving their unity that it tries to manipulate the truth and the true Witness . . . To reject their unity is to reject the truth with the true Witness and *vice versa*.[297]

In sum, it seems evident that Barth opposes conceptualizing the doctrine of reconciliation outside of the Christological lens. The vertical reconciliation

294. Barth, *CD* IV/1:52.
295. Barth, *CD* IV/1:157.
296. Barth, *CD* IV/3.1:440–41.
297. Barth, *CD* IV/3.1:440–41.

between God and humanity is "noetically" and "ontically" in "the history" of Jesus Christ.[298] An abstract notion of vertical reconciliation with God cannot be found in reality. Reconciliation "does not take place, and therefore cannot be seen or understood, apart from Him or in any way in itself."[299] In the previous section, Barth maintained that without vertical reconciliation, there can be no horizontal reconciliation. In this section, Barth's argument is that vertical reconciliation is not obtained through an abstract notion of reconciliation, but only through the concrete history of Jesus Christ, the Reconciler. Therefore, discussing the church's engagement with God's ministry of reconciliation in Barth's thought is appropriate.

The Witness of Reconciliation by The Church

In Barth's view, the church is both a sign of and witness to God's reconciliation. The church is a sign of the people who are reconciled with God and living under the reign of the kingdom of God. This tells the story of God. With some variations, the phrase that Barth uses to illustrate this is "God loves us and we can love Him in return."[300] The church is "a sign of what God is and does for all and what all may be and do for God."[301] It "can and must be" "a reminder" of "the kingdom of God," which is "already set up on earth in Jesus Christ."[302] The church, therefore, "can and should show" the world this divine "order" given by God.[303] As examined above, the reconciled relationships that the church should show to the world include both with God and with fellow humans.[304]

Simultaneously, the church is also a witness; *kerygma* of the church.[305] Barth argues that the world "stands in urgent and painful need of the revelation of Jesus Christ in the power of His Holy Spirit as the revelation of its own true reality."[306] Thus, the church community ought to "proclaim the name of Jesus Christ as the word of reconciliation, as the good news of the kingdom, of the saving *coup d'état* of God within it."[307]

298. Barth, *CD* IV/1:158.
299. Barth, *CD* IV/3.1:39.
300. Barth, *CD* IV/2:812, 813, 814, 816, 818.
301. Barth, *CD* IV/2:814.
302. Barth, *CD* IV/2:721.
303. Barth, *CD* IV/2:721.
304. Barth, *CD* IV/2:828.
305. Barth, *CD* IV/3.1:221.
306. Barth, *CD* IV/3.2:620.
307. Barth, *CD* IV/3.2:620.

Witnessing the Gospel is a primary ministry of the church. According to Barth, the witness of the church "has to confront the world, whether implicitly or explicitly, whether in words or in acts or attitudes, yet unequivocally and resolutely" and "tell it [the witness of Christ] openly to the world."[308] If not, the meaning of the church's existence will be "renounced."[309]

In *The Church Dogmatics*, Barth expounds the meaning and manner of witness by the church in several places. First, witness is the proclamation of the Gospel. This means giving "information" of "the truth and reality."[310] The information that Christians witness—"attest and guarantee"—to their neighbors is that "God loves them, and that they may love Him in return."[311]

Barth's understanding of the church's witness does not merely include but also highlights the proclamation of the Gospel as a primary ministry of the church.[312] Barth states that "the ministry" of the church community is "essentially and in all forms and circumstances" "the declaration of the Gospel," which is the first.[313] Furthermore, he states,

> Whatever else the community may plan, undertake and do, whatever else it may or may not accomplish, it has always to introduce into the sphere of world-occurrence and to disclose to men a human historical fact which, not itself the kingdom of God but indicating it as a likeness, corresponds and points to the divine historical fact which constitutes the content of the Gospel.[314]

In this sense, the Gospel should not simply be "presupposed" or "left far behind" even when the church talks about ethics.[315] According to Barth, "Ethics, too, must testify directly to the atonement which man himself does not make, but which God has made in him as His own work, by giving him direction in Jesus Christ."[316]

The second form of witness by the church is acts of love. Christians' love for their neighbor is basically "a witness of God" because "what can take place on this [horizontal] level . . . can be only a reflection of what takes place on the vertical level" and "can be only a copy of it."[317] It should be a

---

308. Barth, *CD* IV/3.2:621.
309. Barth, *CD* IV/3.2:621.
310. Barth, *CD* IV/2, 812.
311. Barth, *CD* IV/2, 814, 815.
312. Barth, *CD* IV/2, 812–13.
313. Barth, *CD* IV/3.2, 844.
314. Barth, *CD* IV/3.2, 844.
315. Barth, *CD* IV/1, 101.
316. Barth, *CD* IV/1:101.
317. Barth, *CD* IV/2:815.

"true" and "visible" "reflection and imitation" of God's love;[318] otherwise, the church's witness becomes a "lie."[319] In the words of Barth,

> The function of the love for the neighbour and brother which corresponds to God's love and the love for God is thus to be the ministry of human witness in which the one guarantees to the other the turning of God's love to His people and the turning of His people to God, giving him a visible reflection and therefore reminder of the twofold movement of and in which this people and within it all its members live, and thus helping to maintain him in this twofold movement.[320]

If Barth's discussions of witness were to be summarized, the core argument would be as follows: the church, as a witness, should proclaim the Gospel of Jesus "in words and works," or in other words, "speaking or proclamation" and "acting or healing."[321] It seems that Barth intentionally does not distinguish between the two methods in explicating the church's witness to the world. In discussing the church's proclamation of the Gospel, Barth includes the human action of witness as not only telling the story of God's love but also showing God's love to neighbors, through which the Gospel can be declared.[322] Conversely, when explaining the self-giving love of Christians, Barth understands the action will serve as a role of the proclamation of the salvific story of God—"loved by God and may love Him in return."[323] Barth explains this matter as follows:

> No matter how we understand speaking or proclamation on the one side and acting or healing on the other in the ministry of the community, and no matter what the community may think it is commanded to do and may actually try to fulfil along these two lines, there can be no doubt that in the light of its origin, of the Giver of its task who is also its content, its ministry and witness have always to move along these two lines: not merely along either the one or the other, but along both; and no less along the one than the other, but with equal seriousness and emphasis along both. It is not as though it were concerned with something different in the two, but wholly with the same thing though in different ways in both. For its speech is also action and its action

318. Barth, *CD* IV/2:815.
319. Barth, *CD* IV/2:816.
320. Barth, *CD* IV/2:817.
321. Barth, *CD* IV/3.2:622, 863.
322. Barth, *CD* IV/2:815.
323. Barth, *CD* IV/2:815–16.

speech. And for this very reason they are distinct. There is a work of the lips and also of the hands. There is speech and also action, proclamation and also healing; though it must be remembered, of course, that the direction given by Jesus to His disciples displays a clear sequence, the speech always preceding the action, as emerges in what we are told of their actual work.[324]

Thus, the church should serve as a sign and witness of the Gospel in its words and deeds. Because Barth believes the dimensions of reconciliation are indivisible, he seems to understand that being a sign and witness by the church includes both vertical and horizontal dimensions of reconciliation. The words and actions of the church would apply to both our relationship with God—proclaiming the Gospel and loving God in return—and relationships with fellow humans—loving within the disciples and to our neighbor. The church speaks and acts the message that it testifies.

Evaluative Summary

The research focus of this dissertation is to examine the relationship between the vertical and horizontal dimensions of reconciliation. Thus, how would interacting with the works of Karl Barth contribute to the understanding of this relationship in the discourse of mission as reconciliation? Barth's idea of fellow-humanity offers his most suitable answer to the research question. This idea is based on his reflections on the doctrine of the Trinity, reconciliation, Christology, and God's creation of humans.

The core argument of Barth's theological anthropology, presented in the term "fellow-humanity," is that humans are created as relational beings in correspondence with the trinitarian understanding of relationships (*analogia relantionis*; analogy of relation), and thus should reflect the Christological understanding of humanity (fellow-humanity actualized in Jesus Christ). The issue of inhumanity is sinfulness of human-beings, rejecting the ascension of Christ and remaining in the sin of sloth. It can be noticed in light of revelation of Christ, the perfect model of fellow-humanity, and in light of God's commandment. This fellow-humanity can be restored in the reconciliation with God, by the work of the Gospel of Christ in whom the true humanity can be actualized in oneself, and by the quickening power of the Holy Spirit.

Barth's idea of fellow-humanity has much to contribute to the current discourse of mission as reconciliation. Before the researcher addresses this contribution, this section presents a brief evaluation of Barth's theology

324. Barth, *CD* IV/2:863.

and theological methodology because of their relevance in shaping the idea of fellow-humanity.

As one of the most prominent theologians of the twentieth century, Karl Barth has received both praise and criticisms from numerous theologians. John Frame asserts that Barth's works have been controversial, and furthermore, there are "wide differences among scholars" in their evaluations of him because of the "difficulty of interpreting him," which results from "the huge volume and complexity of his writings."[325]

Specifically, concerning Barth's anthropology, Henri Blocher criticizes it as lacking biblical evidence. One can recognize several philosophical grounds upon which Barth developed his theological anthropology, the first of which is socialism.[326] Daniel Price surmises that Barth's "suspicion of Western individualism," which is related to the development of fellow-humanity later, could possibly have been affected by "his earlier interest in Christian socialism."[327] The second is Martin Buber's I and Thou personalism. Barth's anthropology, which describes humans as relational beings of I encounter Thou, seems to be influenced by Buber.[328]

Kenneth Oakes even mentions that there could have been "potential meetings and letters between Barth and Martin Buber."[329] Oakes cites the letter that Barth's friend Eduard Thurneysen wrote to Barth, saying that "it would be good if the two met, even if differences concerning their respective doctrines of revelation might arise."[330]

However, it is not certain to what extent those philosophical ideas played roles in shaping Barth's theology. Oakes argues that although Barth acknowledges "the necessity of philosophical study and engagement for theological work," he "remains convinced of the importance of theology's independence, the freedom and scope of dogmatic inquiry."[331] Even in the midst of continuous engagement with philosophy, Oakes interprets Barth's theology as not having significantly changed, and rather his later thoughts are "remarkably similar to his earlier ones."[332]

As many have noted, Barth's foundational theme is the revelation of God. Wolfhart Pannenberg notices that not only Barth's idea of fellow-humanity

325. Frame, *History of Western Philosophy and Theology*, 365–66.
326. Blocher, "Karl Barth's Anthropology," 107–10.
327. Price, *Karl Barth's Anthropology*, 98.
328. Blocher, "Karl Barth's Anthropology," 106–7.
329. Oakes, *Karl Barth on Theology and Philosophy*, 8.
330. Oakes, *Karl Barth on Theology and Philosophy*, 85.
331. Oakes, *Karl Barth on Theology and Philosophy*, 224.
332. Oakes, *Karl Barth on Theology and Philosophy*, 244.

but also his entire theology of revelation is based on the "logical positivism" of revelation, as "Dietrich Bonhoeffer detected."[333] To Barth, revelation is "presupposed" for every theological inquiry and becomes "the only possible *starting-point.*"[334] Furthermore, it denotes that theology is essentially the "science of revelation" or "faith."[335]

Upon this basis, Barth attempts "to bind the theologian and philosopher together into one sphere of inquiry and dispute," promoting "the confrontation and cooperation of the philosopher and the theologian."[336] In doing so, Barth makes several comments, including the truth, for instance, that fellow-humanity is "greater than both parties" and thus both must be humble.[337] Furthermore, he mentions how "theology uses and needs philosophy just as it uses and needs language."[338] The notion of fellow-humanity is an example of this way of doing theology to Barth.[339]

As John Frame rightly argues, it is difficult to deny that there has been "a strong affinity" between theology and philosophy throughout the history of Christianity.[340] Frame argues that, even including the secular philosophers, "the basic questions of philosophers are religious in character. Both . . . explore the great questions of metaphysics (being), epistemology (knowledge), and value theory (value)."[341]

In short, it seems likely that Barth underwent several influences, from Buber's philosophical conceptualization of I and Thou to (ethical or religious) socialism. However, whether Barth's theology is merely philosophical, lacking biblical or theological grounds, remains debatable. This is because a strong interrelatedness exists between the two disciplines, and Barth himself consistently endorsed the "independence" of theology and the "freedom" of "dogmatics" from other disciplines.[342] As examined in the previous section, the concept of fellow-humanity seems to hold some solid biblical and theological foundations based on essential Christian doctrines, such as the Trinity, creation of humans, and Christology.

---

333. Pannenberg, *Theology and the Philosophy*, 29.
334. Pannenberg, *Theology and the Philosophy*, 266.
335. Pannenberg, *Theology and the Philosophy*, 298.
336. Oakes, *Karl Barth on Theology and Philosophy*, 225.
337. Oakes, *Karl Barth on Theology and Philosophy*, 226.
338. Oakes, *Karl Barth on Theology and Philosophy*, 233.
339. Oakes, *Karl Barth on Theology and Philosophy*, 225.
340. Frame, *History of Western Philosophy and Theology*, 4.
341. Frame, *History of Western Philosophy and Theology*, 7.
342. Oakes, *Karl Barth on Theology and Philosophy*, 224.

To apply the contributions of Barth to the discussion of mission as reconciliation, first, Barth's fellow-humanity highlights *how* the two dimensions are truly inseparable. Second, based on the first, the understanding of horizontal reconciliation can be deepened in light of the significance of vertical reconciliation. This underscores the work of vertical reconciliation in the horizontal dimension.

A noticeable debate within the academic conversation of mission as reconciliation is a disagreement on the extent of emphasis on the vertical dimension (or the understanding of its role) in pursuing the horizontal dimension of reconciliation. As stated in chapter 2, no one seems to reject reconciliation with God being the foundation of reconciliation with other humans, and they are not to be separated.

However, what they mean by the agreed statements seems to vary in nuance, similar to a spectrum: from drawing some of the central principles for horizontal reconciliation from vertical reconciliation to promoting evangelism while expecting the fruit of horizontal reconciliation. In other words, the heart of the debate seems to lie in the issue of how legitimate and acceptable it is for the ministry of the church to pursue horizontal reconciliation without witnessing the message of vertical reconciliation verbally.

Related to this concern, first, Karl Barth would respond that inhumanity is a problem of the sinfulness of humans being separated from God—having no knowledge of God revealed in Christ. The problem of inhumanity would not go away without knowing God in person. It is not resolved by knowing a mere abstract notion of reconciliation, which is because to Barth, an actual and living relationship with God, who has been attested in Jesus, the true human, is the only way that one can truly restore fellow-humanity. It is the work of God that restores this humanity in a person. No horizontal reconciliation without vertical reconciliation, as Barth states.

Second, when the church's history demonstrates hatred, hostility, and even murder against fellow humans, it is evident that church communities have serious problems in their understanding of God and their relationship with Him. As argued above, Barth asserts that the vertical dimension of reconciliation necessarily leads to the horizontal dimension of reconciliation.

The first of Barth's points would more likely be welcomed and supported by evangelical scholars in the dialogue of mission as reconciliation. They are not satisfied when vertical reconciliation is treated as a mere premise from which the church draws some principles for its ministry of horizontal reconciliation. These scholars maintain that horizontal reconciliation can be properly and "most profoundly" achieved when it is sought upon vertical reconciliation with God.[343]

On the other hand, the second point of Barth may more likely be highlighted by conciliar scholars, who consider the church to have traditionally invested effort in vertical reconciliation only in its theology, mission, and liturgy, while largely neglecting the significance of horizontal reconciliation.

In this respect, Barth's fellow-humanity suggests a tighter connection between the two dimensions than do some of the current voices in the discussion of mission as reconciliation. He appeals to take account both *Gabe* (gift) and *Aufgabe* (task), in other words, indicative and imperative of the Gospel, together. Barth would agree with Haddon Willmer's saying, that the works of God, which "may be seen by us as distinguishable vertical and horizontal elements," "*are* in God, simultaneous and in harmony."[344]

As stated previously, there is no horizontal reconciliation without vertical reconciliation—the former initiates, enables, and achieves the latter. Furthermore, and simultaneously, vertical reconciliation necessarily leads to horizontal reconciliation. The genuineness of vertical reconciliation is often discerned by the fruit of horizontal reconciliation.

In addition, in the frame of fellow-humanity, one's understanding of horizontal reconciliation can be deepened in light of the significance of vertical reconciliation. According to Barth's thought, the entire concept and argument of fellow-humanity point to the humanity of Christ. The humanity of Christ not only demonstrates the original form of humanity created by God without being destroyed by sinfulness, but also offers the way through which one's humanity can be restored, as John 15:1–8 illustrates; Jesus is the true vine and humans are the branches that should be connected and remain into him. The fruit of fellow-humanity comes from the source, the humanity of Christ. This is why, in Christian doctrine, vertical reconciliation comes first, because loving God comes before the commandment of loving one's neighbor. This relational and responsible understanding of humanity may be paralleled to Emil Brunner,[345] who is often compared to Barth.

Are there any potential limitations in applying Barth's theology in the practical ministry of reconciliation? When developing theological anthropology as an independent dogmatic domain based on biblical teachings, one still may need to interact more actively with secular (or other religious) views of anthropology in pursuing horizontal reconciliation. In the field of mission as reconciliation, the significance of societal and civic

---

343. Ott et al., *Encountering Theology of Mission*, 97.
344. Willmer, "'Vertical' and 'Horizontal,'" 151.
345. Brunner, *Man in Revolt*, 73–74; 78–79; 104, 107.

engagement inevitably increases. Christian mission ventures into societies and neighborhoods, and the ministry of reconciliation often involves conflicts beyond church congregations.

In this case, the church will be required to interact and develop its theology and missiology as an interdisciplinary study, opening itself to other disciplines. If one resists this type of opening, but attempts to remain in a mainly theological domain, as Barth's theological methodology does, the degree of engagement and the chance of lifting voices may be limited. Barth has intransigently dealt with anthropology as a theological discipline, as well as shaped ethics as dogmatics. Having an independent theological ground for moral suggestions is legitimate considering Barth's intended audience and targeted context, yet when it comes to the church's ministry of mission as reconciliation in the social sphere, it needs to acknowledge secular moral discussions in public as a conversation partner in earnest.

Reinhold Niebuhr may share some of this idea. In *The Nature and Destiny of Man*, he asserts that, "Theologies, such as that of Barth, which threaten to destroy all relative moral judgments by their exclusive emphasis upon the ultimate religious fact of the sinfulness of all men, are rightly suspected of imperiling relative moral achievements of history."[346] Perhaps, recognizing similar needs and attempting to avoid the unwanted isolation of theology in public dialogue, Wolfhart Pannenberg developed his theological anthropology, through conversations with other academic disciplines such as biology, psychology, and sociology.[347]

The church, in delivering its message of reconciliation in the public square, must interact with psychology, biology, cultural anthropology, and sociology on the subject of the nature of humans and their relationships with fellow humans without losing the core theological message it seeks to deliver. This is probably a demand of contextualization for the contemporary discourse of mission as reconciliation.

In the mission contexts, the church faces the fact that it must often cooperate with other organizations (religious and nonreligious) to promote conflict resolution in a society. Today's academic and public discussions of topics such as reconciliation, peaceful coexistence, and conflict-resolution are worthy of the church's attention and involvement. This will provide better opportunities for the church to demonstrate the Christian understanding of reconciliation, participate in peace-making work in society, and eventually witness the Gospel of reconciliation in words and deeds. This is also a civil responsibility of Christians.

---

346. Niebuhr, *Nature and Destiny of Man*, 220.
347. Pannenberg, *What is Man*; Pannenberg, *Systematic Theology*, 2:120, 198.

In conclusion, Barth's reflection on fellow-humanity, which suggests the inseparable connection of the two as well as the significance of the vertical dimension in pursuing the horizontal, makes a significant contribution to the understanding of the relationship between vertical and horizontal reconciliation in the current discussion of mission as reconciliation.

4

Reconciliation in the Theologies of Miroslav Volf, Son Yang-Won, and Desmond Tutu

THIS CHAPTER EXPLORES THREE Christian thinkers and practitioners in the field of reconciliation. The literature related to each person's theology of reconciliation is examined, centering on this book's research focus—the relationship between the vertical and horizontal dimensions of reconciliation. An evaluative summary is presented after each person's theology has been reviewed.

Miroslav Volf

Miroslav Volf's theological reflection on reconciliation was well-presented in his book *Exclusion and Embrace*. Both before and after this book, Volf has continuously developed his thought on the theme of reconciliation, or as he terms it "embrace," in books (both academic and nonacademic), articles, and public speeches, although the gist of his argument has largely remained unchanged. Throughout his works, there are several subjects to which he has consistently paid attention.

First, Volf's theology of embrace is rooted in trinitarian theology and the trinitarian understanding of relationship. Volf's core view of embrace has been shaped by how the Trinity relates to each other and engages humanity. As Volf himself states, "the central thesis" of his discussion on embrace is that "God's reception of hostile humanity into divine communion is a model for how human beings should relate to the other."[1] Similar to Karl Barth, Volf focuses on the correspondence of human relationships to that of the Trinity. In this view, Volf examines the topic of forgiveness, making space for others, and reconciliation. Moreover, based on

1. Volf, *Exclusion and Embrace*, 100.

trinitarian theology, Volf develops his eschatological vision for the social dimension of reconciliation.

Second, Volf engages with the issue of identity, and specifically shaping one's identity in relation to others. Barth established his theological anthropology through engaging with I and Thou personalism. Although Volf fundamentally follows the direction of Barth, he has advanced the relational anthropology, further dealing with violence in light of the issue of identity: individual or collective strife and violence against others, such as "ethnic cleansing." Based on his trinitarian theology, Volf suggests forming one's identity as a catholic personality that welcomes others and is enriched by them.

Third, Volf reviews the issue of justice and the legitimacy and limitation of liberation theology in relation to reconciliation. Volf's reflections on justice and liberation theology are a significant part of his theology of embrace. In *Exclusion and Embrace*, revealing the limitations of both the modern and postmodern understanding of exclusion, embrace, justice, and so forth, Volf often argues for the third way, guided by biblical narratives. Furthermore, although he agrees on the worth of justice, Volf indicates that the framework of liberation theology has a clear limitation and proposes embrace (embedded in justice) as a paradigm and goal. The issue of justice remains a salient challenge of reconciliation, and furthermore, the legacy of liberation theology can be found in the current discourse of mission as reconciliation, as it is in Robert Schreiter's; therefore, Volf's reflections on justice and liberation theology should merit our attention.

Lastly, for the question of *how* humans can embrace each other as God has shown to them, Volf has consistently suggested Christological and pneumatological statements. Based on what Christ has done on the Cross, he focuses on the work of the Holy Spirit that enables a human to be transformed to embracing personhood. In this sense, it can be said that Volf echoes Barth's voice.

In this section, *Exclusion and Embrace* is mainly examined. Volf's other works *After Our Likeness*, *End of Memory*, *Against the Tide*, *Free of Charge*, and journal articles on the issue of embrace are also reviewed.

The Context of Volf's Theology of Reconciliation

At the beginning of *Exclusion and Embrace* and on other occasions,[2] Volf has introduced the context in which his theology of reconciliation

2. For example, his speech at Trinity Institute's 36th National Theological Conference in 2006, which was later published as a journal article and a chapter of the book,

emerged—a series of tragic moments of conflict in his home country. In the Balkans, "ethnic cleansing" was conducted by Serbians against his people, the Croatians, in the early 1990s, which is when his theological reflection became embedded. His personal unfortunate experience in the military service that initiated his noetic journey of reconciliation, however, was in the mid 1980s.

In his compulsory military service, Volf was suspected of being an American spy and unduly imprisoned and threatened by Captain Goranovic because of his Christian faith, American wife, and academic degree from the "West."[3] In his reminiscences, Volf struggles with remembering other's wrongdoings *rightly*, overcoming evil with good (Rom 12:21), and forgiveness. Volf calls to remembrance and explains his inner struggle as follows:

> To triumph fully, evil needs two victories, not one. The first victory happens when an evil deed is perpetrated; the second victory, when evil is returned. After the first victory, evil would die if the second victory did not infuse it with new life. In my own situation, I could do nothing about the first victory. But I could prevent the second. Captain G. would not mold me into his image. Instead of returning evil for evil, I determined to try to heed the apostle Paul by trying to overcome evil with good (Rom. 12:21). After all, I myself had been redeemed by the God who in Christ died for the redemption of the ungodly. And so, once again, now in relation to Captain G., I started walking—and stumbling—in the footsteps of the enemy-loving God.[4]

Out of this personal grief, his theology of embrace began to develop. In connection, as introduced in *Exclusion and Embrace*, there was another struggle for his people. His "preliminary account" of exclusion and embrace "took place" when Volf was staying in Osijek, Croatia "during the fall of 1992" when the (first phase) of the war was over.[5] Volf witnessed a society devastated by war as well as "many deep wounds in the hearts of the people."[6] Volf asserts that, "the war was continuing with even greater brutality in the neighbors' courtyard . . . The feeling of helplessness and frustration of anger and hatred was ubiquitous."[7] These are the contexts of Volf's theology of reconciliation.

The End of Memory, talks about the context of his theology of embrace.
   3. Volf, "God's Forgiveness and Ours," 214–15.
   4. Volf, "God's Forgiveness and Ours," 214–15.
   5. Volf, "Exclusion and Embrace: Theological Reflections," 232.
   6. Volf, "Exclusion and Embrace: Theological Reflections," 232.
   7. Volf, "Exclusion and Embrace: Theological Reflections," 232.

Volf's Reflection on Liberation Theology

In many places in his discussion on reconciliation, Volf identifies both contributions and limitations of liberation theology. Volf's interest in and favor toward liberation theology can be observed through several pieces of information he shares. He shares how (1) his "theological upbringing" was partly "shaped by liberation theology"; (2) he "took a course" with Orlando Costas, "an evangelical liberation theologian" at Fuller Theological Seminary and "continued to study it afterwards"; and (3) he did his doctoral study with Jürgen Moltmann, partly because he is "a granddaddy of liberation theologians."[8]

Volf argues that liberation theologians have provided significant "lessons," placing "the themes of oppression and liberation at the center of theological reflection."[9] Volf considers the issue of justice to be a central topic in his theology of reconciliation. He rejects the term "cheap reconciliation."[10] Affirming the Kairos Document, which states that reconciliation without justice is "not Christian reconciliation" but "sin," Volf claims that "cheap reconciliation sets 'justice' and 'peace' against each other as alternatives."[11] Volf elaborates, "To advocate cheap reconciliation clearly means to betray those who suffer injustice, deception, and violence" because it is to act as though the transgression never happened.[12] It is also "a betrayal . . . of the Christian faith."[13] Furthermore, Volf argues that, "The struggle against injustice is inscribed in the very character of the Christian faith."[14] In Volf's understanding of reconciliation it is evident that "the concern for justice is integral to forgiveness and reconciliation."[15]

As he underlines the necessity and legitimacy of liberation theology, Volf describes the themes of liberation theology as primarily being "designed to handle experiences of economic exploitation and political domination."[16] Nonetheless, Volf finds the categories to be "inadequate" in examining the emerging cultural and ethnic conflicts such as the case of the Balkans and

---

8. Volf and Neufeld, "Conversations with Miroslav Volf," 71.

9. Volf, "Exclusion and Embrace," 234.

10. Volf, "Forgiveness, Reconciliation, and Justice," 867. This is influenced by Dietrich Bonhoeffer's famous expression, "cheap grace."

11. Kairos Theologians (Group), *Kairos Document*, sec. 3.1.; Volf, "Forgiveness, Reconciliation, and Justice," 867.

12. Volf, "Forgiveness, Reconciliation, and Justice," 867.

13. Volf, "Social Meaning of Reconciliation," 168.

14. Volf, "Forgiveness, Reconciliation, and Justice," 868.

15. Volf, "Forgiveness, Reconciliation, and Justice," 869.

16. Volf, "Vision of Embrace," 200.

others.[17] Moreover, Volf problematizes the paradigm of oppression and liberation prioritizing justice more than any other themes in the pursuit of reconciliation, even more so than forgiveness or reconciliation itself, as is shown in the phrase "first justice, then reconciliation."[18]

The first problem that Volf specifies is that the framework of oppression and liberation can hardly put an end to the vicious cycle of endeavor for justice and reach a peaceful agreement. Although it seems that Volf does not attempt to curtail the importance of justice in the process of reconciliation, he seems skeptical that "first justice, then reconciliation" is sufficiently adequate to engender reconciliation. Referring to Fredrich Nietzsche, he discusses the following:

> First, taken seriously, a "first justice, then reconciliation" stance is impossible. As Nietzsche rightly noted, given the nature of human interaction, the pursuit of justice not only rests and feeds on injustices but also creates new injustices. Injustice is the chaff that cannot be removed from the wheat of human interaction—until that eschatological day when the wheat will be gathered into the "barns." Moreover, justice is to some extent linked to particular groups and invariably contested by rival groups. No peace is possible within the overarching framework of strict justice for the simple reason that no strict justice is possible.[19]

Under the theme "first justice, then reconciliation," as Volf rightly indicates, the goal of reconciliation can easily be forgotten and the endless cycle of the pursuit of justice will be launched by both parties. When each side considers themselves oppressed, the "struggle" will not end "until 'our' side has won."[20] Justice can hardly be achieved to the extent that both parties are satisfied and "reconciliation is not even attempted."[21]

According to Volf,[22] liberation theology can offer the motivation and "gear" to fight for justice, but not an answer to the question of how to "live together" with the once-oppressed/oppressor neighbor, even if justice has been achieved. Achieving justice once is not enough because "liberation through

---

17. Volf, "Exclusion and Embrace," 234; Volf, "Vision of Embrace," 200.

18. Volf, "Social Meaning of Reconciliation," 169; Volf, "Forgiveness, Reconciliation, and Justice," 869.

19. Volf, "Social Meaning of Reconciliation," 169; Nietzsche, *Human, All Too Human*, 216.

20. Volf, "Social Meaning of Reconciliation," 163.

21. Volf, "Social Meaning of Reconciliation," 163.

22. Volf, "Exclusion and Embrace: Theological Reflections," 235; Volf, "Vision of Embrace," 200–201.

violence breeds new conflicts."[23] Introducing E. M. Cioran's quote of "the great persecutors are often 'recruited among the martyrs not quite beheaded,'"[24] Volf maintains that the struggle for justice will not end readily.[25]

The second problem is the ambiguity of identifying perpetrators and victims realistically. In many cases of social conflicts, although it is not as difficult as discerning perpetrators and victims in the case of "the Nazis and the Jews during World War Two,"[26] oppressors and victims "are not so clean."[27] There is no "clear perpetrator" and "victim," and "each side perceives itself as oppressed by the other."[28] Regarding the ambiguities of liberation, Volf presents the following discussion:

> If the plot is written around the schema of "oppressed" ("victims") and "oppressors" ("perpetrators"), each party will find good reasons for claiming the higher moral ground of a victim; each will perceive itself as oppressed by the other and all will see themselves as engaged in the struggle for liberation. The categories of oppression and liberation pro vide combat gear, not a pin-striped suit or a dinner dress; they are good for fighting, but not for negotiating or celebrating—at least not until the oppressors have been conquered and the prisoners set free.[29]

This is because any social conflict can often become "very messy."[30] On the predicament and concurrent dilemma, Volf expounds as follows:

> How will we disentangle those who are innocent from those who are blameworthy in the knotted histories of individuals, let alone the narratives of whole cultures and nations? The longer the conflict continues the more both parties find themselves sucked into the vortex of mutually reinforcing victimization, in which the one party appears more virtuous only because, being weaker, it has less opportunity to be cruel. If we organize our moral engagement around the categories of "oppression/ liberation" we will need clear narratives of blame and innocence. Failing to find a blameless victim, however, we will be left with two equally unattractive choices: either to withdraw from

---

23. Volf, "Exclusion and Embrace," 235.
24. Ciroan, *Short History of Decay*, 4.
25. Volf, *Exclusion and Embrace*, 104.
26. Volf, *Exclusion and Embrace*, 104.
27. Volf, "Social Meaning of Reconciliation," 163.
28. Volf, "Exclusion and Embrace," 234; Volf, "Vision of Embrace," 200.
29. Volf, *Exclusion and Embrace*, 103.
30. Volf, *Exclusion and Embrace*, 103.

engagement in moral disgust (and thereby giving tacit support to the stronger party), or to impose clear-cut moral narratives with moral partisanship (and therefore sharing in the ideological self-deception of the one party).[31]

Furthermore, a primary reason that Volf stands against "first justice, then reconciliation" is because he believes that it "is at odds with the core Christian beliefs inscribed in the narrative of the life, death, and resurrection of Jesus Christ," as well as later Pauline writings in which "grace has priority over justice."[32] Citing the two theologians Gustavo Gutierrez and Jürgen Moltmann, Volf asserts that love is the prime theme in Christian faith, not justice or freedom.[33] Volf comments how both have clarified that it is the love of God that shapes our relationships as well as His kingdom.[34]

Volf, therefore, concludes that the "categories" of liberation theology— "oppression" and "liberation"—"seem ill-suited," and thus cannot be "the overarching schema by which to align our social engagement" in the journey of reconciliation.[35] Volf maintains that the "goal must be something that binds conflicting parties together rather than pulling them apart from each other."[36] According to Volf, "we must work towards reconciliation," yet "'liberation' gives us only limited help in this arduous task."[37] Again, however, it does not seem that Volf attempts to "abandon" the issues of liberation and justice, for he understands God "is on the side of the downtrodden," "poor," and "powerless."[38] Rather, he considers the frame of "oppression and liberation" to be "essential dimensions of exclusion and embrace, respectively."[39] Volf explains that to "embrace others in their otherness must mean to free them from oppression and give them space to be themselves. Anything else is either a hypocritical tap on the shoulders or a deadly 'bear hug.'"[40]

In sum, reflecting liberation theology, the central question Volf asks is "How does one remain loyal both to the demand of the oppressed for justice

31. Volf, *Exclusion and Embrace*, 103–4.

32. Volf, "Social Meaning of Reconciliation," 169. Volf yet still comments that "grace, again, that does not negate justice but that *affirms* justice in the act of transcending it" Volf, "Social Meaning of Reconciliation," 169.

33. Volf, *Exclusion and Embrace*, 105.

34. Gutiérrez *Theology of Liberation*, xxxviii; Moltmann, *Trinity and Kingdom*, 56; Volf, *Exclusion and Embrace*, 105.

35. Volf, *Exclusion and Embrace*, 104; Volf, "Exclusion and Embrace," 235.

36. Volf and Neufeld, "Conversations with Miroslav Volf," 72.

37. Volf, "Vision of Embrace," 201.

38. Volf, *Exclusion and Embrace*, 105.

39. Volf, "Exclusion and Embrace," 235.

40. Volf, "Exclusion and Embrace," 235.

and to the gift of forgiveness that the Crucified offered to the perpetrators?"[41] As an answer, Volf "inserts the project of liberation into a larger framework," which is exclusion and embrace.[42] In this sense, Volf presents the paradigm of exclusion and embrace as a superior alternative for the journey of reconciliation that does not negate justice.[43] In the paradigm, Volf argues that "there can be no justice without the will to embrace," and "embrace is part and parcel of the very *definition* of justice."[44]

Exclusion and Embrace

As discussed, Miroslav Volf presents exclusion and embrace as the primary paradigm based on which he has developed his theology of reconciliation. Within the framework of exclusion and embrace, Volf mainly engages the issue of identity and otherness.

Conflicts between Self-Identity and Otherness

Within the paradigm of exclusion and embrace, Volf focuses on the issue of identity and otherness. Volf interprets the issue of identity and otherness as being at the heart of many of serious cases of strife throughout the twentieth and twenty-first centuries, such as those in the Balkans and Rwanda. He claims that, "the problem of ethnic and cultural conflicts is part of a larger problem of identity and otherness."[45] The tragic case of "ethnic cleansing" in the Balkans was an attempt to "wash away" the "ethnic otherness."[46] He also argues that the "will for identity" might have served as the "fuel" for "a good deal of those 50 or so conflicts around the globe."[47] In this respect, Volf analyzes the case of the Balkans as follows: "The practice of ethnic and other kinds of 'cleansing' in the Balkans forces us *to place otherness at the center of theological reflection.* The problem, of course, is not specific to the Balkans."[48]

---

41. Volf, *Exclusion and Embrace*, 9.
42. Volf, *Exclusion and Embrace*, 105; Volf, "Exclusion and Embrace," 235.
43. Volf, "Vision of Embrace," 201; Volf, "Exclusion and Embrace," 235.
44. Volf, *Exclusion and Embrace*, 220.
45. Volf, *Exclusion and Embrace*, 16.
46. Volf, "Exclusion and Embrace," 233.
47. Volf, *Exclusion and Embrace*, 17.
48. Volf, "Exclusion and Embrace," 234.

In the case of Rwanda, following that of Balkans, there was also an attempt to eliminate ethnic otherness. Referring to Alex de Waal's interpretation,[49] Volf explains that Rwanda was "fuel[ed]" by "economic deprivation and lust for power" and "ignited" by "racist ideology."[50] Volf attributes the tragic moment of Rwanda, at least in part, to the distorted understanding of identity and otherness.

In Volf's opinion, the destructive consequences of the issue are not limited to the two regions at that time. Referring to Jacques Derrida's comment on European identity, Volf claims that European history "is full of the worst violences [sic] committed in the name of European identity," which is "totalitarian," and "a monochrome world, a world without the other" is being dreamed, the plan of which has been executed.[51]

In today's world, as Volf indicates, because technological developments and globalization have compressed both space and time, otherness is easily found in one's daily life.[52] It is not something "from distant lands"— the *other* people "are among us; they are part of us."[53] How we should relate other people has increasingly become an urgent issue.[54] Volf warns, "The ghettos and battlefields throughout the world testify indisputably to its importance. It is not too much to claim that the future of not only the Balkans but of the whole world depends on how we deal with ethnic, religious, and gender otherness."[55] From this point of view, Volf contemplates the church's role in the midst of conflicts:

> Rwandas and Bosnias [sic] of today and tomorrow challenge the churches first of all to reflect on their own *identity* as a people of God among the struggling peoples of the world. How should we relate to the cultural communities we inhabit? How should we relate to the multiple cultural communities of our neighbours or our enemies? Second, the resurgence of ethnic strife challenges churches to rethink their *mission* as agents of peace. What vision of the relations between culture do we have to offer to communities at war? What paths to suggest?[56]

---

49. Waal, "Genocide State," 1.
50. Volf, "Vision of Embrace," 195.
51. Volf, "Exclusion and Embrace," 233; Derrida, *The Other Heading*, 82–83.
52. Volf, "Exclusion and Embrace," 234.
53. Volf, "Exclusion and Embrace," 234.
54. Volf, "Exclusion and Embrace," 234.
55. Volf, "Exclusion and Embrace," 234.
56. Volf, "Vision of Embrace," 196.

The questions that Volf raises are related to a main theological question in the academic discourse of mission as reconciliation—how the church as a missional community serves as an agent of reconciliation in the world. With the understanding of *missio Dei*, that the identity of the church has been comprehended as a missional community by nature is agreed by Christians. One indispensable identity of the missional community in contemporary society should be the church as a peacemaker—God's agent of peace. Volf suggests for a Christian to obtain a catholic personality so that a church community can become a catholic community.

Shaping Identity Toward Catholic Personality: Distance and Belonging

Volf basically understands that identity is "shaped by how others relate to persons and by how persons internalize others' relation to them."[57] It has "conscious or unconscious complex relations to culturally situated others."[58] In this sense, in his examination of shaping identity, Volf focuses on how people constitute their identity in their *own* culture. Volf emphasizes the need for both distance and belonging. He argues that if an individual fails to obtain both elements in balance, he or she will end up forming a distorted identity in relation to the otherness of others. He explains the result of missing one of the two as "belonging without distance destroys" while "distance without belonging isolates."[59] The following is an illustration of his personal identity:

> Both distance and belonging are essential. Belonging without distance destroys: I affirm my exclusive identity as Croatian and want either to shape everyone in my own image or eliminate them from my world. But distance without belonging isolates: I deny my identity as a Croatian and draw back from my own culture. But more often than not, I become trapped in tire snares of counter-dependence. I deny my Croatian identity only to affirm even more forcefully my identity as a member of this or that anti-Croatian sect. And so an isolationist "distance without belonging" slips into a destructive "belonging without distance." Distance from a culture must never degenerate into, flight from that culture but must be a way of living in a culture.[60]

---

57. Volf, "Final Reconciliation," 99.
58. Volf, "Final Reconciliation," 99–100.
59. Volf, "Exclusion and Embrace," 236.
60. Volf, *Exclusion and Embrace*, 50.

According to Volf, an identity with both distance and belonging balanced can be formed by Christian faith, which defines believers as "strangers" or "sojourners" in this world.[61] He comments that from "the inception of the Christian church, otherness was integral to Christian ethnic and cultural identity" as it is "explicitly" written as "aliens and exiles" in 1 Pet 2:11.[62] It is thus a "theological" issue to Volf.[63]

The two biblical figures that Volf exemplifies are Abraham and Paul. First, in relation to shaping one's identity, Volf construes the core message of Abraham's narrative of departing from his own culture as "stepping out of enmeshment in the network of inherited cultural relations" because of the "faith in the one God."[64] Then, "the oneness of God implies God's universality, and universality entails transcendence with respect to any given culture."[65] Likewise, Volf stresses that to "be a child of Abraham and Sarah and to respond to the call of their God means to make an exodus, to start a voyage, become a stranger" (Gen 23:4; 24:1–9).[66] This is because "At the very core of Christian identity lies an all-encompassing change of loyalty, from a given culture with its gods to the God of all cultures."[67] However, Volf clarifies that the narrative of Abraham is not about simply being destructive, having no destination, or departing from all relationships.[68] Furthermore, it is not freedom from all types of binding as "modernity seeks"; rather, Volf claims, "Abraham is most radically *bound to God.*"[69]

Likewise, Volf discusses how Apostle Paul was previously a zealous advocate of the God of Torah, and his particular Jewish people had "ingeniously" dealt with the "tension" that was "created by God's universality and the cultural particularity of God's revelation" after conversion to Christ.[70] According to Volf, one can observe in the case of Paul that "the oneness of God requires God's universality," and thus God was no longer the God of Torah, or of a particular genealogy, but the universal God who offered "equal" access to every human in every culture.[71]

---

61. Volf, "Exclusion and Embrace," 236.
62. Volf, "Exclusion and Embrace," 236.
63. Volf, *Exclusion and Embrace*, 37.
64. Volf, *Exclusion and Embrace*, 39.
65. Volf, *Exclusion and Embrace*, 39.
66. Volf, *Exclusion and Embrace*, 39.
67. Volf, *Exclusion and Embrace*, 40.
68. Volf, *Exclusion and Embrace*, 40–41.
69. Volf, *Exclusion and Embrace*, 42.
70. Volf, *Exclusion and Embrace*, 44–45.
71. Volf, *Exclusion and Embrace*, 44–45.

Based on the abovementioned two biblical cases, Volf argues that "Each culture can retain its own cultural specificity"; however, "at the same time, no culture can retain its own tribal deities; religion must be de-ethnicized so that ethnicity can be de-sacralized."[72] The one and only factor that Volf identifies as enabling this radical transformation of one's identity is the faith to God. Volf contends, "Faith in Christ replaces birth into a people" and "the religious irrelevance of genealogical ties and the necessity of faith in the 'seed of Abraham' are correlates of the belief in the one God of all the families of the earth, who called Abraham to depart."[73]

In other words, in Volf's thought, a Christian belongs to one's culture that is differentiated from others, yet at the same time, the Christian, as a sojourner in this world, maintains distance from their own culture for he or she ultimately belongs to God who transcends all cultures. Volf maintains that "the distance" from one's *own* culture can only be "born out of allegiance to God and God's future."[74] Volf explains that Christians need not to be the "outsider" of their own culture, but "when they have responded to the call of the Gospel they have stepped, as it were, with one foot outside their own culture while with the other remaining firmly planted in it. They are distant, and yet they belong. *Their difference is internal to the culture.*"[75]

Belonging to one's culture while maintaining a proper distance from it in fidelity to God in every culture is what Volf calls catholic personality. A catholic personality serves two roles: first, it empowers one to embrace other cultures, and second, it helps one to be prophetic to every culture. Regarding the first role, Volf expounds as follows:

> [I]t *creates space in us to receive the other.* Consider what happens when a person becomes a Christian. Paul writes, "So if anyone is in Christ, there is a new creation" (2 Corinthians 5:17). When God comes, God brings a whole new world. The Spirit of God breaks through the self-enclosed worlds we inhabit; the Spirit re-creates us and sets us on the road toward becoming what I like to call a "catholic personality," a personal microcosm of the eschatological new creation (Volf 1992a).[76]
> A catholic personality is a personality enriched by otherness, a personality which is what it is only because multiple others

---

72. Volf, *Exclusion and Embrace*, 49.
73. Volf, *Exclusion and Embrace*, 45.
74. Volf, *Exclusion and Embrace*, 51.
75. Volf, "Soft Difference," 18–19; Volf, *Exclusion and Embrace*, 49.
76. It is as written as in Volf's book. It indicates his article, "Catholicity of Two or Three: Free Church Reflections on the Catholicity of the Local Church." *Jurist* 52 (1992) 525–46.

have been reflected in it in a particular way. The distance from my own culture that results from being born by the Spirit creates a fissure in me through which others can come in. The Spirit unlatches the doors of my heart saying: "You are not only you; others belong to you too."[77]

In other words, a catholic personality is "porous."[78] It does not exclude other cultures but allows them to enter into one's identity and cultural boundaries.

Regarding the second role, Volf discusses the following:

> The second function of the distance forged by the Spirit of new creation is no less important: it *entails a judgment against evil in every culture* . . . should a catholic personality integrate all otherness? Can one feel at home with everything in every culture? With murder, rape, and destruction? With nationalistic idolatry and "ethnic cleansing"? Any notion of catholic personality which was capable only of integrating, but not of discriminating, would be grotesque . . . there are evil deeds that cannot be tolerated. The practice of "judgment" cannot be given up (see Chapter II). There can be no new creation without judgment.[79]

Here, Volf argues that catholic personality must be both "evangelical" and "ecumenical."[80] It should be evangelical in that it is "brought to repentance and shaped by the Gospel and engaged in the transformation of the world."[81] Furthermore, it should be ecumenical, meaning that "No church in a given culture may isolate itself from other churches in other cultures declaring itself sufficient to itself and to its own culture."[82]

Exclusion

In addition to Volf's concept of catholic personality, he distinguishes "differentiation" from "exclusion."[83] Similar to his depiction of proper process of shaping one's identity as distance *and* belonging, for differentiation Volf

---

77. Volf, *Exclusion and Embrace*, 51.
78. Volf, *Exclusion and Embrace*, 204.
79. Volf, "Exclusion and Embrace," 52.
80. Volf, *Exclusion and Embrace*, 52–53.
81. Volf, *Exclusion and Embrace*, 52.
82. Volf, *Exclusion and Embrace*, 51.
83. Volf, *Exclusion and Embrace*, 65.

defines it as "separating-*and*-binding."[84] He argues that it is "the creative activity" that "results in patterns of interdependence."[85] Volf states, "We are who we are not because we are separate from the others who are next to us, because we are *both* separate *and* connected, *both* distinct *and* related; the boundaries that mark our identities are both barriers and bridges."[86]

On the contrary, exclusion destroys this creative order. Volf defines exclusion as "the sinful activity" that violently reconfigures the "interdependence" of "the creation."[87] Volf considers that exclusion destroys both separation and connection.

> First, exclusion can entail cutting of the bonds that connect, taking oneself out of the pattern of interdependence and placing oneself in a position of sovereign independence. The other then emerges either as an enemy that must be pushed away from the self and driven out of its space or as a nonentity—a superfluous being—that can be disregarded and abandoned. Second, exclusion can entail erasure of separation, not recognizing the other as someone who in his or her otherness belongs to the pattern of interdependence. The other then emerges as an inferior being who must either be assimilated by being made like the self or be subjugated to the self. Exclusion takes place when the violence of expulsion, assimilation, or subjugation and the indifference of abandonment replace the dynamics of taking in and keeping out as well as the mutuality of giving and receiving.[88]

Volf demonstrates that no matter which element is ignored between separation and binding, both cases rearrange the distinctiveness and relatedness of the self to the other, forcibly resulting in the removal of mutual interdependence. Volf claims that the failure to hold both separation and binding would lead to devastating exclusion.

According to Volf, several forms of exclusion exist, namely elimination (assimilation), domination, and abandonment.[89] Elimination is a brutal form of exclusion, violently removing otherness, as in the cases of Bosnia and Rwanda.[90] Assimilation is "the more benign side" of elimination in that

---

84. Volf, *Exclusion and Embrace*, 65.
85. Volf, *Exclusion and Embrace*, 65.
86. Volf, *Exclusion and Embrace*, 66.
87. Volf, *Exclusion and Embrace*, 66.
88. Volf, *Exclusion and Embrace*, 67.
89. Volf, *Exclusion and Embrace*, 75.
90. Volf, *Exclusion and Embrace*, 75.

it allows the other to exist as far as the person "become like us."[91] In domination, the others are "subjugated" and "exploited" to "inflate our egos," as in the examples of India's caste system and South Africa's former apartheid policies.[92] Abandonment denotes ignoring and "passing by" the needs of the others "at a safe distance," unless we find them useful and they help meet our interests, as "the priest and Levite in the story of the Good Samaritan."[93] As noted, all of these forms reject mutual interdependence between the distinctive but related selves in one way or another.

Why is exclusion "so irresistible?"[94] Volf's initial answer is the institutionalized system of exclusion, which has "insuppressible power" over us and even evokes an "uncontrollable chain reaction" of exclusion, even among "mostly decent people."[95] Affirming Walter Wink's words, Volf argues that "the power of evil imposes itself so irresistibly through the operation of a transpersonal 'system' that is both 'institutional' and 'spiritual.'"[96] This system "lures and ensnares" people to "exclude others from scarce goods whether they are economic, social, or psychological."[97] Volf continues: "our very selves have been shaped by the climate of evil in which we live. Evil has insinuated itself into our very souls and rules over us from the very citadel erected to guard us against it."[98]

Volf's second answer is connected to identity. Every self is "dialogically constructed"—"I am who I am in relation to others."[99] However, the problem is that conflicts happen between the self and the other, each of whom asserts oneself "over against" the other.[100] The other self does not often become whom the self wants him or her to be, and vice versa,[101] thereby leading to tension. According to Volf, this situation presents two options: to either (1) accept and "integrate the other into my own will to be myself," or (2) "slip into violence," excluding and eliminating the other self, as the biblical narrative of "Cain's assault" against Abel demonstrates.[102]

91. Volf, *Exclusion and Embrace*, 75.
92. Volf, *Exclusion and Embrace*, 75.
93. Volf, *Exclusion and Embrace*, 75.
94. Volf, *Exclusion and Embrace*, 71.
95. Volf, *Exclusion and Embrace*, 86.
96. Volf, *Exclusion and Embrace*, 87.
97. Volf, *Exclusion and Embrace*, 87.
98. Volf, *Exclusion and Embrace*, 89.
99. Volf, *Exclusion and Embrace*, 91.
100. Volf, *Exclusion and Embrace*, 91.
101. Volf, *Exclusion and Embrace*, 91.
102. Volf, *Exclusion and Embrace*, 91.

Volf's second answer then raises the question of "what *kind* of center the self ought to have."[103] To avoid exclusion, Volf suggests decentering and recentering the self. Referring to Paul's words in Gal 2:20 and Rom 6:5, Volf claims that one's self should be decentered and recentered "by participating in the death and resurrection of Christ through faith and baptism."[104]

Volf states that the new center given by Christ "through faith and baptism" does not eliminate one's old self-identity, which has been connected to one's family, society, and nation, but it rather "transforms" the old self to be "re-made in the image of the Son of God who loved me and gave himself for me."[105] In the self-giving love like Christ, "the new center opens the self up, makes it capable and willing to give itself for others and to receive others in itself."[106] Volf points out that this is the "battle against exclusion."[107]

The only explanation that Volf offers as a way to avoid exclusion in one's self is derived from the Gospel. Volf writes, "The center of the self—a center that is both inside and outside—is the story of Jesus Christ, which has become the story of the self. More precisely, the center is Jesus Christ crucified and resurrected who has become part and parcel of the very structure of the self."[108] Furthermore, Volf argues that the entire process of decentering and recentering can be executed by the work of the Spirit.

> Central to the Christian faith is the belief that the Spirit of the crucified Messiah is capable of creating the promised land out of the very territory the Pharaoh has beleaguered. The Spirit enters the citadel of the self, de-centers the self by fashioning it in the image of the self-giving Christ, and frees its will so it can resist the power of exclusion in the power of the Spirit of embrace. It is in the citadel of the fragile self that the new world of embrace is first created (2 Corinthians 5:17). It is by this seemingly powerless power of the Spirit—the Spirit who blows even outside the walls of the church—that selves are freed from powerlessness in order to fight the system of exclusion everywhere—in the structures, in the culture, and in the self.[109]

This is a discussion by Volf from which his thoughts on the relationship between vertical and horizontal reconciliation can be inferred. In Volf's

---

103. Volf, *Exclusion and Embrace*, 69.
104. Volf, *Exclusion and Embrace*, 69–70.
105. Volf, *Exclusion and Embrace*, 71.
106. Volf, *Exclusion and Embrace*, 71.
107. Volf, *Exclusion and Embrace*, 71.
108. Volf, *Exclusion and Embrace*, 70.
109. Volf, *Exclusion and Embrace*, 92.

thought, through the Gospel of Christ, the way to overcome exclusion and to perform embrace is open to humans. Thus, through the Holy Spirit, one is enabled to participate and practice the way of embrace, thereby imitating Christ. This leads to the discussion of embrace.

Embrace

As previously mentioned, Volf's discussion of embrace centers around the Gospel and the work of the Holy Spirit, from which he continually draws his conclusive inference of the nature and methodology of embrace. He explains, "The central thesis of the chapter [of embrace] is that God's reception of hostile humanity into divine communion is a model for how human beings should relate to the other."[110] This thesis statement implies that Volf's view is fundamentally trinitarian. In addition to focusing on the Gospel and the Holy Spirit, the trinitarian understanding of embrace is connected to his identity theology and eschatological suggestion, which can be deemed part and parcel of his theology of reconciliation. This is discussed separately in a subsequent section. The four "essential moments" of embrace that Volf highlights are "repentance, forgiveness, making space in oneself for the other, and healing of memory."[111]

Repentance

Repentance is a crucial step of embrace to Volf, not only in the sense of sinners' repentance but also of that victims. He understands repentance was at "the very core" of the platform of Jesus's ministry along with love.[112] Volf highlights that "Jesus called to repentance not simply those who falsely pronounced sinful what was innocent and sinned against their victims, but *the victims of oppression themselves.*"[113] Volf contends that the message of Jesus requires profound and radical changes in "moral and religious" senses—concerning sin rather than sociopolitical changes—and Jesus did not divide his audience into two groups, the oppressors and the oppressed.[114]

Evidently, oppressors *must* repent and change their hearts and behaviors. On the other hand, Volf explains that to victims, the call to repentance

110. Volf, *Exclusion and Embrace*, 100.
111. Volf, *Exclusion and Embrace*, 100.
112. Volf, *Exclusion and Embrace*, 112–13.
113. Volf, *Exclusion and Embrace*, 114.
114. Volf, *Exclusion and Embrace*, 113–14.

deals with "inhumane hatred," which is "understandable" but they still must be "released" from it.[115] Referring to Zygmunt Bauman's comment on envy, Volf discusses how victims often also seek "dominant values and practices," and reinforce them through how they were oppressed.[116] Volf argues that it is repentance that emancipates victims from sinful "dominant values and practices," "humanizes" them, and "transforms" their hearts according to "God's vision" for the "new world."[117]

> The dominant values and practices can be transformed only if their hold on the hearts of those who suffer under them is broken. This is where repentance comes in. To repent means to resist the seductiveness of the sinful values and practices and to let the new order of God's reign be established in one's heart. For a victim to repent means not to allow the oppressors to determine the terms under which social conflict is carried out, the values around which the conflict is raging, and the means by which it is fought. Repentance thus empowers victims and disempowers the oppressors. It "humanizes" the victims precisely by protecting them from either mimicking or dehumanizing the oppressors. Far from being a sign of acquiescence to the dominant order, repentance creates a haven of God's new world in the midst of the old and so makes the transformation of the old possible.[118]

In discussing the repentance of victims, Volf asserts that victims ought to also seek a "*change of their heart and behavior.*"[119] Volf calls this "the politics of the pure heart," without which he asserts that "every politics of liberation will trip over its own feet," captured by the seductive power of enmity and jealousy.[120]

Forgiveness

The absence of repentance would make forgiveness more difficult. Volf states that such absence is so common that "both victim and perpetrator are imprisoned in the automatism of mutual exclusion, unable to forgive or repent and united in a perverse communion of mutual hate."[121]

---

115. Volf, *Exclusion and Embrace*, 114.
116. Volf, *Exclusion and Embrace*, 116.
117. Volf, *Exclusion and Embrace*, 114–16.
118. Volf, *Exclusion and Embrace*, 116.
119. Volf, *Exclusion and Embrace*, 114.
120. Volf, *Exclusion and Embrace*, 119.
121. Volf, *Exclusion and Embrace*, 120.

Volf identifies that the "endless turning of the spiral of vengeance" owes its consistency and prevalence to two factors; first is "the predicament of partiality," which implies the disagreement between two groups on "moral significance of their actions."[122] One group would consider their action as "justice or even settling for less than justice," whereas "the other may perceive the same action as taking revenge or perpetrating injustice."[123] This recalls his discussion on the limitations of liberation theology. Volf explains, "As the intended justice is translated by the other party into actual injustice, a 'just' revenge leads to a 'just' counter-revenge."[124]

Another factor is "the predicament of irreversibility," as specified by Hannah Arendt.[125] This denotes that one's action cannot be undone—it is "irreversible" and thus "the urge for vengeance seems irrepressible."[126] As Arendt insists, Volf asserts that "forgiveness is also the only way out of" the predicament.[127] Volf interprets forgiveness "as a genuinely free act," which "breaks the power of the remembered past and transcends the claims of the affirmed justice and so makes the spiral of vengeance grind to a halt."[128] Similarly, in *The End of Memory*, as mentioned in his personal story, Volf underscores the significance of forgiveness, expressing the following: "To triumph fully, evil needs two victories, not one. The first victory happens when an evil deed is perpetrated; the second victory, when evil is returned."[129] In *Free of Charge*, he writes that, "Revenge multiplies evil. Retributive justice contains evil—and threatens the world with destruction. Forgiveness overcomes evil with good."[130]

However, Volf accentuates how forgiveness does not replace justice. He comments that forgiveness "is not a substitute for justice" because without justice, one would not know what to forgive; therefore, "no justice, no forgiveness."[131] Forgiveness does not attenuate justice; instead, "every act of

---

122. Volf, *Exclusion and Embrace*, 121.
123. Volf, *Exclusion and Embrace*, 121.
124. Volf, *Exclusion and Embrace*, 121.
125. Arendt, *The Human Condition*, 212, as quoted in Volf, *Exclusion and Embrace*, 121.
126. Volf, *Exclusion and Embrace*, 121
127. Volf, *Exclusion and Embrace*, 121.
128. Volf, *Exclusion and Embrace*, 121.
129. Volf, *End of Memory*, loc. 91–92.
130. Volf, *Free of Charge*, 161.
131. Volf, *Exclusion and Embrace*, 122–23.

forgiveness enthrones justice; it draws attention to its violation precisely by offering to forego its claims."[132]

Volf then raises a noteworthy question: "How will we satisfy our thirst for justice and calm our passion for revenge so as to practice forgiveness?"[133] As the biblical example of "imprecatory Psalms" demonstrates, Volf argues that "rage belongs before God."[134]

> [. . .] by placing unattended rage before God we place both our unjust enemy and our own vengeful self-face to face with a God who loves and does justice. Hidden in the dark chambers of our hearts and nourished by the system of darkness, hate grows and seeks to infest everything with its hellish will to exclusion. In the light of the justice and love of God, however, hate recedes and the seed is planted for the miracle of forgiveness. Forgiveness flounders because I exclude the enemy from the community of humans even as I exclude myself from the community of sinners. But no one can be in the presence of the God of the crucified Messiah for long without overcoming this double exclusion—without transposing the enemy from the sphere of monstrous inhumanity into the sphere of shared humanity and herself from the sphere of proud innocence into the sphere of common sinfulness. When one knows that the torturer will not eternally triumph over the victim (Chapter VII), one is free to rediscover that person's humanity and imitate God's love for him. And when one knows that God's love is greater than all sin, one is free to see oneself in the light of God's justice and so rediscover one's own sinfulness.[135]
>
> In the presence of God our rage over injustice may give way to forgiveness, which in turn will make the search for justice for all possible (see Chapter V). If forgiveness does take place it will be but an echo of the forgiveness granted by the just and loving God—the only forgive ness that ultimately matters, because, though we must forgive, in a very real sense no one can either forgive or retain sins "but God alone" (Mark 2:7).[136]

---

132. Volf, *Exclusion and Embrace*, 123.

133. Volf, *Exclusion and Embrace*, 123.

134. Volf, *Exclusion and Embrace*, 124.

135. Volf adds a footnote here saying: "Situating ourselves in the presence of God is, of course, not all we need to do in order to learn to forgive. We also need to situate ourselves in a community of forgiveness, a community that will help us learn the craft of forgiveness." Volf, *Exclusion and Embrace*, 124.

136. Volf, *Exclusion and Embrace*, 124-25.

It seems that the forgiveness suggested by Volf is based upon that of God. God's forgiveness enables one to acknowledge the truth that everyone has sinned, to be free from revenge, and to forgive the enemy *miraculously*. According to Volf, it is before God that justice and forgiveness can be achieved together.

In *Free of Charge*, Volf offers further discussions on *how* one can forgive as God does. The gist of the discussion can be summarized as follows: first, Volf focuses on the experience of being forgiven by God—acknowledging God's forgiveness in the Gospel. Volf also underlines the intrinsic gap between God's forgiveness and humans sayings—humans can only "imitate" God's forgiveness with "similarity" in their "own way."[137]

Volf notes that, "Because God has forgiven, we also have to power to forgive. We don't forgive in our own right. We forgive by making God's forgiveness our own."[138] Here, Volf explains that when one says "I forgive you," in effect one says "Because God in Christ doesn't count your trespasses against you and because God has removed your guilt from you, I too don't count against you the fact that you've wronged me, I consider you innocent."[139]

Second, Volf highlights God's empowerment to forgive those who have accepted God's forgiveness. Volf reminds readers that God has not only forgiven us, but also "we are not independent" from Him: God is with us, "in us," and "lives through us."[140] Volf asserts that God "can transform us," enabling us to also forgive; thus, "We forgive because Christ forgives through us."[141] Volf therefore argues, "we respond to God's forgiveness by 'passing on' forgiveness to others."[142]

These two points in Volf's discussion on forgiveness are parallel to the two previously identified theological emphases—that his theology of embrace centers around the Gospel and the work of the Holy Spirit. As is demonstrated in the section on forgiveness, the significance of the vertical dimension of reconciliation, which includes acknowledging and accepting the Gospel and the transformative work of the Holy Spirit within believers, can hardly be overestimated in Volf's theology of embrace.

---

137. Volf, *Free of Charge*, 164–65.
138. Volf, *Free of Charge*, 196.
139. Volf, *Free of Charge*, 196.
140. Volf, *Free of Charge*, 165.
141. Volf, *Free of Charge*, 201–2.
142. Volf, *Free of Charge*, 154.

In sum, Volf concludes, "God's forgiveness and our forgiveness go hand in hand."[143] That being said, if one does not forgive, it "manifests" how the person has not "allowed" him or herself "to receive God's pardon"[144].

> [. . .] when we forgive we make God's forgiveness our own; God forgives, and we take that divine forgiving and, in a sense, put our own signature underneath God's . . . when we forgive it is Christ who forgives through us. Even that activity of making God's forgiveness our own is God's work. Put simply, our forgiveness is but an echo of God's. That's why we are able to forgive, and that's why our forgiving makes sense.[145]

Making Space for Others

Volf addresses forgiveness as an important and necessary step in reconciliation, but not a sufficient one. Volf illustrates forgiveness as "the boundary between exclusion and embrace," which "heals the wounds that the power-acts of exclusion have inflicted and breaks down the dividing wall of hostility."[146] However, reconciliation itself can be achieved when one goes further than "the absence of hostility."[147] Volf argues that *"peace is communion between former enemies"* as it is manifested by God.[148]

> At the heart of the cross is Christ's stance of not letting the other remain an enemy and of creating space in himself for the offender to come in. Read as the culmination of the larger narrative of God's dealing with humanity, the cross says that despite its manifest enmity toward God humanity belongs to God; God will not be God without humanity. "While we were enemies, we were reconciled to God through the death of his son," writes the Apostle Paul (Romans 5:10). The cross is the giving up of God's self in order not to give up on humanity; it is the conscience of God's desire to break the power of human enmity without violence and receive human beings into divine communion. The goal of the cross is the dwelling of human beings "in the Spirit," "in Christ," and "in God." Forgiveness is therefore not the culmination of Christ's relation to the

---

143. Volf, *Free of Charge*, 156.
144. Volf, *Free of Charge*, 156.
145. Volf, *Free of Charge*, 202.
146. Volf, *Exclusion and Embrace*, 125.
147. Volf, *Exclusion and Embrace*, 126.
148. Volf, *Exclusion and Embrace*, 126.

offending other; it is a passage leading to embrace. The arms of the crucified are open—a sign of a space in God's self and an invitation for the enemy to come in.[149]

Similar to his statement of catholic personality, Volf's reflection on making space for others is grounded in a trinitarian understanding of relationships. Regarding the *"perichoresis"* or "mutual-interiority" of trinitarian relations, Volf contends that "the life of God is a life of self-giving and other-receiving love."[150] Similar to Barth, Volf maintains that the "self-giving love" of God and receiving "estranged humanity" by "creating space" "are the two essential moments in the internal life of Trinity."[151] Volf further states the following:

> When God sets out to embrace the enemy, the result is the cross. On the cross the dancing circle of self-giving and mutually in dwelling divine persons opens up for the enemy; in the agony of the passion the movement stops for a brief moment and a fissure appears so that sinful humanity can join in (see John 17:21). We, the others—we, the enemies—are embraced by the divine persons who love us with the same love with which they love each other and therefore make space for us within their own eternal embrace.[152]

Volf suggests that the trinitarian understanding of the Cross "should shape our relations to the other."[153] He claims those "who have been embraced by the outstretched arms of the crucified God" can "make space" in themselves for others and "invite them in" "so that together we may rejoice in the eternal embrace of the triune God."[154]

Volf finds the Eucharist to contain this message precisely. On the Eucharist, Volf contends that believers celebrate this divine "making-space-for-us-and-inviting-us-in" of the Trinity.[155] Volf continues as follows: "In the Eucharist, then, we celebrate the giving of the self to the other and the receiving of the other into the self that the triune God has undertaken in the

---

149. Volf, *Exclusion and Embrace*, 126.
150. Volf, *Exclusion and Embrace*, 127.
151. Volf, *Exclusion and Embrace*, 127.
152. Volf, *Exclusion and Embrace*, 129.
153. Volf, *Exclusion and Embrace*, 127.
154. Volf, *Exclusion and Embrace*, 131.
155. Volf, *Exclusion and Embrace*, 129.

passion of Christ and that we are called and empowered to live such giving and receiving out in a conflict-ridden world."[156]

Trinitarian Understanding of Embrace

Related to the previous discussion, Volf's trinitarian understanding of embrace merits further attention in the present study because it is an essential point of view of Volf's regarding reconciliation. Volf highlights the mutual interiority of the Trinity. His comprehension of the trinitarian relationship may be explained as follows:

> [In Trinity,] The one divine person is not only itself, but rather carries within itself also the other divine persons, and only in this indwelling of the other persons within it is it the person it really is. The Son is Son only insofar as the Father and the Spirit indwell him; without this interiority of the Father and the Spirit, there would be no Son. The same applies to the Father and to the Spirit.[157]

In his article titled "The Trinity is Our Social Program," Volf demonstrates that his social vision is rooted in the self-donating and mutual-welcoming relationship—*perichoresis*—of the Trinity.[158] Volf would agree with Barth's clarification that "human community" can merely be "analogous" of the Trinity because he acknowledges that humans who are sinful "can correspond to the Triune God only in *historically* appropriate ways" until the world to come.[159] Volf proposes that the *perichoresis* of the Trinity, which reveals that "the divine persons" "are *personally interior* to one another," can transform one's identity to become "porous" to and "embracing" of others, thereby becoming enriched by others' identities.[160]

In the same article, regarding the triune God's coming "out of the circularity of divine love" to "embrace" humanity, Volf suggests "a social practice" that is "modeled on God's passion for the salvation of the world."[161] Based on this "downward movement" from the Trinity to humanity, Volf claims that "Jesus Christ empowers his followers to participate" in this "movement

---

156. Volf, *Exclusion and Embrace*, 130.
157. Volf, *After Our Likeness*, 209.
158. Volf, "Trinity is Our Social Program," 409–12.
159. Volf, "Trinity is Our Social Program," 405.
160. Volf, "Trinity is Our Social Program," 409–10.
161. Volf, "Trinity is Our Social Program," 417.

of divine love."¹⁶² Here, again, Volf's core argument on *how* one can imitate God's embrace is referred to—that one can follow and participate in the Gospel of Christ, in which the triune God has embraced humanity, through the work of the Holy Spirit.

> The resurrected Christ appeared to his disciples, breathed on them, and said, "Receive the Holy Spirit" (John 20:22). The Spirit whom the disciples received was the same Spirit whom John the Baptist saw descending upon Jesus when he identified Jesus as "the Lamb of God who takes away the sin of the world" (John 1:29–34). The one who went to the cross in the power of the Spirit, now dispenses the same Spirit to empower his followers to participate in the downward movement of God's love which forgives sins and creates a community of joy in the midst of suffering (John 20:19–23). The "Breath" of Christ risen from the dead gives birth to the "body of Christ" offered to the world —a people whose social vision and social practices image the Triune God's coming down in self-emptying passion in order to take human beings into the perfect cycle of exchanges in which they give themselves to each other and receive themselves back ever anew in love.¹⁶³

Similarly, in the book *After Our Likeness*, Volf also explains the Spirit as the main agent enabling the openness of personhood:

> The Spirit presents in all Christians 'opens' each of them to all others. It starts them on the way to creative mutual giving and receiving, in which each grows in his or her own unique way and all have joy in one another. This path issues in common eschatological communion with the triune God. One can enjoy communion with the triune God at the end of this path, however, only because the triune God already stood at its beginning.¹⁶⁴

In *After Our Likeness*, Volf further argues for the catholic personality and ecclesiology based on his understanding of the church as the image of the Trinity.¹⁶⁵ Volf's trinitarian perspective in the book illustrates some sig-

162. Volf, "Trinity is Our Social Program," 418.
163. Volf, "Trinity is Our Social Program," 418–19.
164. Volf, *After Our Likeness*, 189.
165. Both *After Our Likeness* and *Exclusion and Embrace* share the same root, which is Volf's trinitarian theology. They both thus seek to bear the fruits of embrace. The former mainly engages inside the church (within different traditions and forms of the church; trinitarian and ecumenical ecclesiology) while the latter primarily outside the church context (church's engagement in the violent world; trinitarian theology of embrace).

nificant points related to the present research focus. First, Volf accentuates the horizontal dimension of the church based upon a relational understanding of personhood. Volf says, "It is *the Spirit* who constitutes the church ... however, *they* [the members of the church] must come together, and *they* must remain together."[166] In one's relation to God, Volf discusses how one does not "stand as an individual isolated from other human beings" and "from" one's "environment."[167] Volf argues, "even though every human being is constituted in his or her personhood exclusively by God, that person's inner 'makeup' is till that of a social and natural being. Without other human beings, even God cannot create a human being!"[168]

Second, Volf describes this horizontal open relationship with other humans in the church as the church's analogous correspondence to trinitarian communion. He says, "The relations between the many in the church must reflect the *mutual* love of the divine persons."[169] According to Volf, this correspondence of the church to the Trinity is "ontological" since "it is soteriologically grounded" as it is appeared in "Jesus' high-priestly prayer."[170] Therefore, the fellowship of the church is intrinsically trinitarian.

In the words of Volf, "Like the divine persons, so also ecclesial persons cannot live in isolation from one another; Christians are constituted as independently believing persons through their relations to other Christians, and they manifest and affirm their own ecclesial personhood in mutual giving and receiving (see Phil. 4:15)."[171]

Citing Jürgen Moltmann,[172] Volf also says, "The Spirit dwelling through faith in the hearts of human beings 'himself issues from his fellowship with the Father and the Son, and the fellowship into which he enters with believers corresponds to his fellowship with the Father and the Son and is therefore a *trinitarian fellowship.*'"[173]

These two points by Volf illustrate that he advocates relational anthropology, which mainly comes from his trinitarian theology. Volf describes how the creation and redemption of the triune God toward humanity has occurred in a human within fellowship with other humans, not merely as an individual. This relates to Volf's identity theology, and

---

166. Volf, *After Our Likeness*, 176.
167. Volf, *After Our Likeness*, 182.
168. Volf, *After Our Likeness*, 183.
169. Volf, *After Our Likeness*, 195.
170. Volf, *After Our Likeness*, 195.
171. Volf, *After Our Likeness*, 206.
172. Moltmann, *Spirit of Life*, 218.
173. Volf, *After Our Likeness*, 189.

this thought seems to serve as the foundational idea in both *Exclusion and Embrace* and *After Our Likeness*.

However, as discussed previously, Volf argues that an inevitable limitation exists in the church's correspondence to the Trinity. The church "can correspond to God only in a creaturely fashion,"[174] which he explains as follows: "The correspondence of ecclesial to trinitarian communion is always lived on the path between baptism, which places human beings into communion with the triune God, and the eschatological new creation in which this communion is completed."[175] Owing to this limitation, the church's correspondence has "acquired an inner dynamic, moving between the historical minimum and the eschatological maximum."[176] Regarding the minimum, Volf states that it is "being from others," or "being together with others," whereas the maximum is "being toward others," "in which they give of themselves to one another and thereby affirm one another and themselves."[177] Volf explicates that if the church "remains at a statically understood minimum," it "misses possibilities God has given it along with its being."[178] On the other hand, "if it reaches for a statically understood maximum," the church "risks missing its historical reality . . . its self-understanding turns into ideology."[179] The maximum Volf notes is connected to his eschatological understanding of reconciliation, about which he argues the following: "The final reconciliation is the eschatological side of the vision of social transformation contained in the movement of the Triune God toward sinful humanity to take them up into the circle of divine communal love."[180] The eschatological view of Volf is clearly revealed in his discussion of memory, which is presented after this section.

To discuss the topic of the church's correspondence to the *perichoresis* of the Trinity, the framework of Volf's view is basically trinitarian, while simultaneously being pneumatologically emphasized, at least for the matter of how. Volf states, "In a strict sense, there can be no correspondence to the interiority of the divine persons at the human level."[181] This is the case because "The Spirit indwells human persons, whereas human beings by contrast indwell

---

174. Volf, *After Our Likeness*, 199.
175. Volf, *After Our Likeness*, 199.
176. Volf, *After Our Likeness*, 199.
177. Volf, *After Our Likeness*, 207.
178. Volf, *After Our Likeness*, 199.
179. Volf, *After Our Likeness*, 199–200.
180. Volf, "Final Reconciliation," 108.
181. Volf, *After Our Likeness*, 210.

the life-giving ambience of the Spirit, not the person of the Spirit."[182] Volf's main opinion can be observed in the following statements:

> Human beings can be in the triune God only insofar as the son is in them (John 17:23; 14:20); and if the Son is in them, then so also is the love with which the Father loves the Son (John 17:26). Because the Son indwells human beings through the Spirit, however, *the unity of the church is grounded in the interiority of the Spirit*—and with the Spirit also in the interiority of the other divine persons—*in Christians*.[183]

Volf's explanation of how to obtain unity in the church is established upon the interiority of the Holy Spirit. Embracing within the church becomes possible through the work of the Holy Spirit. Volf comments that it is "not the mutual perichoresis of human beings, but rather the indwelling of the Spirit common to everyone that makes the church into a communion corresponding to the Trinity."[184]

Notably, Volf contends that the trinitarian correspondence of the church can only be established after other theological understandings are founded. Volf comments that the "correspondences between church and Trinity can be demonstrated only after the development of anthropology, soteriology, and ecclesiology (even though both anthropology and ecclesiology must be developed in the light of trinitarian doctrine)."[185] It can be inferred that Volf understands that the correspondence is built upon the knowledge of what humanity is and what God has done for humanity, which can be grasped in the light of God. This recalls Barth's argument of the knowledge of God which, he claims, enlightens humans to understand both. Furthermore, Volf mentions trinitarian correspondence *after* the development of other understanding, which is similar to Barth's categorization of fellow-humanity under the section of sanctification.

The Issue of Memory

The final step of embrace that Volf suggests is the issue of memory, about which he comments that it is "perhaps the most difficult act to take place."[186] As described by the phrase "forgive, don't forget," Volf mentions that "the

---

182. Volf, *After Our Likeness*, 211.
183. Volf, *After Our Likeness*, 212.
184. Volf, *After Our Likeness*, 213.
185. Volf, *After Our Likeness*, 200.
186. Volf, *Exclusion and Embrace*, 131.

summons to remember has in recent decades become almost ubiquitous in Western culture."[187] However, Volf insists that forgetting is an eventual goal of reconciliation, although he adds that it is "a *certain kind of forgetting.*"[188] The forgetting that Volf stands for is that of the issue of "truth" and "justice" already having "been taken care of."[189]

The main framework of forgetting by Volf is eschatological. As God's final judgement has occurred, which ultimately satisfies all thirst for justice, one can forget the memory of being trespassed against. Thus, Volf states that it can occur *"only together with* the creation of 'all things new.'"[190] Volf's main idea can be inferred from the following words:

> Since no final redemption is possible without the redemption of the past, and since every attempt to redeem the past through reflection must fail because no theodicy can succeed, the final redemption is unthinkable without a certain kind of forgetting. Put starkly, the alternative is: either heaven *or* the memory of horror. Either heaven will have no monuments to keep the memory of the horrors alive, or it will be closer to hell than we would like to think. For if heaven cannot rectify Auschwitz, then the memory of Auschwitz must undo the experience of heaven. Redemption will be complete only when the creation of "all things new" is coupled with the passage of "all things old" into the double *nihil* of nonexistence and nonremembrance [*sic*]. Such redemptive forgetting is implied in a passage in Revelation about the new heavens and the new earth. "Mourning and crying and pain" will be no more not only because "death will be no more" but also because "the first things have passed away" (21:4)—from experience as well as from memory, as the text in Isaiah from which Revelation quotes explicitly states: "the former things shall not be remembered or come to mind" (65:17; cf. 43:18).[191]

From the perspective of redemptive and eschatological forgetting, Volf claims that remembering is indispensable until the ultimate justice is achieved on the Day of the Lord. Volf asserts that "we do not forget that, as long as the Messiah has not come in glory, for the sake of the victims, we must keep alive

---

187. Volf, *End of Memory*, loc. 117.
188. Volf, *Exclusion and Embrace*, 131.
189. Volf, *Exclusion and Embrace*, 131.
190. Volf, *Exclusion and Embrace*, 131.
191. Volf, Exclusion and Embrace, 135–36.

the memory of their suffering; we must know it, we must remember it, and we must say it out loud for all to hear."[192]

However, this remembering "should be guided" by the redemptive and eschatological vision that the Bible declares.[193] Volf elucidates this as follows: "We remember now in order that we may forget then . . . Though we would be unwise to drop the shield of memory from our hands before the dawn of the new age, we may be able to move it cautiously to the side by opening our arms to embrace the other, even the former enemy."[194] This is Volf's call—remembering *rightly*. In *The End of Memory*, which contains his personal struggle of overcoming the memory of abuse, Volf says that remembering rightly is "neither to hate nor to disregard but to love the wrongdoer."[195]

Volf's thought has its basis on the Cross, which he regards as "a paradoxical monument to forgetting" to achieve "God's all-embracing memory," where He "forgives humanity's sin.[196] The understanding that forgetting is "what God does with our sins" seems to guide Volf to advocate eschatological forgetting as the final form of reconciliation.[197]

Not only for embrace but for the entire church's engagement with society, Volf takes the eschatological view. Similar to the previous warning that the church's correspondence to the Trinity should not lean to either the minimum or maximum extent, in *A Public Faith*, Volf says "No" to "total transformation" by the church, which attempts to "transform the *whole culture they inhabit*."[198] He insists that it is not "possible" nor "desirable" because "the new Jerusalem Revelation describes" it as "coming down out of heaven from God" (Rev 21:2), "not designed and built by Christians."[199]

Eschatological Understanding of Reconciliation

In relation to the above discussion, several points of Volf's eschatological view are explored in this section. First, Volf has continually argued that the final reconciliation is God's—it is what "God will accomplish" by Himself.[200] In *Exclusion and Embrace*, Volf says that "the final reconciliation is not a work

192. Volf, *Exclusion and Embrace*, 138–39.
193. Volf, *Exclusion and Embrace*, 139.
194. Volf, *Exclusion and Embrace*, 139.
195. Volf, *End of Memory*, loc. 100–101.
196. Volf, *Exclusion and Embrace*, 140.
197. Volf, *Free of Charge*, 173.
198. Volf, *Public Faith*, 93.
199. Volf, *Public Faith*, 94.
200. Volf, "Final Reconciliation," 94.

of human beings but of the triune God . . . it is not an apocalyptic end of the world, but the eschatological new beginning of this world."²⁰¹ In "Final Reconciliation," Volf draws a picture of final reconciliation as "the divine embrace" of God to which both parties of once-enemies are invited to come together.²⁰² He asserts, "Reconciliation with one's estranged neighbors is integral to the reconciliation with God."²⁰³ The final reconciliation is "included" in "the eschatological consummation of salvation" by God.²⁰⁴

Second, Volf simultaneously underscores the human agency corresponding to the divine act of God, saying humans are "involved" not only for vertical reconciliation but also horizontal reconciliation.²⁰⁵ Referring to Matt 25:34, he states, "Just as God's action of preparing the children for the kingdom is indisputable, so God's 'not-acting-in-them-without-them' is indispensable."²⁰⁶ In response to the call by God to enter the kingdom He has prepared, Volf argues, "the final reconciliation is an essential dimension of this entry."²⁰⁷ Volf places "inter-human" relations, a form of "human participation" with God's embrace, in the "overarching account of the eschatological transition accomplished by the power of the Spirit."²⁰⁸ Volf concludes as follows:

> The combined emphasis on divine grace as the defining origin and sustaining power of the whole process, on human participation as a fruit and indispensable medium of that grace that transforms sinful persons and their relationships, and on the community of love in the Triune God as the goal of the process explains the introduction of the category "social reconciliation" into the transition from a world of sin to the world of perfect love.²⁰⁹

Third, in Volf's thought, the final reconciliation in the eschatological view should include "*appropriation* by persons on whom it is effected."²¹⁰ He explicates this as follows:

---

201. Volf, *Exclusion and Embrace*, 109–10.
202. Volf, "Final Reconciliation," 101.
203. Volf, "Final Reconciliation," 101.
204. Volf, "Final Reconciliation," 101.
205. Volf, "Final Reconciliation," 106.
206. Volf, "Final Reconciliation," 107.
207. Volf, "Final Reconciliation," 107.
208. Volf, "Final Reconciliation," 107.
209. Volf, "Final Reconciliation," 107–8.
210. Volf, "Final Reconciliation," 103.

The divine judgment will reach its goal when, by the power of the Spirit, all eschew attempts at self-justification, acknowledge their own sin in its full magnitude, experience liberation from guilt and the power of sin, and, finally, when each recognizes that all others have done precisely that—given up on self-justification, acknowledged their sin, and experienced liberation.[211]

Based on this work from God, people can "no longer condemn" each other but treat them in "the grace of forgiveness" that they have received from God.[212] As Volf distinguishes the will to embrace and embrace itself, he mentions that this forgiveness of God and of each other will not be enjoyed by those who reject the embrace of God. Volf comments, "For those, however, for whom the judgment day does not become the day of giving and receiving grace, it will become a day of wrath leading to a hellish world of indifference and hate."[213]

Christian Faith and Embrace

In this section, along with the previous discussions, the two topics in Volf's theology of embrace that are evidently shaped by Christian faith are reviewed: nonviolence and the will to embrace. To begin with, Volf contends that Christian faith promotes nonviolence. Throughout history, opinions have denounced religious forms of violence, and the Christian faith has not been exempted from being the target. As Volf develops his theology of embrace, he engages with the criticisms against Christianity. Volf admits that the history has often shown that "Churches, the presumed agents of reconciliation, are at best impotent and at worst accomplices in the strife."[214] One major factor in churches' complicity in violence that Volf identifies is the strong affiliation to their cultural and ethnic identity through which their religious identity as agents of peace is often overridden.[215]

In addition to his argument about shaping catholic identity, Volf basically asserts that the Christian faith will and should cherish peace and repress violence. To the critique of religious violence in Christianity, Volf claims that "the cure against religiously induced or legitimised violence is not less religion, but in a carefully qualified sense, more religion."[216] Respond-

---

211. Volf, "Final Reconciliation," 103.
212. Volf, "Final Reconciliation," 103.
213. Volf, "Final Reconciliation," 103.
214. Volf, *Exclusion and Embrace*, 36.
215. Volf, *Exclusion and Embrace*, 37.
216. Volf, "Forgiveness, Reconciliation, and Justice," 862.

ing to the censure that Christian faith is monotheistic, which intrinsically promotes violence, he presents the trinitarian understanding of Christian faith and love.[217] Volf considers the religiously motivated violence from Christianity as "malfunctions" of Christian faith, particularly in the form of "coerciveness."[218] According to Volf, it is derived from "a thinned out faith," which can be overcome by "thick faith."[219] Volf thus argues, "'Thick' practice of the Christian faith will help reduce violence and shape a culture of peace . . . at Christianity's heart, and not just at its margins, lie important resources for creating a culture of peace."[220] The thesis of Volf is as follows:

> The more we reduce faith to vague religiosity that serves primarily to energize, heal, and give meaning to the business of life whose course is shaped by factors other than faith (such as national or economic interests), the worse off we will be. Inversely, the more the Christian faith matters to its adherents as faith that maps a way of life, the more they practice it as an ongoing tradition with strong ties to its origins and history, and with clear cognitive and moral content, the better off we will be.[221]

Volf clearly rejects any form of violence and advocates for nonviolence, saying that it cannot be justified theologically and morally based on his reflection on the Cross of Jesus.[222] In the chapter titled Violence and Peace in *Exclusion and Embrace*, he insists that legitimate violence only belongs to God because just violence can only be executed by Him, not anybody else.[223] Volf expounds that the New Testament consistently demonstrates this message.

> The suffering Messiah and the Rider on the white horse do indeed belong together . . . They are not accomplices in spilling blood, but partners in promoting nonviolence. Without entrusting oneself to the God who judges justly, it will hardly be possible to follow the crucified Messiah and refuse to retaliate when abused. The certainty of God's just judgment at the end of history is the presupposition for the renunciation of violence in the middle of it. The divine system of judgment is not the flip

217. Volf, *Public Faith*, 41–43; Volf, "Forgiveness, Reconciliation, and Justice," 865.
218. Volf, *Public Faith*, 39–40.
219. Volf, *Public Faith*, 19–20, 39–40.
220. Volf, "Forgiveness, Reconciliation, and Justice," 862.
221. Volf, *Public Faith*, 40.
222. Volf, *Exclusion and Embrace*, 291; Volf and Neufeld, "Conversations with Miroslav Volf," 82.
223. Volf, *Exclusion and Embrace*, 301.

side of the human reign of terror, but a necessary correlate of human nonviolence.[224]

Second, Volf stands for the will to embrace, which should not be discriminative or conditional because God opens his arms to everyone in the crucified Messiah. However, he comments that the embrace itself can be discriminative and conditional for there would be those who reject the will to embrace, as some do to the salvific arms of God.[225] Volf's discussion of embrace mostly concentrates on the will to embrace, which he considers the primacy.[226] Based on the Christian traditional view that all humans are sinful, Volf claims that the will to embrace must be placed in primacy over "the moral mapping of the social world into 'good' and 'evil.'"[227] It is because one's perception of good and evil is incomplete unlike God's. In this respect, Volf also insists "enlarged thinking" and "the double vision" which includes the others' perspectives.[228]

According to Volf, the will to embrace has priority and is a key factor in overcoming exclusion. He comments that "such nonexclusionary judgements passed by persons willing to embrace the other are what is needed to fight exclusion successfully"[229].

Evaluative Summary

The core argument of Miroslav Volf's theology of reconciliation (embrace) can be summarized as follows. Christian faith can shape one's identity as an embracing identity of others based on the trinitarian understanding of relationships—the mutual interiority of the Trinity, the decentering and recentering process of the self by the Gospel of Christ, and the power of the Holy Spirit that enables one to overcome the dominance of exclusion in sinful humanity. Also, this embrace formed by Christian faith intrinsically includes (an enlarged perception of) justice, social dimension, and eschatological hope.

Volf's theology of embrace makes several contributions to the discourse of mission as reconciliation, the first of which is his theological

---

224. Volf, *Exclusion and Embrace*, 302.
225. Volf, *Exclusion and Embrace*, 29.
226. Volf, *Exclusion and Embrace*, 29; Volf, "Forgiveness, Reconciliation, and Justice," 872.
227. Volf, "Forgiveness, Reconciliation, and Justice," 872.
228. Volf, *Exclusion and Embrace*, 212–13.
229. Volf, *Exclusion and Embrace*, 65.

discussion of identity. In terms of the research focus in this study, what Volf argues is that the vertical dimension of reconciliation shapes and enables the horizontal dimension of reconciliation. Volf's argument is elaborated demonstrating how one's identity can be transformed by the vertical dimension of reconciliation.

The issue of identity is placed at the center of numerous cases of conflict that the church faces today: ethnic, national, or religious identity (usually amalgamated to each other) is often found to play a key role in numerous cases of strife worldwide. As Volf notes, among the multiple identities, Christian identity is sometimes subdued by others such as ethnic or national identities, and unfortunately churches end up uncritically echoing the message or actions of societies they belong to, often missing the prophetic voice.

The Gospel essentially deals with the hearers' identities for it defines them as they are created as the image of God, but at the same time, sinners who need to turn to Christ. Accordingly, as Volf rightly focuses on, horizontal reconciliation would not be profound enough unless it engages with the issue of identity in any form. In particular, Volf's argument on obtaining both distance and belonging from one's own culture and suggestion of establishing a catholic personality and community are relevant to the discussion of identity and reconciliation, not only in the church context but also as the church's voice of reconciliation in the public arena. This is because, although Volf's consideration of identity is largely theological and philosophical, it seems that his analysis may have points that correspond with observations of social scientists.

In brief, among social scientists such as psychologists, anthropologists, and sociologists, an issue of debate has been to what extent the two factors— one's autonomous self-consciousness and social interactions—influence the formation of one's identity.[230] Volf includes both as crucial factors in his theology of identity. As he engages with this issue, it seems that he intentionally takes dual focuses on both the individual and community, for example, catholic personality and catholic community, probably owing to the nature of the topic of reconciliation and his social frame for discussing it.

Volf does not explicitly engage the identity theories of social science; however, some of his examination does not seem too distant or irrelevant. For example, when explaining why conflict easily occurs, Volf states that every self is "dialogically constructed"—"I am who I am in relation to others."[231]

---

230. Further discussions with examples are given in the following evaluation section.

231. Volf, *Exclusion and Embrace*, 91.

Conflicts arise as the self and the other both assert oneself "over against" the other.[232] This understanding seems to be germane to what George Herbert Mead[233] or Charles Cooley[234] discuss regarding identity, that self-consciousness cannot be established without social interactions.

Furthermore, Volf's observations about ethnic conflicts, that individual identities are often conquered by the group identity, sounds similar to the view of social identity theory founded by Henri Tajfel and developed by John Turner. This theory explains how an individual becomes depersonalized and enhanced through in- and out-group boundaries by stereotyping and ethnocentrism through such processes as the social cognitive process and social categorization.[235]

Furthermore, Volf's argument about transforming one's ethnic and cultural identity into a porous identity has its basis, at least partially, in what a renowned anthropologist, Fredrik Barth, argued in *Ethnic Groups and Boundaries*. Fredrik Barth's explanation of forming ethnicity, which is well-known as "Constructivism," rejects the idea that ethnicity is "biologically self-perpetuating" or naturally given, but contends that it is a continuous "social process" selected within the circumstances it is placed and through "interdependent" interactions with other ethnic groups.[236]

All of the abovementioned points of his theology of identity that correspond to different social scientific disciplines can be considered as strengths of Volf's theology of reconciliation. Volf's theology of identity can draw attention from secular societies when the church lifts its voice of reconciliation in the public dimension. The paradigm of exclusion and embrace by Volf is largely built upon his theological reflection on identity. The thesis of Volf, which maintains that Christian faith can shape an embracing identity, may open up more possibilities for the church's involvement in peace-making works in society, as well as elicit more willingness among public society to hear the church's message of reconciliation.

Another contribution is Volf's reflection on liberation theology and justice. Volf has argued that reconciliation must include justice, yet the paradigm of liberation theology is not adequate to many cases of conflict today. It deserves attention in the current discourse on mission as reconciliation, which has dealt with the issue of justice. The theology of reconciliation of a leading scholar in the discourse, Robert Schreiter, seems to at least partially

---

232. Volf, *Exclusion and Embrace*, 91.
233. Mead, *Mind, Self, and Society*.
234. Cooley, *Human Nature and the Social Order*.
235. Hogg et al., "Tale of Two Theories," 259–61.
236. Barth, *Ethnic Groups and Boundaries*, 11–13, 15–16, 18–19.

share the legacy of liberation theology, which takes the paradigm of oppression and liberation. As Volf rightly identified, with seldom exceptions, the predicaments of partiality and ambiguity of victims and perpetrators do not allow the pursuit of justice to become an easy process and lead to the final goal of reconciliation. A legitimate concern of Volf is how today's church should discern and adopt the heritage of liberation theology, which has been a prophetic voice for justice.

Last but not least, regarding the central research concern of this dissertation—the relationship between the vertical and horizontal dimensions of reconciliation—it can be said that according to Volf, horizontal reconciliation can be achieved *based on* and *through* vertical reconciliation. In Volf's theology of embrace, it is clear that the vertical reconciliation shapes and enables the horizontal reconciliation. This is what "the crucified Messiah" has achieved in his "self-giving . . . for many"—he has removed the wall of "enmity" between humans.[237] The following words of Volf illustrate the point again:

> The practice of "embrace," with its concomitant struggle against deception, injustice, and violence, is intelligible only against the backdrop of a powerful, contagious, and destructive evil I call "exclusion" . . . and is for Christians possible only if, in the name of God's crucified Messiah, we distance ourselves from ourselves and our cultures in order to create a space for the other.[238]

> With that mutual embrace, made possible by the Spirit of communion and grounded in God's embrace of sinful humanity on the cross, all will have stepped into a world in which each enjoys the other in the communion of the Triune God and therefore all take part in the dance of love freely given and freely received.[239]

Furthermore, Volf comments that catholic personality must be both evangelical and ecumenical.[240] He continues, "Unaware that our culture has subverted our faith, we lose a place from which to judge our own culture. In order to keep our allegiance to Jesus Christ pure, we need to nurture commitment to the multicultural community of Christian churches."[241] Based on this comment, it can be inferred that the primary reason to be ecumenical is to be more evangelical. Churches in each local and cultural context have to

---

237. Volf, *Exclusion and Embrace*, 47.
238. Volf, *Exclusion and Embrace*, 30.
239. Volf, "Final Reconciliation," 104.
240. Volf, *Exclusion and Embrace*, 52–53.
241. Volf, *Exclusion and Embrace*, 53.

embrace each other in order to become able to examine weaknesses in their own understanding of faith and practice, and be more faithful to Christ. In this case, horizontal reconciliation among churches, enabled and shaped by vertical reconciliation, now promotes vertical reconciliation, thereby strengthening each church's loyalty to Christ conversely. This deepens churches' understanding of vertical reconciliation as both the beginning and end of horizontal reconciliation. The significance of the vertical reconciliation and its effect on the horizontal reconciliation in Volf's thought should be noted. In the current academic discourse in mission studies of mission as reconciliation, Volf's view of the relationship between the two dimensions would once again highlight these crucial points.

After examining Volf's writings, further practical discussions are still required, such as a discussion of what would enhance and accelerate the process of decentering and recentering of the self in Christ as well as the work of the Holy Spirit in vertical reconciliation, which would eventually bear the fruit of horizontal reconciliation. What will help or hinder the process? The following discussion of Son Yang-Won demonstrates a representative example of this issue.

Son Yang-Won

In the previous discussions, Karl Barth and Miroslav Volf have offered elaborated theological discussions of reconciliation. The inquiry of necessity for the practical steps of reconciliation based on theology of reconciliation is still an appropriate concern. In this regard, the theology and practice of reconciliation by Son Yang-Won[242] are explored in this section.

Even though Son Yang-Won has often been considered one of the most influential early church leaders in Korea along with Ju Gi-Chul and Kil Sun-Ju, his life and theology have not been thoroughly studied.[243] It was in more recent years that church historians and theologians began comprehensive research on Son Yang-Won's life and theology.

The present study engages with both primary and secondary sources. Korean historians and historical theologians have recently published the handwritten works of Son Yang-Won that have been found thus far, which

---

242. As mentioned in Introduction, Korean names will be ordered as: last names, then first names, in order to avoid confusion, and also in accordance with the prevalent academic custom in Korean historical studies among both Korean and international scholars.

243. Lee, "Son Yang-Won's Life and Work," 220.

are mostly preserved in the Rev. Son Yang-Won Martyrdom Memorial Hall in Yeosu, South Korea.

In terms of primary sources, the researcher reviewed the following materials written by Son: 221 sermons transcripts and abridgments, forty personal letters, and 1129 personal diaries in from 1928, 1930, 1931, 1934, 1938, and 1949. Most of his diaries discuss the major events of the day, the people he met, and the titles of the sermon and Bible passages that he delivered, but some diaries also contain Son's theological reflections. Furthermore, the letters that Son received from others were explored when deemed necessary. Other types of historical records were also reviewed, such as the protocol of examination of Son and the protocol of the witness examination of the church elders and colleagues by Japanese police and prosecutors. In terms of secondary sources, the researcher reviewed academic literature by Korean historical theologians.

A Brief Discussion of the Life, Ministry, and Reconciliation of Son Yang-Won

Rev. Son Yang-Won (1902–1950), a Korean Christian leader, is an icon of love and reconciliation in Korean Christianity known for his forgiveness and adoption of a man who killed his two sons. Following a brief explanation of Son's background of faith, the account of Son's life, ministry, and reconciliation is outlined by three major events: (1) his ministry at Aeyangwon;[244] (2) his refusal of Shinto worship and consequent imprisonment during the Japanese colonial period; and (3) the martyrdom of him and his two sons following his forgiveness and adoption of their murderer.

Son's Background of Faith

Son first became a Christian through his father, Son Jong-Il, who experienced a radical conversion to Christianity, and subsequently endured persecution from family and neighbors because of his refusal to participate in the ancestor veneration of Confucianism.[245] Son had difficulties attending school because he refused to worship the Japanese emperor, which was mandatory before classes, and furthermore, his father was imprisoned for

---

244. It literally means the Garden of Loving Care. It is a church community for the leprosy patients in Yeosu which is located in southwestern part of South Korea. It was established by Robert M. Wilson, a medical missionary of Southern Presbyterian Mission Board in USA. D. Son, *Rev. Son Yang-Won, My Father*, 16; Ahn, *Seed Must Die*, 9.

245. Son, *Rev. Son Yang-Won, My Father*, 22–31.

his independence movement. Son eventually went abroad to study in Japan, where he had a strong spiritual experience.[246]

In Japan, Son was influenced by such Japanese Christian leaders as Nakada Juji,[247] a Japanese holiness evangelist, and Uchimura Kanzo,[248] a Japanese nonchurch movement leader.[249] Later, in the first protocol of examination, Son announced that he "realized the true meaning of Christian faith by listening to Nakada Juji's sermons in Japan when he was twenty years old."[250]

Son's Ministry at Aeyangwon

Son was invited to preach at Aeyangwon, South Korea, in the fall of 1937 which served as the momentum for him to begin his ministry there in July 1939.[251] Aeyangwon was more of a hospital community at that time; however, Robert Wilson, the founding missionary, wanted to deal with both the spiritual and physical dimensions of patients because he considered that leprosy, or Hansen's disease, involved the problem of sin.[252] Thus, Son tried to guide the patients in Aeyangwon spiritually, transforming it into a faith community.[253]

---

246. Ahn, *Triumph of Pastor Son*, 13; Lee, "Son Yang-Won's Life and Work," 223; Park, "Rev. Sohn Yang-Won," 117–19.

247. Nakada Juji opposed the Shinto worship of Japanese Imperialism, which Son would probably esteem. It seems that the eschatological view (urgent coming of the millennial kingdom of Christ) that Son had was shaped under Nakada Juji's theological influence. Son's eschatological conviction served as a key role to resist strongly Shinto worship until the Independence. It can be inferred from reviewing the protocol examination of Son, the protocol of witness examination of the elders of Aeyangwon as well as Keum Suk-Ho and Lee Sang-Ho. Yi, *Selected Collection*, 457, 463, 469, 477, 500–501, 504–5, 521–26. Keum and Lee actively participated Shinto worship criticizing Son's eschatology as "mystical" and "dangerous." Yi, *A Selected Collection*, 523, 526.

248. Uchimura Kanzo "opposed Japanese colonial rule over Korea," and also "inspired national consciousness" to many Korean Christians, Park, "Rev. Sohn Yang-Won," 118. Son read Uchimura's books in Japan, and later subscribed *Sungsuh Chosun* (*The Bible Korea*), a nonchurch magazine, published by Kim Kyo-Shin, a Korean nonchurch movement leader: Kim, "Son Yang-Won's Resistance," 224; Lee, "Son Yang-Won's Life and Work," 223; Park, "Rev. Sohn Yang-Won," 118.

249. Lee, "Theological Thoughts of Rev. Sohn Yang-Won," 162–63; Lee, "Son Yang-Won's Life and Work," 223; Park, "Rev. Sohn Yang-Won," 117–19.

250. Yi, *Selected Collection*, 454–55.

251. Son, *Rev. Son Yang-Won, My Father*, 51.

252. Choi, "Son Yang-Won and Leprosy," 194–96.

253. Choi, "Son Yang-Won and Leprosy," 208; Park, "Rev. Sohn Yang-Won," 133.

Son's ministry at Aeyangwon can be divided into two main focuses: spiritual formation and loving care. After Son started his ministry, he vitalized the Bible studies and prayer meetings.[254] Choi Byung-Taek (2011, 205) introduces an interview with Lee Gwang-Il,[255] who said that according to the church's records "they did Bible study intensely. Also . . . [Aeyangwon] church rewarded those who memorized Westminster Shorter Catechism, and thirty people received the reward. It means they studied hard." In Aeyangwon, reading the Bible and prayer soon became revitalized movements.[256] Son Dong-Hee, a daughter of Son Yan-won, similarly recalls that "one can hear the sound of prayer and singing praise everywhere in Aeyangwon. Early morning prayer meetings, family worship meetings, and all-night prayer meetings."[257]

Regarding loving care, numerous stories are reported of how Son treated the leprosy patients as humans with dignity and hoped to join their suffering with Christ's love. Son "removed the dividing screen between staffs and patients of Aeyangwon," "took off the gloves when he touched the lepers," and "had meals sitting next to them."[258] Son Dong-Hee introduces elder Baik Il-Hong's eyewitness, who was in charge of nursing room number 14 where the most critical patients stayed, that "some patients were in so awful situation . . . discharge from the wounds, blood, and sweat got congealed all over the room . . . it was so hard to enter the room and take care of the patients."[259] Baik continues, however, that Son "entered the room" and "grasped their hands with love," "touched them," "comforted them," and "prayed for them."[260] The song that Son wrote and used to sing, "Let me love Aeyangwon,"[261] reflected his inner efforts of love toward the patients.

254. Choi, "Son Yang-Won and Leprosy," 205.

255. The sixth senior pastor of Aeyangwon. Son Yang-Won was the second senior pastor.

256. Ahn, *Atomic Bomb of Love*, 36–37.

257. Son, *Rev. Son Yang-Won, My Father*, 52.

258. Lee, "Son Yang-Won's Life and Work," 228.

259. Son, *Rev. Son Yang-Won, My Father*, 57–58.

260. Son, *Rev. Son Yang-Won, My Father*, 58–59.

261. The lyrics is as follows:

1. Lord, let me love Aeyangwon genuinely. Give me love as the Lord loves them. They are abandoned by their parents and siblings, and disliked by all people in the world, but oh Lord, help me love them truly.

2. Oh, Lord, let me love them, love them more than my parents, siblings, and wife and children . . . If I become like one of them, I will be pleased and spend my life with them. As you love and touch them, let me love them truly.

3. Lord, even if they don't like me and betray me, let me still truly love them and do not dislike them until the end . . .

Son's Refusal of Shinto Worship and Imprisonment

When Son became the lead pastor at Aeyangwon, Korean Christianity was facing the problem of Shinto worship more seriously than ever. Approximately 1 year later, Son was arrested and imprisoned by the Japanese colonial rulers because he refused to participate in Japanese Shinto worship, which he considered clear idolatry.[262] Son was imprisoned for approximately five years.[263] The Japanese colonial government expelled American missionaries and threatened the people in Aeyangwon that if they refused Shinto worship, no medical supplies would be dispatched.[264] The remaining family members of Son Yang-Won had to leave Aeyangwon as the new Japanese director, Anto, was appointed.[265] A number of patients and members of Aeyangwon left and went into the streets and mountains to escape the Japanese authorities.[266] They suffered persecution, keeping their faith and resisting Shinto worship.[267] They were influenced by Son, who had set an example by showing firm resistance to Shinto worship and consequently being imprisoned.[268]

---

4. Oh, Lord, I say I love them, but do not let my love be artificial and man's love. Let me not love for men, but for you, Lord. Let me not love them more than You. It is the love from You and my love for them is for You, then how can I love them more than You . . .

5. Lord, let my love not become a love of desire which is for worldly reputation, or reward at the end of the world. Let it be a simple love that love these poor spirits and bodies only through the love of Christ. . . Son, *Rev. Son Yang-Won, My Father,* 52–54.

262. Ahn, *Seed Must Die*, 24–28.

263. Son was arrested September 25, 1940. He was imprisoned in detention centers before the trial. Then, he served his sentence, one and half years as the punishment execution for resisting Shinto worship which ended in May 17 1943. However, the release was postponed. His appeal was dismissed and Son was transferred to several prisons and was sentenced to life due to his continuous refusal of Shinto worship. He was finally discharged in August 17, 1945, two days after the national independence from Japan. Lim et al., *Letters in Prison by Rev. Son,* 186, 191; Yi, *A Selected Collection,* 545.

264. Choi, "Son Yang-Won and Leprosy," 205–8.

265. Son, *Rev. Son Yang-Won, My Father,* 107–9.

266. Choi, "Son Yang-Won and Leprosy," 207.

267. Choi, "Son Yang-Won and Leprosy," 207.

268. Park, "Rev. Sohn Yang-Won," 133–34.

The Martyrdom of Son's Two Sons, and His Adoption of Their Murderer

After Korean national independence, Son's first and second sons, Dong-In and Dong-Shin, were murdered in the midst of national turmoil by communist rebel forces in the Yeosu and Suncheon areas of Korea in October 1948.[269] Leftists soldiers and students killed those who "showed pro-American attitude, especially Christians."[270] The rebel army was finally repressed by the South Korean army, and the murderer[271] of his two sons was arrested and sentenced to death.[272] Son begged for his life multiple times through various channels, and ultimately saved him from being executed.[273] Arch Campbell discusses the colonel who was in charge was deeply impressed so that he released the murderer.[274] Campbell comments Son was even trying to "send a request to President Syngman Rhee," whom Son knew "personally" in order to save the murderer.[275] George Thompson Brown, who was missionary of Korea, also writes "Pastor Sohn's great act of forgiveness went from mouth to mouth throughout Korea."[276]

Son forgave and adopted the person as his own son. Rhie Deok-Joo construes that such forgiveness by Son was derived from him "practicing Jesus' commandment that love your enemy, a sense of duty as a pastor to evangelize an unbeliever who is about to be executed, and his hope to reconcile the nation cutting the vicious circle of revenge and strife between the left and right."[277]

Later, during the Korean War, while many fled to southern areas seeking shelter, Son Yang-Won remained with the leprosy patients who were unable to escape the area, and he was killed by communist soldiers

---

269. Cha, *Aeyangwon and Martyr of Love*, 180–81.

270. Cha, *Aeyangwon and Martyr of Love*, 181.

271. Although the name of the murderer is known, it is not indicated here. It is because the concern of Son Dong-Hee. She comments that it is unfortunate and unnecessary that his real name was written in Ahn Yong-Choon's book, considering the sense of guilt that his descendant may have who knew nothing about the incident. Son, *Rev. Son Yang-Won, My Father*, 288–89. Son Dong-Hee wrote his false name in her memoirs. A son of the murderer later became a pastor.

272. Son, *Rev. Son Yang-Won, My Father*, 256–59.

273. Son, *Rev. Son Yang-Won, My Father*, 265–73.

274. Campbell, *Christ of the Korean Heart*, 53.

275. Campbell, *Christ of the Korean Heart*, 53.

276. Thompson, *Mission to Korea*, 185.

277. Rhie, "From 'White Martyrdom,'" 170.

because of his Christian faith.[278] Based on his life and ministry, Son becomes an icon of reconciliation of Korean Christianity, and has been referred to as "an atomic bomb of love."[279]

The Essential Features of Son's Theology of Reconciliation

Several features require attention when examining Son Yang-Won's theology of reconciliation. First, the starting point of Son's theology of reconciliation is the love of God revealed on the Cross toward sinners. Son repeatedly describes himself as a sinner who has been forgiven. Second, based on God's love, Son's theology centers around sanctification. His endeavor and eagerness for sanctification can easily be observed in many of his letters and sermons. It was all the fruits of his unending effort toward sanctification—loving neighbors and patients with leprosy who were not welcomed by many, and forgiving the person who killed his sons and adopting him as a son. Third, the main method to be sanctified to which Son devoted himself the most was prayer. Son's theology is prayer-oriented; unsurprisingly, along with the Gospel of Christ, receiving the grace of the Holy Spirit is a central focus in Son's theology in his emphasis on prayer. Fourth, Son considered Christian faith to be disciplined as a genuine faith in the midst of suffering and persecution. The culmination in which his theology was well-represented was Son's forgiveness and adoption of the person who killed his two sons. This was demonstrated in Son's memorable speech at the funeral service of his sons, entitled "Nine Things that I am Thankful for":

> Ladies and gentlemen, how can I possibly give a long reply? Instead I would like to talk about several items of thanksgiving that I came to reflect upon in response to my sons' martyrdom.
>
> First, I thank the Lord for producing martyrs out of the lineage of a sinner like me.
>
> Second, I thank the Lord for having had entrusted these two precious jewels to me, of all the saints out there.
>
> Third, I thank the Lord for blessing me so that I could dedicate my beautiful two sons to you, the oldest and the second, out of my six children of three sons and three daughters.

---

278. Cha, *Aeyangwon and Martyr of Love*, 197–98.
279. Lee, "Son Yang-Won's Life and Work," 219.

Fourth, they say that it is glorious to have one son die as a martyr. Still how much more glorious are the deaths of two sons? I thank you for this blessing.

Fifth, they say it is glorious to die in sleep while believing in Jesus. Still, how much more glorious is it to be shot to death while carrying out the work of evangelism.

Sixth, they were preparing to go and study abroad in America. However, they went to a far better place in heaven. I thank you for this peace within me.

Seventh, I thank the Lord for giving me this heart of compassion and conviction to embrace as my son the enemy who killed my two sons and help him turn to God in repentance.

Eighth, I thank the Lord for giving me the assurance that, through the martyrdom of my sons, many more sons of heaven would be generated.

Ninth, I thank the Lord for giving me the eight truths, the heart of joy that seeks God's love, and the faith that is generous [even in the midst of this adversity[280]].[281]

Before Son delivered this speech, in the funeral march when people of Aeyangwon and Son's family followed the bier singing hymns, Son Dong-Hee recalls that her father Son's "praise became sobbing and sobbing became praise again," which she interpreted as an inevitable expression of Son's feeling that oscillated between "bodily sadness and spiritual faith."[282]

Self-Identity as a Forgiven Sinner

To begin with, the self-identity that Son often demonstrated himself is that of a forgiven sinner. Not just on ordinary occasions but also in the midst of praise for him, Son reveals the identity without reserve. In his diary of June 20, 1949, when Son was invited to speak about the martyrdom of his two sons at the Second Army Hospital, he wrote,

---

280. The quote comes from the English translated edition of Cha Jong-soon's book. It seems that the phase is omitted. It exists in the publication by Son Dong-Hee in both original (1999) and revised edition (2016), however not in Cha's book which refers to Son's.

281. Cha, *Aeyangwon and Martyr of Love*, 183–84; Son, *Rev. Son Yang-Won, My Father*, 245–46.

282. Son, *Rev. Son Yang-Won, My Father*, 244.

It seems that many people revere me as if I did something great and consider me as a saint, but I hope people don't ask to me speak about the martyrdom anymore. Some even sell our three father and sons' pictures as saints pictures, and I feel extremely painful and uncomfortable about this. I am truly a big sinner . . . all good deeds are what the Lord has done, and I am powerless and weak who had never overcome even a little sin by myself and do not know how to cope with this treatment. So, I cry a lot privately . . . Therefore, I am very careful of what I say to avoid of boasting words. Oh, Lord, hold my tongue and hold my reputation so that they never become excessive, but they serve only to the glory of God . . . hide me in your embrace.[283]

Similar words can easily be found in his diary.[284] A few examples are presented as follows. On June 3, 1949, when Son preached to a young adult revival meeting in the Busan area of South Korea, which was highly successful and people praised him, Son wrote, "I don't know how to thank the grace of God that has worked through a sinner like me."[285] Furthermore, on June 11, 1949, he wrote, "I do not care of my own eternal reward, but I am only moved by the grace that has been given to me so that all I want is to be loyal to God to pay back the debt of grace and my sin no matter what."[286] In addition, on July 1, 1949, he wrote, "At 4 o'clock in the morning, as I woke up due to coughing, I instantly went to the sanctuary and I thanked God for giving the great grace of prayer to a sinner like me."[287] Similarly, on July 7, 1949, he wrote in his diary, "Oh, Lord, I do not understand why you are using a sinner like me . . ."[288] Lastly, on July 26, 1949 he wrote, "I believe there is a forgiving grace for a great sinner like me and I give thanks and glory to the Lord alone."[289]

It seems that the idea of being forgiven by God was a core identity of Son Yang-Won. Not only his diaries but also his sermons and letters explicitly and implicitly indicate this. For example, in his sermon on May 30, 1948, entitled "Why I came to believe in Jesus," Son described his personal experience as follows: "initially my faith was blind, I heard the

---

283. Yi, *Selected Collection*, 125.

284. The diaries before the year of 1949, as mentioned, they are briefly written only about major events and sermons that he preached. From May 1949, he began to write longer diaries.

285. Yi, *Selected Collection*, 121.

286. Yi, *Selected Collection*, 123.

287. Yi, *Selected Collection*, 126.

288. Yi, *Selected Collection*, 126.

289. Yi, *A Selected Collection*, 127.

heaven is simply good . . . later I became half in doubt . . . eventually as I utterly realized that I am a sinner, I repented and after that, unfathomable joy came to me."[290] Furthermore, it seems that this personal experience of conversion in company with the influence of Nakada Juji shaped Son's identity as a forgiven sinner. The influence of Juji and the holiness church continued as Son focused on the issue of sanctification, which is discussed in the following paragraphs.

Sanctification-Focused

As the second feature, Son concentrates on sanctification. His endeavor for sanctification can be observed in (1) his strong warning against committing sins in his sermons and letters; (2) his concern and wish to receive the grace of holiness in his spirit, mind, and body; and (3) his desire to live according to the words of God.

First, in various writings, Son expresses his very cautious attitude to sin. In his sermon on June 20 and August 13, 1937, he said, "sin is a scarier thing than a plague and even death."[291] In this regard, in a letter to his son Dong-In in August, 1945 (dates assumed),[292] Son advised, "more than anything, I'm concern if you commit a sin by any chance. Of course, I do not doubt that you would not sin, but I'm concerned if the temptation of demons come to you . . . the seed of sin is so scary and strong that I cannot emphasize enough about it."[293] In the same letter, Son wrote the following to his son:

> All the time, we have to pursue the complete holiness. The three great enemies of humans: 1) the desire of flesh, 2) vanity of the world, and 3) temptation of the devil. One has to fight and win over these three, and to win, efforts and perseverance are required. Also, to persevere, the will power should be strong, otherwise a human cannot persevere to the end . . . old saints all had frighteningly intense efforts and strong will power. You should have persevering volition that even bleeding and determined to the extent that "even if I die." Some might say "I have weak will power by nature, so I can't." But that is a cowardly excuse, trying to avoid the fight against sin and suffering . . . Therefore,

290. Yi, *A Selected Collection*, 290.

291. Yi, *A Selected Collection*, 171.

292. The same letter has been assumed as written in August 1945 by Yi Man-yeol. Yi, *Selected Collection*, 164.

293. Son strongly advises not to sin to his children in the letters of June 13, 1942, and December 7, 1942 Lim et al., *Letters in Prison by Rev. Son*, 72–77, 120–30. Lim et al., *Letters in Prison by Rev. Son*, 222–23, 229–33.

discipline your will always. My beloved children, do not emulate your father by all means. I am the worst sinner of all and the most foolish of foolish people.[294]

Second, he places receiving the grace of holiness as one of the top priorities in his spiritual life. In a diary entry from June 24, 1949, mentioning John Wesley, he wrote, "I have been praying for the grace of holiness in my spirit, mind, and body until today since I started the prayer in Tokyo, Japan, twenty seven years ago."[295] To Son, the life of holiness is what Christians' life looks like based on the Gospel of Christ.

On July 14, 1946, Son preached on Christians' life that "Christians are crucified so that they cannot do and eat as they want. Every life should be crucified. It is painful during the moment of being crucified, but after that . . . there is no pain for those even whose passions and desires are crucified."[296] A few months later, in a sermon on Christians' holy life on September 8, 1946, Son declared that "Christian life" is "the life of holiness."[297] In a sermon on "Reproof and Discipline" on March 23, 1947, Son preached that "hating sin is evidence of loving God . . . Without fail, hate sin, keep yourself away from sin . . . be zealous and repent. Passionate repentance. Do it thoroughly."[298] On multiple occasions, Son evidently emphasized the significance of holiness in Christian faith.

Kwak In-Sub notes that "the two characteristics of Son Yang-Won in his inner and spiritual life are sensitivity to sin and total commitment to prayer."[299] Kwak describes how "before the martyr that Son already committed his life, Son committed his life first to the prayer fighting against his sinful desires and the prayer for the intimate relationship with God."[300]

It was based on this sensitive acknowledgement and resistance against sin and seeking holiness that Son resisted the Shinto worship of the Japanese empire. While the majority of Christian leaders attempted to compromise their faith and performed Shinto worship, pastors such as Son and Ju Gi-Chul rejected it, viewing it as clear idolatry worship.[301] In this sense, Cha

---

294. Lim et al., *Letters in Prison by Rev. Son*, 223–24, 231–33.
295. Yi, *Selected Collection*, 125.
296. Yi, *Selected Collection*, 234.
297. Yi, *Selected Collection*, 237–38.
298. Yi, *Selected Collection*, 418.
299. Kwak, "Reformed Life Theology and Rev. Son," 40, 52–54.
300. Kwak, "Reformed Life Theology and Rev. Son," 40.
301. Not only about Shinto worship, but also about a salutation to the Korean national flag after the Independence, Son strongly argued against, and thus a salute has never been enacted as the ROK government accepted the resistance of Christian

Chong-Soon comments that "the most visible virtues of Rev. Son's life of faith were faithfulness and integrity."[302] As Son refused Shinto worship, he anticipated and accepted the concomitant persecutions against him and his family. In a sermon (dates unknown), Son said, "it is natural for a Christian to be persecuted if he or she tries to live a holy life . . . [referring to the people of faith in the past] it is not a new thing."[303]

Another factor to consider here is Son's eschatological faith. According to the protocol of examining Son and others, Son constantly mentions that Jesus will return and reign the millennial kingdom on Earth, which meant that all other regimes and kingships including Japanese would be overthrown eventually. Son asserts that because it is true he cannot worship other emperors. By contrast, Keum Suk-Ho and Yi Sang-Ho, who participated in Shinto worship and later provided testimony in Son's investigation, had a dispute with Son on this matter. All three knew each other because they had graduated from the Pyeongyang Theological Seminary.[304]

According to the protocol of witness examination, both Keum and Yi claimed that they did not believe in Jesus's return and rule on Earth, but they only believed in the afterlife, which made them perceive Shinto worship as compatible with Christian faith.[305] Considering the witness accounts of the elders of Aeyangwon regarding Son's teaching on the millennial kingdom of Christ on Earth, Son's resistance to Shinto worship was based on not merely faith to one true God, but at least partially on his eschatological vision of Christ's kingdom on Earth soon.[306]

Third, being sensitive to committing sin, Son disciplined himself to keep the commandments of God thoroughly. It seems that keeping God's commandments was a fundamental rule for Son's life, theology, and sermons. It was a core principle for himself to live accordingly to God's words. For instance, when Son sent his daughter to his friend Rev. Na Duk-hwan to save the murderer, Son Dong-Hee witnessed how she refused to follow her father's order. Son, "after a sigh," explained,

> [. . .] why did I suffer in prison knowing that you were suffering outside? It was to keep the first and second commandments of God . . . the commandment of love that your enemy is also

leaders. Yi, *Selected Collection*, 121, 281.

302. Cha, *Aeyangwon and Martyr of Love*, 154.

303. Yi, *Selected Collection*, 426.

304. It was the former Presbyterian seminary that later divided into Presbyterian University and Theological Seminary and Chongsin Theological Seminary.

305. Yi, *Selected Collection*, 521–27.

306. Yi, *Selected Collection*, 132, 497–521.

the commandment of God. If I obey one and disobey another, it is a huge contradiction. If I don't obey the commandment of love your enemy now, my 5 years in prison and our suffering are in vain . . . your two brothers are in heaven, but the murderer will go to hell. As an evangelist, how can I see this happening and do nothing?[307]

Emphasis on Prayer

Third, to Son, prayer is the main method of sanctification. His sermons frequently highlight that a prayerful life is the way to receive the grace of holiness. Not only in sermons but also in all of Son's writings, the emphasis on prayer appears widely. He was known as a man of prayer who led numerous revival meetings in Korea. His nickname was "Son-Bul" (Son the fire), which means "a man of blazing prayer."[308] A sermon topic that he felt "most confident" with and "most frequently delivered" was prayer.[309] In a sermon on prayer (dates unknown), Son stated that "prayer is like a breathing of spiritual humans."[310] He continued, "prayer is not easy, but like a war so that one should devote all of one's energy into prayer . . . prayer is the source of all strength and the most significant job."[311]

As stated above, a feature to notice in Son's understanding of prayer is that prayer is like a war and a strenuous labor—but one of the most valuable—of Christians.[312] In Son's view, prayer is not an option but a "duty."[313] He deals with the issue of prayer with determined resolution instead of an easy mind.

Referring to the meaning of Gethsemane, Son said "prayer is truly something that squeezes human's essence."[314] In "Let us be a person of prayer" (dates unknown), Son also characterized prayer as follows: "desperate prayer means relying on God totally and longing for God to achieve something with His power. However, if there is no prayer, that means one

---

307. Son, *Rev. Son Yang-Won, My Father*, 260–61.

308. Son, *Rev. Son Yang-Won, My Father*, 48; Kim, "Rev. Son Yang-Won," 283; Rhie, "From 'White Martyrdom,'" 153.

309. Yang, "Analysis of Sermons of Rev. Sohn," 135; Kwak, "Reformed Life Theology and Rev. Son," 59.

310. Yi, *Selected Collection*, 337.

311. Yi, *Selected Collection*, 337.

312. Yi, *Selected Collection*, 322, 337, 340.

313. Yi, *Selected Collection*, 339.

314. Yi, *Selected Collection*, 323.

is acting by his or her own will and ignoring God, which makes the person like a prodigal son. In everything and every deed, prayer should be the head and tail."[315]

Son Dong-Hee, Son's daughter, recalls his prayer life as follows: "father often went to a mountain to pray. There was a place where he always prayed. When father went to the mountain to pray, he usually did not return for a few days, but prayed in the mountain. He brought rice with him, soaked it in water and ate a handful of rice while he was praying there."[316]

There are three different aims in Son's understanding of prayer: (1) to surmount the desire of flesh and win the spiritual war; (2) to obey God's words and live a godly life (including loving one another); and (3) to endure and overcome persecution and suffering.

For the first aim, in relation to the fight against sin, Son identifies prayer as the main weapon. Numerous examples of this understanding exist in Son's writings. For instance, in a sermon titled "Let us be a person of prayer" (dates unidentified), Son claimed that "every sin occurs in the absence of prayer."[317] Furthermore, in his sermon on "Gethsemane Prayer" (dates unknown), Son argued that "prayers drive out worldly thoughts... and conquer devils. It is easy to be defeated unless the prayer is desperate."[318] In the same sermon, Son encouraged his audience by saying, "we should do a prayer that wins over our flesh and rebukes devils."[319]

Similarly, in a sermon on the Lord's Prayer on June 29, 1947, Son stressed that the "devil tries to tempt us by any chance" with "worldly things," and "the world wicked and devil are also wicked, but I am weak, so I do this prayer [being united with Jesus] hard every day."[320] On January 18, 1948, in "Two ways of life" (Ps. 1), Son warned, "why a Christian is depraved... one dies because the person does not eat prayer and the Bible."[321] Evidently, Son understood and practiced the life of prayer for victory in his spiritual battle.

For the second aim, Son argued in a sermon titled "Let us be a person of prayer" (dates unknown) that "the will of God is achieved by prayer and the real worth of life is related to existence and nonexistence of prayer."[322] In addition, on February 7, 1932, in a sermon on "those who are

---

315. Yi, *Selected Collection*, 339.
316. Son, *Rev. Son Yang-Won, My Father*, 47.
317. Yi, *Selected Collection*, 340.
318. Yi, *Selected Collection*, 322.
319. Yi, *Selected Collection*, 322.
320. Yi, *Selected Collection*, 268.
321. Yi, *Selected Collection*, 286.
322. Yi, *Selected Collection*, 338.

blessed," Son proclaimed that "how to keep the words of God? Through prayer."[323] Similarly, in a sermon titled "Live according to the Bible" (dates unknown), the following words of Son demonstrate the first and second goals of prayer well:

> [. . .] the only way that can make one's life of faith correspond to the teaching of the Bible is prayer . . . Christianity is the religion of prayer, and a Christian is a person of prayer . . . Without prayer, it is impossible to live a Christian life . . . the strength to have victory over the devil and the secular world comes from prayer only . . . Prayer is a war. In a war, the enemy does not die, then I die. It is a war: flesh vs. I, and the secular world and the devil vs. I. It absolutely depends on one's victory in prayer life that he or she can live a life of faith corresponding to the teachings of the Bible . . . Let us die while praying. In order to live according to the Bible![324]

According to Son, a great commandment of God is to love as He does, and he asserted that prayer is a primary method of becoming a person who loves as God does.[325] In December 1948, when Son preached on "the end of all things is near" (1 Pet 4:7–11) at Cho-Ryang church after his two sons were martyred, Son emphasized the significance of prayer once again:

> If a Christian does not pray, that is like a living being without breathing. Of course, his or her own life is lost, and furthermore the person is guilty of paying no attention to the life given by God. Therefore, we sometimes do not pray, considering it without scruple, but never forget that it is a great sin.[326]

In the same sermon, as he described the relationship between prayer and loving, Son preached the following:

> The most important thing in one's relationship with other humans is love. But how come we rarely see Christians are loving others, which is the most valuable thing? The fountain of loving does not well up in the prayer-less hearts that are dried up and stubborn. Prayer . . . is the booster in the fountain of love that provokes love . . . The hidden meaning in "Keeping loving one another earnestly" [1 Peter 4:8] is that it indicates the love in the

---

323. Yi, *Selected Collection*, 201–2.
324. Yi, *Selected Collection*, 373.
325. Yi, *Selected Collection*, 246.
326. Yi, *Selected Collection*, 306.

heart of Jesus Christ that has loved the church and forsaken his own body for sinners.[327]

Based on these words, one can infer that the forgiveness and reconciliation that Son showed to his sons' murderer was possible because he was man of prayer who steadily and desperately prayed as if he was in a fierce battle between being conquered by his sinfulness and receiving the power of God in his struggle to follow Christ.[328]

The third aim of prayer concerns the context of Son himself and his family; persecution and imprisonment for five years due to Son's denial of Shinto worship, and the martyrdom of his two sons after the independence. Eventually, Son himself was martyred by North Korean soldiers during the Korean war.

To overcome such suffering and persecution, Son contended that what one needs is prayer. Multiple times, Son preached that one should pray to endure and overcome persecution and suffering. For example, on August 3, 1947, in his sermon on "lead us not into temptation" (Jas 1:2–4, 12, 15), Son said, "do not be afraid of trials . . . [God] makes us overcome them through the power of the Holy Spirit . . . during my prayer time . . . Here is a reason for the failure of Peter . . . due to the absence of prayer . . . one can overcome only when one's will and resolution are combined with prayer."[329]

Similarly, in his sermon on Gethsemane Prayer, Son explained Matt 26:41 by saying that "all trials come in as they seize an opportunity of prayerlessness. To disciples, that Jesus was captured and crucified is a big trouble and the greatest trial. Nothing except prayer can overcome this trial."[330] Yang Nak-Hong offered an interpretation that "the first secret that Rev. Son Yang-Won could endure the suffering faithfully was his prayerful life."[331] Kwak In-Sub also comments that it was prayerful life that made Son overcome "inner anxiety and distrust caused by suffering" in his realities, even in prison.[332]

---

327. Yi, *Selected Collection*, 306.
328. Yi, *Selected Collection*, 337, 339.
329. Yi, *Selected Collection*, 274.
330. Yi, *Selected Collection*, 322.
331. Yang, "Analysis of Sermons of Rev. Sohn," 136.
332. Kwak, "Reformed Life Theology and Rev. Son," 62.

Son's View on The Holy Spirit

Unsurprisingly, along with his emphasis on prayer, Son acknowledges the significance of the work of the Holy Spirit. Son commented in a sermon titled "Do not receive the grace in vain" on January 26, 1931, that "the grace of the Holy Spirit" is a way "to gain the power of prayer," "the power of evangelism," and "the power to defeat the devil."[333] Similarly, in a sermon about the "conception of the Holy Spirit" (July 13, 1947), Son said, "as one prays more, reads the Bible more, one can be filled with the Holy Spirit. Do not commit a sin against the Spirit. He would leave you."[334] Referring to 1 Thess 5:19, he continued,

> Do not quench the inspiration of the Holy Spirit. The inspiration motivates one to pray, to read the Bible, to perform relief, and to visit other fellow Christians. When you have this type of inspiration, do not quench, but do it immediately. To pray in one accord and with united efforts is the only way to receive the Holy Spirit and to be filled with the inspiration of the Spirit (Acts 1:8). Just pray.[335]

It can be noted that his sensitivity toward the work of the Holy Spirit goes together with his cautious attitude against committing sin. Prayer is often emphasized as a central method for these issues in his teachings. A prayerful life means having deeper communion with the Holy Spirit. In a sermon titled "Only a bottle of oil left—receive the oil" (2 Kgs 4:1–7; dates unidentified), Son said, "the oil is prayer, that is to say, the Holy Spirit. The Holy Spirit, that is to say, a prayerful life . . . . prayerfulness is, in other words, being filled with the Holy Spirit. One prays to receive the Holy Spirit, and the person who has received the Spirit also prays through the Spirit."[336] Therefore, Son argued that, "The genuine faith is the faith that receives the Spirit" (in December 7, 1947, "about the baptism of the Holy Spirit").[337]

Suffering

The last feature of Son's theology concerns suffering, which has been embedded in his context. Similar to the discussion for the third aim of prayer,

---

333. Yi, *Selected Collection*, 198.
334. Yi, *Selected Collection*, 271–72.
335. Yi, *Selected Collection*, 272.
336. Yi, *Selected Collection*, 350.
337. Yi, *Selected Collection*, 283.

Son defines how Christian faith becomes a genuine faith in the midst of suffering. In his letters to his family from prison, Son encouraged them to overcome suffering with faith. For example, in a letter to his sister (August 12, year unidentified), Son advised, "suffering itself is not treasure, but it becomes one only when you withstand it."[338]

Because suffering disciplines one's faith, it seems that Son saw there are some positive aspects of suffering in an ironic manner. In a letter to his wife, Jung Yang-Soon, dated October 14, 1942 (presumed), Son wrote, "as I have always said, suffering is truly a huge blessing. Let's treat it as honey . . . suffering disciplines us."[339] In the same letter he said, "hardships help one realize one's sin . . . lead the person to come close to God."[340] The letter was to embolden his wife not to worry. Son commented that anxiety comes from "disbelief" and the "thought of flesh."[341] Then, Son asked his wife "earnestly to pray and stay without anxiety."[342]

In a letter (September 4, 1943) to his sister, Son similarly wrote,

> beloved sister, I perceive that the suffering of Job is more precious than the wealth of Solomon, and the perseverance of Job is more beautiful than the wisdom of Solomon. Solomon later committed sin caused by the wealth and wisdom he received, but the suffering and perseverance of Job later became final bliss. One's happiness should be examined at the last and true wisdom is being distant from sin . . . Therefore, please cast all the anxiety to God and be thankful and rejoice always.[343]

Son described Christian faith in the same manner in a letter to his son, Dong-In (July 27, 1945; presumed). He said, "Christians' life of faith is to give thanks and rejoice in suffering and adversity."[344] According to the witness account of Son Dong-Hee, Son said "all the time that Christian faith is disciplined through suffering only."[345]

This understanding of suffering reflects Son's life and context, not only individuals and family but also national circumstances. Son's sermons often

---

338. Lim et al., *Letters in Prison by Rev. Son*, 461, 465.
339. Lim et al., *Letters in Prison by Rev. Son*, 94–95, 99–101.
340. Lim et al., *Letters in Prison by Rev. Son*, 95, 101.
341. Lim et al., *Letters in Prison by Rev. Son*, 94, 99.
342. Lim et al., *Letters in Prison by Rev. Son*, 95, 103.
343. Son wrote a letter to his wife with almost the same message in August 18, 1943. Lim et al., *Letters in Prison by Rev. Son*, 158, 161, 163. Lim et al., *Letters in Prison by Rev. Son*, 170, 173.
344. Lim et al., *Letters in Prison by Rev. Son*, 442, 445.
345. Son, *Rev. Son Yang-Won, My Father*, 189.

emerged during his prayer time in the midst of suffering. Son reinterpreted the situation of suffering in the light of his faith, which became primarily renewed during his prayer time before God. The hope that he found in his relationship with God made him endure and rejoice in Him. The issue of suffering has been a main theme of the academic discussion of reconciliation. One of the greatest hindrances to achieving reconciliation is the suffering that the victims have experienced at the hands of the perpetrators. This often defines the depth and seriousness of reconciliation, and it is certainly a complex issue that is never easily resolved.

In Son's case, vertical reconciliation with God, which was continuously enhanced during his prayer time, was his perpetual source of strength of endurance and offered a new perspective for interpreting the situation and an eschatological hope for the end. Moreover, in becoming a disciple of Christ, Son wished to participate in the suffering of Christ who suffered for humanity.[346]

Evaluative Summary

The life, ministry, and theology of Son Yang-Won can be best described as sanctification-focused, Gospel-centered, and prayer-driven. Son's theology of reconciliation centers around sanctification. It is a core idea that not only characterizes Son's theological focus but also illustrates his understanding of the relationship between vertical and horizontal reconciliation. Son's life was a pursuit of sanctification. The forms of sanctification include keeping oneself away from sin, obeying God's commandment, and becoming a Christ-like person who is holy and loves others as He did. Son's concept of sanctification thus can be summed up through two topics: holiness and love. It was these two aspects that Son focused on in his ministry at Aeyangwon. Horizontal reconciliation—loving others—is an essential form of sanctification in Son's theology.

In Son's thought, sanctification is Gospel-centered and prayer-driven. First, for Son, sanctification is a proper response to God as a forgiven sinner. It inseparably lingers on the love and forgiveness of God revealed in the Gospel of Christ. The salvific story of God toward humanity continuously motivates a person to be sanctified who is being moved by the divine reconciliation. Second, sanctification is driven by prayer. In Son's perception, prayer is the main force that empowers oneself to overcome sinful desires, temptations, and suffering, and to commit oneself to follow God's will. The three characteristics

---

346. Son, *Rev. Son Yang-Won, My Father*, 321.

of Son's theology of reconciliation—sanctification-focused, Gospel-centered, and prayer-oriented—are closely interrelated.

The practical example of living a life of reconciliation that Son manifested indicates that being overwhelmed by the meaning of vertical reconciliation is a key element in forgiveness and reconciliation in one's horizontal dimension. Understanding the depth of the meaning of reconciliation with God transforms one's heart and redefine one's identity to be able to practice forgiveness and reconciliation as God did. This is what Miroslav Volf elaborated in discussing how Christian faith affects a person to be able to embrace and overcome exclusion through the power of the Gospel and the Holy Spirit. Furthermore, it is exactly what Son demonstrated in his life and ministry through emphasizing a significant practical method, prayer as a cooperative tool from human agency to the work of God.

As depicted by the testimony of Son Dong-Hee, in Son's mind, it seems that the horizontal dimension of reconciliation was not grasped and pursued as a separate task; rather, it was comprehended in the light of vertical reconciliation as one of the most important of God's commandments.[347] This sounds very close to what Karl Barth suggested, who shaped ethics as dogmatics. As examined in chapter 3, Barth viewed sinful humans' own moral consciousness as intrinsically incomplete, and ethics is not self-evident apart from God's standard. Thus, he claimed that "the ethical reflection" can be understood "in awareness of the absolute *givenness* of the command" from God, which is "itself the truth of the good."[348] That is, "*Good* means *sanctified by God*."[349] Therefore, again, John Webster construes Barth's ethics as follows: "the significance of the notion of divine judgment in the *Ethics* can hardly be overestimated."[350]

Barth's view of ethics corresponds to the case of reconciliation by Son. Son's relationship with God, in which his understanding of the Gospel both moved his heart and compelled him to keep God's commandments, enabled

---

347. As it is written previously, when Son Yang-Won sent Son Dong-Hee to his friend Rev. Na Duk-hwan to save the murderer from the military execution, she refused to go. Then, she witnessed that Son Yang-Won, "after a sigh," and said: "why did I suffer in prison knowing that you were suffering outside? It was because to keep the first and second commandments of God . . . the commandment of love your enemy is also the commandment of God. If I obey one and disobey another, it is a huge contradiction. If I don't obey the commandment of love your enemy now, my five years in prison and our suffering are in vain . . . your two brothers are in heaven, but the murderer will go to hell. As an evangelist, how can I see this happening and doing nothing?" Son, *Rev. Son Yang-Won, My Father*, 260–61.

348. Barth, *Ethics*, 76.

349. Barth, *Ethics*, 16.

350. Webster, *Barth's Moral Theology*, 45.

him to forgive and love the murderer as his own son. As demonstrated by his suffering imprisonment for resisting Shinto worship, keeping God's commandments could not be compromised, nor was it optional for him based on his attitude toward God and the Scripture.[351]

For example, in a sermon on "only he who does the will of my Father will enter the heaven," (Matt 7:15–27; dates unidentified), Son claimed that the will of God means three things: "1) one should believe in Jesus, 2) one should be sanctified by the life of Jesus, and 3) one should become a person who lives by loving others."[352] On loving life, Son argued that because God himself is love and every deed of Him is love . . . He looks for those who love and those who do not love will not enter into the heaven."[353] Son additionally asserted, "Unlike the fake love and selfish love of the world . . . the love in the great commandment of Jesus can only be done by those who received the new life."[354]

The story of reconciliation and the theology of Son Yang-Won should merit more attention not only from Korean Christianity, which currently struggles with the issue of reconciliation in many aspects of society and the nation, but also from the international Christian community in whatever concerns the church's understanding and practice of reconciliation.

One of the main contributions of Son's life and theology is providing an actual example of how vertical reconciliation can empower horizontal reconciliation in the life of someone who truly sought to be faithful to God. Specifically, this involves such ideas as what kind of spiritual and theological emphases would help a person be prepared for reconciliation with fellow humans. This indicates that (1) the issue of self-identity formation in light of the Gospel including its effect in reconciliation with others; (2) understanding of

---

351. As briefly reviewed previously, Son had a very high view of Scripture. It seems that keeping God's commandments is a very significant issue to Son. Even though one should consider the time when Son lived, the theology of Son Yang-Won may be considered as strong "evangelical" by many of contemporary Christians. Son defines a Christian as "a person who tries to live according to the Bible, 66 books of the Old and New Testaments." Yi, *Selected Collection,* 369. Son once said "I witness with my life that this Bible is the Word of God. If anyone doubts that, I do not want to associate with the person." Yi, *Selected Collection,* 370. In a sermon of "Let us believe Jesus well" in March 9, 1947 (John 6:22–40), Son addressed that "today the theologians of new theology interpret the bible with their own wisdom and knowledge. Traditional theologians interpret through the Holy Spirit by faith. Faith is the Bible as it is. Believing well means to believe the Bible as it is, and the Holy Spirit as He is. Disregarding my own will and ability, but the Bible as it is. Do not adjust the Bible with anything else." Yi, *Selected Collection,* 255.

352. Yi, *Selected Collection,* 353.
353. Yi, *Selected Collection,* 352.
354. Yi, *Selected Collection,* 352.

sanctification, for example, what its nature is and aspects are; and (3) practical steps for enhancing reconciliation in both dimensions such as prayer. All of these issues can be inferred from the example of Son.

The practical step, in particular, can be helpful. The advice that Son presents is simple. Through prayer one can reflect better upon God's reconciling character. Robert Schreiter, a leading voice in mission as reconciliation, also recognizes spirituality as a key in the ministry of reconciliation, yet Son demonstrates how one's spirituality can facilitate reconciliation in reality. Through total commitment to prayer and reliance on the Holy Spirit, Son was able to be faithful to God's commandments of love and forgiveness. Son's life of prayer not only reveals the significance of prayer but also how much and how deeply one should pray as well.

In short, it is evident in Son's case that vertical reconciliation—God's love revealed in the Gospel of Christ—had continuously been the main motivation and empowerment for him to overcome human's sinfulness, practice love for his marginalized neighbors at Aeyangwon, and forgive and adopt the enemy as his own son. In other words, because sanctification before God was a clear focus of his life and ministry, a life of reconciliation was possible. Horizontal reconciliation can be observed in Son's life as much as vertical reconciliation can. Love God and love your neighbor are the two inseparable commandments in Son's theology.[355] As Barth explains about Jesus, He was the man "for God" so that could be "for us" with fellow-humanity.[356] Resembling Jesus, being described by his nicknames, Son could be an "atomic bomb of love" because he was "Son-Bul" (a man of blazing prayer).

Desmond Tutu

Over the last four decades, Archbishop Desmond Mpilo Tutu has been one of the most influential Christian figures of reconciliation. As an Anglican clergyman, he has devoted his life to multiple types of social activism and human rights movement, the most well-known being the anti-apartheid movement in South Africa, which led to him being awarded the Nobel

---

355. In relation to this, it is noteworthy that Son views that a Korean traditional idea, 경천애인, (Gyung-Chun-Ae-In; worship the heaven and love humans), which was allegedly announced by the founder (Dan-gun) of the first ancient Korean nation (Go-Chosun), has connection to the greatest commandments of the Bible. Yi, *Selected Collection*, 245, 440, 442. Son considers the idea corresponds to "love God and love neighbor," and Korea people had been prepared to receive the Gospel by this thought. Yi, *Selected Collection*, 331.

356. Barth, *CD* III/2:201, 207, 208, 216, 217.

Peace Prize in 1984. In the post-apartheid period, Tutu is widely known for his work as the chair of the Truth and Reconciliation Committee (TRC).[357] The committee has attempted to investigate, publicly reveal the truth, and achieve forgiveness and reconciliation for the human rights abuses committed during the apartheid period by both pro- and anti-apartheid groups in South Africa.

Tutu's commitment to Christian faith has been visible since his youth.[358] It can be argued that Tutu's views on justice and reconciliation, as well as other social issues, are based on his Christian faith and theology.[359] This section reviews how Tutu's theology has shaped his idea and practice of horizontal reconciliation. After a brief examination of Tutu's ministry of reconciliation, his theology of reconciliation is reviewed regarding to the relationship between the vertical and horizontal dimensions of reconciliation. Furthermore, both literature written by Tutu himself as well as academic literature on Tutu's ministry and theology are explored.[360]

A Brief Explanation of the Ministry of Reconciliation by Desmond Tutu

The Ministry of Social Engagement

Desmond Mpilo Tutu (born on October 7, 1931) has served in quite a few representative offices during his religious career, including as the Director of the Theological Education Fund (TEF) in Africa, the General Secretary of the South African Council of Churches (SACC), the Bishop of Johannesburg, and the Archbishop of Cape Town, South Africa. During his career, from the early phase,[361] Tutu has consistently been engaged in

---

357. Tutu was appointed by Nelson Mandela, after Mandela was elected as the first African president of South Africa.

358. Gish, *Desmond Tutu*, 23.

359. Du Boulay, *Tutu*, 140–41; Allen, *Rabble-Rouser for Peace*, 164, 169–70, 179, 342; Gish, *Desmond Tutu*, 73, 83–84.

360. As Johnny Bernard Hill notes, among the writings by Tutu, "No single text . . . provides adequate insight into . . . [his] theological understandings of reconciliation." Hill, *Theology of Martin Luther King, Jr. and Desmond Tutu*, 5. Hill evaluates Michael Battle's writing—*Reconciliation: The Ubuntu theology of Desmond Tutu* "provides the most rigorous account of" Tutu's theology of reconciliation "to date." Hill, *Theology of Martin Luther King, Jr. and Desmond Tutu*, 7. About Battle's another book on Ubuntu theology, Tutu wrote a foreword saying that he "strongly encourages the readers' trust" in Battle "to teach . . . about *Ubuntu*." Battle, *Ubuntu: I in You and You in Me*, vii.

361. Even when Tutu was an educator before he became a clergy, he opposed the national discriminative policy, Bantu Education Act, which prohibited black people's

socio-political activism against racial segregation and discrimination.[362] Tutu became more visible in anti-apartheid activism because he was positioned in offices with more responsibility.

To list a few exemplary cases, during his office as the Dean of St. Mary's Cathedral, Johannesburg (1975-1978), Tutu publicly appealed against apartheid: he wrote columns in newspapers, sent a letter to John Vorster,[363] and "publicly supported an economic boycott to put pressure on the government."[364] Tutu recalls that "he felt called by God"—the "pressure" to write "a personal plea" to Vorster.[365] The letter contained warnings and concerns from Tutu that he is "dreadfully frightened" of a devastating moment coming to them, which was ultimately realized as the Soweto uprising occurred "six weeks later."[366]

In addition, Tutu publicly engaged with the issue of violence observed in the civil movement such as some groups in the Black Consciousness movement and the military wing of the African National Congress, Umkhonto we Sizwe.[367] When he was the General Secretary of the SACC (1978-1985), in spite of his own conviction of nonviolence,[368] Tutu spoke in court on behalf of Tokyo Sexwale, who was arrested for an armed liberation.[369] Tutu defended him as follows: "We are not violent people but we have . . . tried everything that is nonviolent and have failed . . . I can understand

---

education opportunity, and resigned his job as a teacher. Allen, *Rabble-Rouser for Peace*, 59-61, 64.

362. According to Tutu's reminiscence, it seems that this tendency was formed, at least partially, by the mentors such as Trevor Huddleston, and his own experience of liberation when Tutu was studying abroad in UK.

363. A pro-apartheid politician of South Africa who served as the seventh Prime Minister and fourth State President.

364. Allen, *Rabble-Rouser for Peace*, 153-55.

365. Allen, *Rabble-Rouser for Peace*, 153-54; Tutu, *Rainbow People of God*, 6-13.

366. Allen, *Rabble-Rouser for Peace*, 154; Tutu, *Rainbow People of God*, 10.

367. Tutu spoke at the funeral of Steve Biko, when he was killed by security police, a notable leader of the Black Consciousness movement, founding such organizations as South African Students' Organization (SASO) and Black People's Convention (BPC). Tutu, *Rainbow People of God*, 15-21.

368. In 1986, Tutu said, "I abhor all violence. I condemn the violence of an unjust system such as apartheid and that of those who want to overthrow it. But it is absolutely important for South African whites to know that the ANC and the PAC were nonviolent for most of their history . . . It is important when talking about violence to note that the primary violence in this country is the violence of apartheid." Tutu, *Rainbow People of God*, 125.

369. Allen, *Rabble-Rouser for Peace*, 172.

when . . . people feel they have exhausted all nonviolent avenues," which allegedly helped Sexwale avoid the death penalty.[370]

Tutu's preferred choice of resistance was more peaceful. It was an international call for economic pressure "in the form of disinvestment and sanction" against the South African government.[371] Tutu considered it as "necessary to bring about fundamental change" despite the national disadvantage that it entails.[372] Because of these actions, Tutu was placed under strict surveillance by government security agencies and his passport was "seized."[373] However, the persecution by the government raised Tutu's profile higher instead, and Tutu's petition and support for Nelson Mandela, who was not yet the "icon" of liberation, but a "terrorist," was widely known.[374] As the General Secretary of the SACC, Tutu led the organization and the churches of membership to become "visible" in the civil anti-apartheid movement.[375]

In 1989, the anti-apartheid movement faced a new era with the support of the "international community," which increased the pressure on the South African government.[376] On August 17, 1989, when the election was imminent, as the Archbishop of Cape Town, Tutu contributed to organizing a massive civil march movement, the "Defiance Campaign," which followed "an Ecumenical Defiance Service" at St. George's Cathedral, which he led.[377] Subsequent civil movements took place in different areas. Eventually, as F. W. de Klerk became the new president and with the start of his government, the social system of apartheid began to be dismantled.

370. Allen, *Rabble-Rouser for Peace*, 172.

371. Tutu, *Rainbow People of God*, 105; Allen, *Rabble-Rouser for Peace*, 175; Du Boulay, *Tutu*, 242.

372. Allen, *Rabble-Rouser for Peace*, 179.

373. Allen, *Rabble-Rouser for Peace*, 181–82; Du Boulay, *Tutu*, 186–87, 191.

374. Allen, *Rabble-Rouser for Peace*, 181–83.

375. Gish, *Desmond Tutu*, 72; Allen, *Rabble-Rouser for Peace*, 184, 188–89; Du Boulay, *Tutu*, 184. As discussed, the active engagement in social dimension by Tutu has its root in his spiritual convictions and theology. As the general-secretary of SACC, Tutu's a salient focus was spiritual formation of the organization. Shirely Du Boulay evaluates Tutu's leadership at this moment as: "One of the Tutu's great contribution to SACC, something he gave from the very centre of his being, was his emphasis on the spiritual foundation of its work. On a formal level he introduced daily prayers, insisting that the entire staff come together as a community from 8.30 to 9.30pm. every morning; once a month there was a Eucharist . . . During these periods everything, from staff birthdays to the most recent national or international event, was considered in the light of the Gospel, prayer about, placed before God." Du Boulay, *Tutu*, 140.

376. Allen, *Rabble-Rouser for Peace*, 299.

377. Allen, *Rabble-Rouser for Peace*, 301–8.

Truth and Reconciliation Commission

After the Promotion of National Unity and Reconciliation Act in 1995, Tutu was named the chairman of the TRC by Nelson Mandela, the newly elected first black president of South Africa, who felt the strong need for forgiveness and reconciliation in the nation.[378] The TRC had "quasi-judicial powers to grant individual amnesties, with subpoena powers and hearings in public," which enabled the commission to reveal what happened in detail.[379] John Allen explains the work of the TRC as follows:

> The TRC's task was to investigate and report on gross violations of human rights—defined as killing, abduction, torture, and severe ill-treatment—in the period between the Sharpeville massacre of 1960 and Mandela's inauguration in 1994; to consider applications for amnesty; and to make recommendations to the government on reparations.[380]

To do so, the commission operated three committees for each task respectively.[381] A number of hearings of witnesses and confessions took place and were broadcasted publicly. Sparks and Tutu state, "These hearings were presided over by three judges in a committee that operated independently within the TRC and whose findings were final and had the force of law."[382] The atrocities witnessed by the victims and confessions of perpetrators for amnesty during the hearings were so shocking that they profoundly disturbed South Africans and the international community; some reached a limit and almost failed to be redeemed unless Tutu intervened.[383]

Under the leadership of Tutu, the TRC investigated cases of human right abuses by *both* the proponents and opponents of apartheid. As representative examples, Tutu personally persuaded[384] P. W. Botha, the

---

378. Allen, *Rabble-Rouser for Peace*, 345; Sampson, *Mandela*, 521, 524.

379. Sampson, *Mandela*, 521.

380. Allen, *Rabble-Rouser for Peace*, 346.

381. The third committee, "reparation for victims," is considered as "the least successful" Sparks and Tutu, *Tutu*, 215. Sparks and Tutu, *Tutu*, 215; Allen, *Rabble-Rouser for Peace*, 346.

382. Sparks and Tutu, *Tutu*, 215.

383. Allen, *Rabble-Rouser for Peace*, 352–55. About the murder cases confessed by thirty policemen of the Northern Transvaal security, Tutu said, "Yes indeed these people were guilty of monstrous, even diabolical, deeds [but] that did not turn them into monsters or demons. To have done so would mean that they could not be held morally responsible for their dastardly deeds. Monsters have no moral responsibility." Allen, *Rabble-Rouser for Peace*, 355.

384. Reviewing the personal words from Tutu to Botha and Mandela indicates

eighth Prime Minister and sixth President of South Africa, who advocated apartheid, and Winnie Mandela[385] (Madikizela-Mandela after divorce from Nelson Mandela), a leader of anti-apartheid, to present at the public hearing, when they were accused of being involved in violence.[386] There were undeniable limitations in both cases;[387] however, TRC members including its Deputy Chair Alex Boraine and journalists such as Antijie Krog and Max du Preez, "who were close to the process," doubted that even those "limited" successes could happen without Tutu.[388]

As the cases of Botha and Mandela demonstrate, Tutu tried to be unbiased and did not pursue socio-political revenge against pro-apartheid politicians (i.e., retributive justice), but he "advocated restorative justice."[389] This was not only against pro-apartheid groups, as the final report of the TRC "included serious accusations against the ANC [African National Congress, an anti-apartheid group]" as well.[390] Allen introduces Tutu's further discussion of his vision of restorative justice as follows:

> Here the central concern is not retribution or punishment but, in the spirit of *Ubuntu*, the healing of breaches, the redressing of imbalances, the restoration of broken relationships. This kind of justice seeks to rehabilitate both the victim and the perpetrator, who should be given the opportunity to be reintegrated into the community he or she has injured by his or her offence.[391]

In that sense, Sparks and Tutu similarly indicate that "Tutu's main contribution to the TRC" is that he presented "a clear ethical framework in which to operate"; this was "not only to establish the truth of what had

---

that Tutu made a very humble and kind request to them to attend the hearing, showing his favor, appreciation, and expectation to them, rather than being authoritative or threatening with law enforcement. Allen, *Rabble-Rouser for Peace*, 357; Sparks and Tutu, *Tutu*, 228.

385. She was accused due to the violence and murder of Stompie Seipei by Mandel United Football Club, "a gang of tough youths based at Winnie Mandela's home" and "operated" under her leadership. Sparks and Tutu, *Tutu*, 225–26.

386. Allen, *Rabble-Rouser for Peace*, 355–57; Sparks and Tutu, *Tutu*, 225–29.

387. P. W. Botha denied to attend public hearing and spoke privately to Tutu and Mandela. Allen, *Rabble-Rouser for Peace*, 356. Later, Botha was convicted, sentenced of a twelve-month prison, and suspended at the court. Allen, *Rabble-Rouser for Peace*, 357. On the other hand, Winnie Mandela publicly apologized, convinced by Tutu, in "a soft monotone, speaking as if by rote," rather than "heartfelt apology," which made "the audience" be "outraged." Sparks and Tutu, *Tutu*, 228.

388. Allen, *Rabble-Rouser for Peace*, 370; Sparks and Tutu, *Tutu*, 214.

389. Allen, *Rabble-Rouser for* Peace, 347.

390. Sampson, *Mandela*, 523.

391. Allen, *Rabble-Rouser for Peace*, 347.

happened during those years of vicious racial violence but to lay the basis for the start of an ongoing process of national reconciliation."[392] This ethical framework of Tutu is rooted in his theology, the rainbow people of God and *ubuntu*, which highlight the harmonious coexistence and interdependence of different ethnic groups.[393]

The core argument of Tutu's theology corresponds to "the African concept of *Ubuntu*, which idealizes the interdependence of the whole community."[394] Tutu's theology is further reviewed in the following section. The TRC led by Tutu is evaluated as successful on the issue of justice—making "a single history," not double (one by victims and one by oppressors, which is not uncommon).[395] It is still controversial, however, to what extent reconciliation was successful. When he submitted the final report of the TRC to Mandela in 1998, Tutu admitted its "limitations," yet "urged that it be seen as the beginning, not the end, of a process of national reconciliation."[396] Likewise, Mandela commented, "They have done not a perfect but a remarkable job and I approved everything they did."[397]

Desmond Tutu's Theology of Reconciliation

Desmond Tutu's theology can be described as *ubuntu* theology. Under this expression, the core argument of Tutu's theology of reconciliation is that we ought to appreciate the dignity of other humans because they are also God's people[398] who are created in the image of God and forgive (and ask forgiveness for) each other's wrongdoings. Human beings can peacefully coexist and be interdependent in our humanness without violence. This is based on Tutu's

---

392. Sparks and Tutu, *Tutu*, 214.
393. Sparks and Tutu, *Tutu*, 215.
394. Sparks and Tutu, *Tutu*, 215.
395. Allen, *Rabble-Rouser for Peace*, 369–70; Sparks and Tutu, *Tutu*, 229.
396. Sparks and Tutu, *Tutu*, 229.
397. Sampson, *Mandela*, 524.
398. Tutu personally demonstrate this belief to Botha about whom Tutu comments, "God did not call me to be a pastor of black people, God called me to be a pastor of his children . . . Mr. Botha . . . is my brother because that is the interpretation of my faith and my baptism . . . He is a member of my family." Allen, *Rabble-Rouser for Peace*, 357. It should be noted that this argument assumes, at least partially, "the others" would also have Christian faith, which applies to the context of Tutu, South Africa, in which Christianity has the largest adherents including Afrikaners. However, considering Tutu's view of humanity revealed in many cases of Tutu's social engagement, the core idea may still apply to every human being as they are created by God. Also, Tutu's ministry, especially the latter part of it, seem to go beyond the Christian basis in discussing reconciliation, interacting with other religious leaders such as Dalai Lama.

own view of humans as the image of God and a relational and interdependent being: humans are humans through other humans.

As stated, this idea of Tutu has its roots in the spirit of *ubuntu*, an African traditional concept. Out of the notion of *ubuntu*, Tutu draws the essential element of being a human.[399] The fact that Tutu draws his theology from an African concept demonstrates that the foundation of his theology in which he has "rejected" the idea that "any theology, Western or other, could be universally applicable" and advocated contextual theology, which "takes into account the context in which believers live."[400] This is because any theology should engage the public matters of society. In this sense, Tutu acknowledges the issues of liberation and justice as major theological themes for developing the theology of reconciliation in the South African sociopolitical context.

In the following paragraphs, Tutu's theological reflections, which are closely interrelated, are reviewed in the following order: (1) contextual theology (African and black theology) and the social dimension of theology, which are foundational understandings of his theology; (2) liberation, which is a prerequisite in his theology of reconciliation; (3) *Ubuntu* theology, forgiveness, and reconciliation, which are Tutu's main theological contributions; and (4) Tutu's discussion of spirituality and its role in his ministry of reconciliation.

Contextual Theology and The Social Dimension of Theology

According to Tutu, "Western theologians . . . were looking for answers to questions that Africans were not asking."[401] Unlike the philosophical struggle of existence of God in Western churches in the 1960s, Tutu identified "two all-consuming questions for African Christians": (1) "how to replace an alien, imported way of expressing their faith with one that was authentically African," and (2) "how to liberate people from bondage."[402]

Tutu considers there are components in African culture that correspond to the Old Testament, for instance, between the African understanding of ancestors and the biblical concept of ancestors, which is hardly found in "Western" ideas.[403] However, Tutu claims that African Christians lose their

---

399. Allen, *Rabble-Rouser for Peace*, 347.
400. Allen, *Rabble-Rouser for Peace*, 135.
401. Allen, *Rabble-Rouser for Peace*, 135–36.
402. Allen, *Rabble-Rouser for Peace*, 136.
403. Du Boulay, *Tutu*, 115; Allen, *Rabble-Rouser for Peace*, 136–37.

"African-ness" and become "Western" when they become Christians.[404] To rebuild African theology, Tutu tried to "graft black theology onto African theology."[405] While he admitted some dissimilarities, as did John Mbiti,[406] Tutu nevertheless considered how "both African and black theology have arisen as reactions against a situation in which black humanity has been defined in the terms of the white man."[407] For Tutu, it is about identity as African Christians. In other words, it is a matter of incarnation—"Christianity for the African must be incarnated in Africa, speaking to the African from an African context."[408] Thus, Tutu hoped to see African theology "address contemporary problems" in the African context as "black theology"[409] has done.[410]

In his address before "the Styne Commission on the media" on February 2, 1982, Tutu demonstrated his black theology in the African context as follows:

> Black theology merely incarnates the Christian faith for blacks, just as German, Scandinavian and other types of theology incarnate the Christian faith for their various peoples. Black theology is firmly biblical . . . Black consciousness is of God. Our Lord said the two major laws are "Love God and thy neighbor as thyself." A proper self-love is an indispensable ingredient to love of others. Black consciousness seeks to awake in the black person an awareness of their worth as a child of God. Apartheid, oppression, and injustice are blasphemous and evil because they have made God's children doubt that they are God's children. Black consciousness is deeply religious.[411]

404. Allen, *Rabble-Rouser for Peace*, 136–37.

405. Allen, *Rabble-Rouser for Peace*, 137.

406. John Mbiti distinguished African theology from black theology, saying the latter "cannot and will not become African theology." Mbiti, "African Views American Black Theology," 43. Mbiti viewed black theology as a "specifically American phenomenon." Mbiti, "African Views American Black Theology," 43. In that sense, Mbiti criticized such move of Tutu as "a foreign import" which has "no direct relevance to Africa." Allen, *Rabble-Rouser for Peace*, 137; Du Boulay, *Tutu*, 115.

407. Du Boulay, *Tutu*, 116.

408. Du Boulay, *Tutu*, 116.

409. In his speech at Union Theological Seminary in New York in 1973, Tutu addressed on black theology as: "Black theology seeks to make sense of the life experience of the black man, which is largely suffering at the hands of rampant white racism . . . Black theology has to do with whether it is possible to be black and continue to be Christian . . . it is to be concerned about the humanisation of man because those who ravage our humanity dehumanise themselves in the process." Allen, *Rabble-Rouser for Peace*, 138–39.

410. Du Boulay, *Tutu*, 116.

411. Battle, *Ubuntu*, 67–68.

Within the grain of contextual theology, Tutu develops his theology by engaging such social issues as liberation, justice, and reconciliation. Hill indicates that, "Tutu's view on community and reconciliation were very much engrained in the sociopolitical and cultural context of South Africa."[412]

Stated differently, it is Tutu's firm belief that theology should always engage with the sociopolitical dimension of society, the very reality of the people. Tutu rejects the account of the privatization of Christianity, asserting that, "Christianity can never be a merely personal matter. It has public consequences and we must make public choices."[413] Hill comments, "Tutu views human social relations as not simply a social fact, but a theological mandate of God's divine purposes for humanity."[414]

When some criticized the active involvement of the SACC in social issues, Tutu defended its position and said, "Indeed, the liberation is to be set free from sin, the most fundamental bondage, but Jesus was a Jew and he would have known nothing about an ethereal act of God—God's liberation would have to have real consequences in the political, social and economic spheres or it was no Gospel at all."[415]

Later, in *God has a Dream*, he recalls the criticism against him and responds,

> To oppose injustice and oppression is not something that is merely political. No, it is profoundly religious. Can you imagine what the gospel means to people whose dignity is trodden underfoot every day of their lives . . . ? Can you think of anything more subversive of a situation of injustice and oppression? Why should you need Marxist ideology or whatever? The Bible is dynamite in such a situation . . . I was often criticized during the struggle to end apartheid for being 'political' . . . but we are involved in the struggle because we were being *religious*, not political. It was because we were obeying the imperatives of our faith.[416]

Thus, when the first nonracial election took place in 1994, Tutu perceived "the first election" by black people as "a deeply spiritual," "religious," and "transfiguration experience."[417] Tutu's theology has a strong association with the sociopolitical dimension of the South African context. According to Hill, "Tutu's theology, though profoundly theological, is very concerned with

---

412. Hill, *Theology of Martin Luther King, Jr. and Desmond Tutu*, 92.
413. Tutu, *Crying in the Wilderness*, 34.
414. Hill, *Theology of Martin Luther King, Jr. and Desmond Tutu*, 94.
415. Tutu, *Rainbow People of God*, 37.
416. Tutu, *God Has a Dream*, 63–64.
417. Tutu, *God Has a Dream*, 7.

the social makeup of human beings" having connections with such sociologists as Charles Horton Cooley, Emile Durkheim, and T. H. Green.[418] It is because his theology "was shaped and formed" in the midst of "his involvement with the church, in its resistance to the apartheid regime."[419]

Liberation From Injustice

Based on these convictions, Tutu identifies the issue of liberation as an "all-consuming question" for African Christians,[420] as mentioned previously.[421] From 1948 onward, the white Dutch Reformed Churches in South Africa theologically "legitimized the policies of apartheid."[422] Against this move, South African theologians began to discover the "hermeneutics" of liberation thanks to liberation theologians, and "embarked" upon their theology and praxis "on a social analysis" in the following decades.[423] This was the emergence of the indigenous liberation theology of South Africa, "breaking through established ideologies, challenging entrenched elites and destabilizing their power structure."[424]

Tutu was a noticeable voice in this stream. For Tutu, God is a liberator God. In his speech at the funeral of Steve Biko (Sept. 25 1977), a notable public appearance of his, Tutu argued that Jesus is "the great liberator" for "the oppressed, the poor, [and] the exploited," quoting Isa 61:1–4.[425] It is liberation from suffering, oppression, and injustice.

Tutu emphasizes God as a God who is partial to the marginalized. In their qualitative analysis of Tutu's message, Hendrik Pieterse, Peer Scheepers, and Fred Wester discover that the most frequently used phase in his entire public messages is "*God is on the side of the oppressed*," especially in the early 1980s and 90s.[426]

Tutu asserts that God has "a bias for the weak."[427] According to Tutu, a salient message of the Old and New Testaments is that God liberates his

418. Hill, *Theology of Martin Luther King, Jr. and Desmond Tutu*, 92.
419. Hill, *Theology of Martin Luther King, Jr. and Desmond Tutu*, 98.
420. In his mind, black theology as well is in a sense "a component" of the "spirituality of liberation." Battle, *Ubuntu*, 67.
421. Allen, *Rabble-Rouser for Peace*, 136.
422. Walshe, "Evolution of Liberation Theology," 299.
423. Pieterse, "South African Liberation Theology," 28.
424. Walshe, "Evolution of Liberation Theology," 311.
425. Tutu, *Rainbow People of God*, 18.
426. Pieterse et al., "Structure of Thought," 50.
427. Tutu, *God Has a Dream*, 66.

people: God of the Exodus, and the Incarnate God, Jesus is "ransom" (meaning, who "is paid") to "set free those who are kidnapped."[428]

> Liberation is what the Gospel of Jesus Christ spells out in a situation of injustice, oppression and deprivation, such as most blacks experience in the land of their birth. Liberation is through and through biblical and evangelical. You would have to scrap a substantial section of the biblical and Christian tradition if you marginalized liberation.[429]

That is, Christians should "reflect the character of this God" and "have no option but to have a like special concern for those who are pushed to the edges of society, for those who because they are different seem to be without a voice. We must speak up on their behalf . . ."[430] Pieterse, Scheepers, and Wester discuss how Tutu's view of "God on the side of the oppressed *gives guidance to the role of the church.*"[431] The church should "identify" itself "with the poor" in their suffering and do anything possible "to alleviate [their] suffering," even if it comes to facing "vilification and ostracism."[432] According to Johannes van der Ven, Tutu's concept of morality is "entirely dominated" by this conviction.[433]

Tutu explicitly opposes the idea that the church should be neutral in politics and remain a simply religious gathering.[434] He contends that the church should "always be critical of all political systems, always testing them against Gospel standards."[435] In the South African context of apartheid, this means that if the church "chooses" to be neutral and not "to oppose," Tutu argues that it is "in fact to have chosen to side with the powerful, with the exploiter, with the oppressor."[436]

At the same time, for Tutu, liberation is a prerequisite of humanity, and eventually reconciliation. He asserts, "It was liberation from bondage and liberation for the service of God and of his creation, liberation so that we might become fully human with a humanity to be measured by nothing less than the humanity of Christ himself."[437] In his thought, only after both

---

428. Tutu, *Rainbow People of God*, 36–37.
429. Tutu, *Rainbow People of God*, 36.
430. Tutu, *God Has a Dream*, 66.
431. Pieterse et al., "Structure of Thought," 39.
432. Tutu, *Crying in the Wilderness*, 32–33.
433. Ven, "Moral and Religious Self," 95.
434. Tutu, *Crying in the Wilderness*, 34.
435. Tutu, *Crying in the Wilderness*, 33.
436. Tutu, *Crying in the Wilderness*, 34.
437. Tutu, *Rainbow People of God*, 37–38.

parties obtain humanity being liberated from oppression can they accept each other and be reconciled.

Therefore, it can be argued that Tutu's understanding of *Ubuntu*, the subject of the following section, offers a theoretical foundation for the pursuit of liberation, along with the idea that God is a liberator God. This is because "a person of ubuntu," who believes in intrinsic connections with fellow humans, knows that "he or she" "is diminished when others are humiliated or diminished, when others are tortured or oppressed, or treated as if they were less than who they are."[438] Liberation is a prerequisite of *Ubuntu* in Tutu's theology.

Ubuntu Theology. The concept of *ubuntu* plays a key role in Tutu's theology of reconciliation. The term *Ubuntu* can roughly be translated as "humanity" or "humaneness" in English.[439] It comes from the Xhosa phrase, "*Ubuntu ungamntu ngabanye abantu*" ("Each individual's humanity is ideally expressed in relationship with others").[440] In *The Rainbow People of God*,[441] Tutu describes *ubuntu* as follows:

> It has to do with what it means to be truly human, it refers to gentleness, to compassion, to hospitality, to openness to others, to vulnerability, to be available for others and to know that you are bound up with them in the bundle of life, for a person is only a person through other persons . . . A person is a person because he recognizes others as person.[442]

> Our humanness, caring, hospitality, our sense of connectedness, our sense that my humanity is bound up in your humanity.[443]

In *God has a Dream*, Tutu expounds the concept further.

> According to *ubuntu*, it is not a great good to be successful through being aggressively competitive and succeeding at the expense of others. In the end, our purpose is social and communal harmony and well-being. *Ubuntu* does not say, "I think, therefore I am." It says rather: "I am human because I belong. I participate. I share." Harmony, friendliness, community are

---

438. Tutu, *Rainbow People of God*, 31.
439. Battle, *Reconciliation*, 39.
440. Battle, *Reconciliation*, 39; Battle, *Ubuntu*, 3.
441. It is a collection of "key speeches, letters, sermons, interview extracts, submissions to government and off-the cuff remarks" by Tutu (from 1976 to 1994) which was edited by John Allen, the authorized biography writer. Tutu, *Rainbow People of God*, xxi.
442. Tutu, *Rainbow People of God*, 125.
443. Tutu, *Rainbow People of God*, 229.

great goods. Social harmony is for us the *summum bonum*—the greatest good.[444]

As he defines in *In God's Hands*, for Tutu, *ubuntu* is "the essence of being human."[445] Tutu has "turned the concept of ubuntu into a theological concept."[446] It draws its core belief from the theological foundation of *imago Dei*, and it is based on the *perichoresis* relationship of the Trinity. In other words, based on his trinitarian theology, the core idea of Tutu's *ubuntu* is humans as an image of God.

For Tutu, the "interdependent" relationship that God "created" in humans is derived from the "divine fellowship of the holy and blessed Trinity."[447] Johnny Bernard Hill recognizes that a close relationship exists "between Tutu's concept of ubuntu and the affirmation of the Trinitarian God."[448]

Battle also comments, "Indeed, such human interdependence is built into our very creation by our being created in God's image, our common *imago Dei*."[449] The claim leads him to identify apartheid as explicitly unchristian and evil.[450] In his acceptance speech for the Nobel Peace Prize, Tutu concisely addresses this conviction as follows:

> When will we learn that human beings are of infinite value because they have been created in the image of God, and that it is blasphemy to treat them as if they were less than this . . . They need each other to become truly free, to become human. We can be human only in fellowship, in community, in *koinonia*, in peace.[451]

This view entails two different implications for Tutu. The first is that humans are obliged to seek the liberation of other fellow humans, as stated in the previous section. Hill explains the relationship between trinitarian theology and liberation as follows:

> At the center of Tutu's conception of God is a communitarian ethos founded on a Trinitarian model. Tutu rejects the notion of an individualistic transcendent God that is detached from

---

444. Tutu, *God Has a Dream*, 27.
445. Tutu, *In God's Hands*, 34.
446. Battle, *Reconciliation*, 64.
447. Tutu, "My Credo," 235 as cited in Battle, *Ubuntu*, 31–32.
448. Hill, *Theology of Martin Luther King, Jr. and Desmond Tutu*, 101.
449. Battle, *Reconciliation*, 40.
450. Battle, *Reconciliation*, 47.
451. Tutu, "Nobel Peace Prize Lecture," 38.

community and the other . . . God is not so aloof that God is not intimately connected and sensitive to suffering humanity.[452]

The second implication is that any person should basically be treated with dignity as an image of God, even when it seems to be destroyed. Tutu does not apparently lose hope that one can restore his or her own imageness of God and be transformed as a person of *ubuntu* even if it has seemed otherwise. Tutu believes in the possibility of transforming people and society. In *God has a Dream*, in which he shows his "hope in the nobility of the human spirit,"[453] Tutu writes based on the Bible, history, and his own experience that he has a "deep conviction" that "transformation can be recognized and experienced" "regardless" of "faith and religion."[454] Two underlying messages of the book are that transformation is possible,[455] and "we are the agents of transformation that God uses to configure His world."[456] Tutu describes this type of understanding as the "spirituality of transformation."[457]

In *No Future Without Forgiveness*, Tutu similarly addresses how the TRC operated "on the premise that people could change, could recognize . . . the error of their ways . . . at the very least, remorse . . . confess . . . and ask for forgiveness . . . In this theology, we can never give up on anyone because our God was one who had a particularly soft spot for sinners."[458]

In this sense, Battle describes Tutu's *ubuntu* theology as follows: it is formed "around the knowledge that there is so much about another person which both cannot be known and cannot be known *responsibly* by human beings. Tutu turns the concept of Ubuntu into a theological concept in which human beings are called to be persons because we are made in the image of God . . ."[459]

Similarly, Hill describes Tutu's anthropology as follows:

> The core of Tutu's view of human nature is that human beings are made in the image of God. Hence individuals are constituted by their relationship to others. To be in insolation as a human being means to not be fully human . . . Tutu declares that to be

---

452. Hill, *Theology of Martin Luther King, Jr. and Desmond Tutu*, 101.
453. Tutu, *God Has a Dream*, ix.
454. Tutu, *God Has a Dream*, viii.
455. Tutu, *God Has a Dream*, 3.
456. Tutu, *God Has a Dream*, 15.
457. Tutu, *God Has a Dream*, 75.
458. Tutu, *No Future Without Forgiveness*, 83–84.
459. Battle, *Ubuntu*, 53.

made in the image of God means to share in a common humanity and fellowship.[460]

For Tutu, the dignity of humans comes from God. He observes a human as a "God carrier" who "acknowledges" "God" in others as well.[461] Therefore, as stated, it is "blasphemy to treat" humans "less than" they are.[462] Tutu expounds this as follows:

> [. . .] it is the fact that each one of us has been created in the image of God. This is something intrinsic. It comes, as it were, with the package. It means that each one of us is a God-carrier, God's viceroy, God's representative. It is because of this fact that to treat one such person as if he or she were less than this is veritably blasphemous. It is like spitting in the face of God.[463]

Thus, Tutu's *ubuntu* theology is based on the understanding of humans as the image of the triune God. This is the essential theological rationale of Tutu's anthropology. Furthermore, it is one of the most significant Christological understandings of Tutu because he views Jesus as "the man for others."[464] Tutu refers to it as "the humanity of Jesus Christ Himself."[465]

Forgiveness and Reconciliation

On many occasions, forgiveness and reconciliation come together in Tutu's mind. The nature and process of forgiveness that Tutu supports is much similar to that of reconciliation. Tutu describes the church as "a community of reconciliation, a forgiving community of the forgiven," which should be able to "offer the remedy to the world's hatreds and divisions, which is not possible when the church itself is 'divided.'"[466]

The core foundation of Tutu's theology of forgiveness is built upon his *ubuntu* anthropology and the concept of humanity. His main argument is that forgiveness and asking for forgiveness can restore and reestablish, respectively, the humanity of victims and perpetrators, whereas revenge destroys it and dehumanizes everyone.

In *No Future Without Forgiveness*, Tutu states,

460. Hill, *Theology of Martin Luther King, Jr. and Desmond Tutu*, 106.
461. Tutu, *God Has a Dream*, 63.
462. Tutu, "Nobel Peace Prize Lecture," 38.
463. Tutu, *No Future Without Forgiveness*, 92–93.
464. Tutu, *Rainbow People of God*, 29.
465. Tutu, "Nobel Peace Prize Lecture," 38.
466. Tutu, *Crying in the Wilderness*, 31.

Anger, resentment, lust for revenge, even success through aggressive competitiveness, are corrosive of this good [social harmony, friendliness, and community]. To forgive is not just to be altruistic. It is the best form of self-interest. What dehumanizes you inexorably dehumanizes me. It gives people resilience, enabling them to survive and emerge still human despite all efforts to dehumanize them.[467]

This corresponds to the fact that he advocates restorative justice instead of retributive justice. Tutu denounces retributive justice as in fact having "little consideration for the real victims and almost none for the perpetrator."[468] Rather, he suggests restorative justice, "which was characteristic of traditional African jurisprudence."[469] Tutu argues,

> Here the central concern is not retribution or punishment. In the spirit of ubuntu, the central concern is the healing of breaches, the redressing of imbalances, the restoration of broken relationships, a seeking to rehabilitate both the victim and the perpetrator, who should be given the opportunity to be reintegrated into the community he has injured by his offense.[470]

However, restorative justice is *still justice*. The forgiveness that Tutu refers to never abandons telling the truth nor does it forget wrongdoings. Tutu states,

> Forgiving and being reconciled are not about pretending that things are other than they are. It is not patting one another on the back and turning a blind eye to the wrong. True reconciliation exposes the awfulness, the abuse, the pain, the degradation, the truth. It could even sometimes make things worse. It is a risky undertaking but in the end it is worthwhile, because in the end dealing with the real situation helps to bring real healing. Spurious reconciliation can bring only spurious healing.[471]

In addition, forgiving does not forget. He continues, "In forgiving, people are not being asked to forget. On the contrary, it is important to remember, so that we should not let such atrocities happen again. Forgiveness

---

467. Tutu, *No Future Without Forgiveness*, 31.
468. Tutu, *No Future Without Forgiveness*, 54.
469. Tutu, *No Future Without Forgiveness*, 54.
470. Tutu, *No Future Without Forgiveness*, 54–55.
471. Tutu, *No Future Without Forgiveness*, 270–71.

does not mean condoning what has been done. It means taking what happened seriously and not minimizing it . . ."[472]

Tutu requires anyone who dreams of reconciliation to face and tell the truth from which liberation as well as forgiveness can result. He argues that, "True reconciliation is based on forgiveness, and forgiveness is based on true confession, and confession is based on penitence, on contrition, on sorrow for what you have done."[473] When the perpetrators admit their wrongdoings and ask for forgiveness, this "helps the process of forgiveness and reconciliation immensely;"[474] however, "it is not absolutely indispensable,"[475] and forgiveness still can take place.

In addition, repentance should include action, which is because often any wrongdoing "has affected the victim in tangible, material ways;" as the white were privileged through apartheid, the repentance should be demonstrated in the same way as well.[476] Otherwise, "confession will be considered to be nil."[477]

Tutu's book *No Future Without Forgiveness* proclaims his own thoughts, but simultaneously introduces multiple stories of forgiveness and reconciliation by "ordinary" people in which Tutu finds hope. Based on his hope for people's humanity, Tutu states that ordinary people "living down the street" "have demonstrated noteworthy instances of the capacity to forgive," and "Wonderfully, forgiveness and reconciliation are possible anywhere and everywhere and have indeed been taking place, often unsung, unremarked."[478]

For Tutu, forgiveness can take place through humility. He comments that forgiveness "obviously requires a fair measure of humility."[479] Tutu further discusses how the "ability to forgive others ultimately comes from the humble recognition that we are all flawed and all human and if the roles were reversed we could have been the aggressor rather than the victim. Humility is so important for seeing with the eyes of the heart that it bears elaboration."[480]

---

472. Tutu, *No Future Without Forgiveness*, 271.
473. Tutu, *God Has a Dream*, 53.
474. Tutu, *No Future Without Forgiveness*, 269.
475. Tutu, *No Future Without Forgiveness*, 272.
476. Tutu, *No Future Without Forgiveness*, 273.
477. Tutu, *No Future Without Forgiveness*, 57, 273.
478. Tutu, *No Future Without Forgiveness*, 155.
479. Tutu, *God Has a Dream*, 56.
480. Tutu, *No Future Without Forgiveness*, 81.

Why does Tutu claim humans should pursue forgiveness and reconciliation? In theological anthropology, it has been discussed that Tutu views humans as relational beings who become fully human through other humans. Furthermore, it is commandment given by Jesus. Tutu says, "Theologically, we knew that the gospel of our Lord and Savior constrained us to be ready to forgive when someone asked for forgiveness."[481]

Moreover, as the book title suggests, Tutu asserts that only through forgiveness, which sufficiently and properly deals with the past as he suggests, can humans have a future and "a new beginning."[482] In his words, "without forgiveness without reconciliation there is no future."[483] He further discusses this as follows:

> In the act of forgiveness, we are declaring our faith in the future of a relationship and in the capacity of the wrongdoer to make a new beginning on a course that will be different from the one that caused us the wrong. We are saying here is a chance to make a new beginning. It is an act of faith that the wrongdoer can change . . . because we are not infallible . . . we will always need a process of forgiveness and reconciliation to deal with those unfortunate yet all too human breaches in relationships. They are an inescapable characteristic of the human condition.[484]

In *God has a Dream*, Tutu similarly argues,

> Forgiveness gives us the capacity to make a new start . . . That is the power, the rationale, of confession and forgiveness. It is to say, "I have fallen but I am not going to remain there. Please forgive me." And forgiveness is the grace by which you enable the other person to get up, and get up with dignity, to begin anew. Not to forgive leads to bitterness and hatred, which just like self-hatred and self-contempt, gnaw away at the vitals of one's being. Whether hatred is projected our or projected in, it is always corrosive of the human spirit.[485]

In sum, reconciliation in Tutu's terms includes all the concepts described thus far. The existence of fellow humans is indispensable for defining the humanity of any self. It begins with acknowledging the dignity of other humans, and liberates those who are being treated without dignity, because

---

481. Tutu, *No Future Without Forgiveness*, 276–77.
482. Tutu, *No Future Without Forgiveness*, 273.
483. Tutu, *No Future Without Forgiveness*, 165.
484. Tutu, *No Future Without Forgiveness*, 273.
485. Tutu, *God Has a Dream*, 54.

they are the divine image of the triune God. It thus becomes a societal matter and deserves the work of the church as well as the entire community. For the matter of injustice, facing the truth is significant and repentance is expected, pursuing restorative justice, rather than retributive justice which will not reestablish humanity in anyone. In this process of reconciliation, the role of forgiveness is crucial for it makes a new start possible for the community as a reconciled one.

Tutu perceives this reconciliation as a "a long-drawn-out process with ups and downs, not something accomplished overnight."[486] It is a journey of a generation to another generation. However, with hope, he asserts that " . . . in our experience nothing was wasted, for in the fullness of time, when the time was right, it would all come together and those looking back would realize what a critical contribution they had made. They were part of the cosmic movement toward unity, toward reconciliation, that has existed from the beginning of time."[487] Tutu believes his hope is derived from the dream of God. He considers that reconciliation illustrates "God's dream for humanity."[488] God's dream for Tutu is that human beings are "indeed members of one family" as the rainbow people of God, "bound together in a delicate network of interdependence."[489]

Spirituality and Reconciliation

As briefly mentioned previously, Tutu has committed himself to spiritual formation, particularly prayer (along with reading the Bible), and emphasized doing the same to other Christians such as his staff in "insisting the importance of prayer."[490] For instance, as General Secretary of the SACC, he began "compulsory daily staff prayers; regular Bible study; monthly Eucharist; and . . . silent retreats."[491] Notably, it was Tutu's time in the SACC that he became prominent in the anti-apartheid movement. Although he shared his commitment to prayer elsewhere, one of the most representative records of Tutu about prayer was then, when he addressed SACC staff as follows:

> He [Jesus] was a man of prayer, a man of God . . . Prayer and communion with the father were like breathing to him . . . So we

---

486. Tutu, *No Future Without Forgiveness*, 274.
487. Tutu, *No Future Without Forgiveness*, 263.
488. Tutu, *No Future Without Forgiveness*, 274.
489. Tutu, *No Future Without Forgiveness*, 274.
490. Du Boulay, *Tutu*, 140–41.
491. Allen, *Rabble-Rouser for Peace*, 169.

concluded that prayer and spirituality were central in the life of our Lord and that indeed he could have been the man for others only because first and foremost he had been the man of God.[492]

He continued as follows:

> For us, his followers, it cannot be otherwise. This twofold movement and pattern in our Lord's life must be ours as well. And so for the Council of Churches an authentic spirituality is central and crucial. Prayer and worship and the sacraments and Bible reading take first place in the life of the South African Council of Churches. Our belief is that a relevant and authentic spirituality cannot but constrain us to be involved, as we are involved, in the sociopolitical realm. It is precisely our encounters with Jesus in worship and the sacraments, in Bible reading and meditation, that force us to be concerned about the hungry, about the poor, about the homeless, about the banned and the detained, about the voiceless whose voice we seek to be. How can you say you love God whom you have not seen and hate the brother whom you have? He who loves God must love his brother also.[493]

Introducing Tutu's comments at that time, Allen adds,

> The church exists first and foremost to praise and glorify god and it cannot be otherwise for a council of churches. That is our first priority . . . So for us prayer, meditations Bible reading are not peripheral to our operations. These things are at the centre of our lives. We are not embarrassed that we put God first.[494]

It seems that a prayerful life is something that Tutu himself abides by: "a full hour" daily prayer in early morning, "occasional fasting," "a quiet day" every month, and "three to seven days retreat" every year in order to "listen" to God.[495] He spent hours "in silence" every day.[496] It was reported that one day, when there was "a particularly tense time," Tutu "came into the office" and said "I am going to fast for a week, this is what God has said to me," and then he "spent all day in the chapel."[497]

Tutu himself has also shared personal stories about how prayer time and prayerful reflection either urged him to engage in sociopolitical issues

---

492. Tutu, *Rainbow People of God*, 30.
493. Tutu, *Rainbow People of God*, 30–31.
494. Allen, *Rabble-Rouser for Peace*, 169–70.
495. Du Boulay, *Tutu*, 141; Allen, *Rabble-Rouser for Peace*, 275.
496. Sparks and Tutu, *Tutu*, 127.
497. Du Boulay, *Tutu*, 141.

under the Vorster regime (liberation and social justice) or shaped his view of embracing people such as Botha, who was not cooperative with the work of the TRC (i.e., forgiveness and reconciliation).[498]

Again, attention should be paid to the fact that the fruit of Tutu's prayer time has always comprised of active engagement in the sociopolitical dimension, which he considers the divine work of God. Tutu once mentioned that, "Jesus is reported as saying that some demons could not be exorcised except by prayer and fasting. The demons of injustice, oppression and exploitation can be exorcised only by prayer and fasting."[499]

Unlike some public observations, Tutu stated in an interview that he is "not a politician" but "a pastor" and "a church person."[500] Answering a question about his determined and continuous involvement in sociopolitical matters, he stated that he "believes that religion does not just deal with a certain compartment of life. Religion has a relevance for the whole of life and we have to say whether a particular policy is consistent with the policy of Jesus Christ or not . . ."[501]

In the same vein, he explains his view on the relationship between the vertical and horizontal dimensions of reconciliation. Tutu argues that,

> Our God does not permit us to dwell in a kind of spiritual ghetto, insulated from real life out there. Jesus used to go out and be alone with God in deep prayerful meditation, but he did not remain there. He refused to remain on the Mount of Transfiguration but descended to the valley beneath to be involved with healing the possessed boy . . . That is our paradigm. He did not use religion as a form of escapism . . . That is why he could say we must love God and love our neighbor as well, quoting from the Old Testament. These were two sides of the same coin. The one without the other was unacceptable. Love of God was authenticated and expressed in and through love of our neighbor. That is what is often referred to as the vertical dimension (relationship with God) and the horizontal dimension (relationship with neighbor) in our Christian faith.[502]

Tutu grounds his argument in recalling the parable of Jesus of the Final Judgment in Matt. 25 (separating sheep from goats), which modifies being

---

498. Tutu, *Rainbow People of God*, 6–13; Allen, *Rabble-Rouser for Peace*, 153–54, 357.
499. Tutu, *Rainbow People of God*, 118.
500. Tutu, *Rainbow People of God*, 204.
501. Tutu, *Rainbow People of God*, 204.
502. Tutu, *Rainbow People of God*, 70.

"religious in the narrow sense" and "firmly" announces that God is with "the downtrodden, the oppressed, [and] the marginalized ones."[503] He also maintains that the Old Testament "prophets are deeply involved in politics because politics is the sphere where God's people demonstrate their obedience and their disobedience."[504] Lastly, Tutu highlights the God-driven motivation to resist unjust society as follows:

> Where there is injustice, exploitation and oppression, then, the Bible and the God of the Bible are subversive of such a situation. Our God, unlike the pagan nature gods, is not God sanctifying the status quo. He is a God of surprises, uprooting the powerful and unjust to establish his Kingdom. We see it in the entire history of Israel.[505]

Furthermore, according to Tutu,[506] the reason for the Holy Spirit descending upon us is not "to luxuriate [oneself] in its possession," rather it is "to goad him or her into action, to prepare him for the stern business of loving God and loving neighbor, not in a nebulous fashion but in flesh-and-blood terms . . . in the harsh reality . . ."

In conclusion, for Tutu, spirituality, and particularly prayer, has played a significant role in shaping his theology of reconciliation, and conducting the work of reconciliation as a Christian agent in the societal domain.[507] According to the appraisal of Allen, "The foundations of Tutu's stature and his moral authority are to be found in his spirituality and his faith."[508] The following section presents an evaluation of Tutu's theology of reconciliation.

Evaluative Summary

The most significant feature of Tutu's theology of reconciliation is that it centers around the concept of *ubuntu* humanity, that humans are relational beings who are created in the image of the triune God and can be fully human through others. His reflections on liberation, forgiveness, and reconciliation are all rooted in this understanding.

It seems that Tutu's thoughts echo, at least partially, Karl Barth's trinitarian theology and relational anthropology. However, unlike Barth who

---

503. Tutu, *Rainbow People of God*, 70–71.
504. Tutu, *Rainbow People of God*, 71.
505. Tutu, *Rainbow People of God*, 72.
506. Tutu, *Rainbow People of God*, 114.
507. Battle, *Reconciliation*, 100.
508. Allen, *Rabble-Rouser for Peace*, 394.

deals with the issue of inhumanity as a form of sin, in particular sloth, under the redemption of God, Tutu rather focuses God's creation of humans, and its implications on the social dimension, as it condemns the system of apartheid. Battle notes that "God the Creator is the most definitive African conception for Tutu's theology."[509] In explaining Tutu's theological epistemology, Battle further argues that "Tutu's theology is characterized by deep reflection on creation and the image of God."[510]

For Barth, as he holds the position that inhumanity is humans' sinful resistance against the ascension of Christ (sanctification), he illustrates the significance of one's conversion to Christ, knowing the reconciler, and imitating the fellow-humanity of Christ. By contrast, although Tutu would agree strongly with Barth, he primarily targets the inhumane social system against humanity and dignity given by God, the Creator.

Certainly, one should contemplate at least two factors when examining and comparing their theologies. The first is that Tutu has never attempted to publish academically systematic treatise on the issue of reconciliation. Most crucial sources are his public speeches and writings, although to be fair, this should not be recognized as a comprehensive representation of his theology of reconciliation. The second factor is that their contexts were different. Even though parallels can be drawn between Karl Barth's involvement in the Barmen Declaration and Tutu's anti-apartheid movement and the Kairos Document by South African theologians (despite Tutu himself allegedly not signing the document), the personal and collective experiences of Tutu and his people under the discriminative regimes and policies are largely absent in that of Barth.

Nevertheless, some observations and examinations grounded in repeated emphases of Tutu's words are still possible. As noted, in Tutu's theology, God's creation of humans in the image of Himself is the fundamental foundation and repeatedly highlighted. This has explicitly breathed and empowered his fatigueless voice to fight against inhumane and blasphemous realities and policies. However, because the idea has become the most significant foundation, it seems that the necessity of conversion has been weakened and the centrality of God's reconciliation in Christ with humanity has been dimmed.

For example, in *God is not a Christian*, Tutu makes such statements as "if God is *one*, as we believe, then he is the only God of all his people,

---

509. Battle, *Reconciliation*, 58.
510. Battle, *Reconciliation*, 69.

whether they acknowledge him as such or not."[511] Likewise, in *God has a Dream*, he states,

> In God's family, there are no outsiders. All are insiders. Black and white, rich and poor, gay and straight, Jew and Arab, Palestinian and Israeli, Roman Catholic and Protestant, Serb and Albanian. Hutu and Tutsi, Muslim and Christian, Buddhist and Hindu, Pakistani and Indian—all belong . . . Yes, George Bush and Osama bin Laden belong together. God says, All, all are My children. It is shocking. It is radical.[512]

Tutu further argues that living in "harmony" as "God's family" regardless of one's religion is "God's dream."[513] Another quote from Tutu is as follows: "We try to claim God for ourselves and for our cause, but God's love is too great to be confined to any one side of a conflict or to any one religion."[514] Battle interprets Tutu's theology related to this matter as Tutu "adheres" to the fact that "human salvation is participation in the life of God," which appears closer to the Eastern church tradition.[515] Battle continues, for Tutu, "If one truly participate in the claim of being made in the image of God, a transformation occurs in which an individual becomes a person or personality"—it is the "mystery" that "is known in Christ."[516] This means that if a person acknowledges him or herself as well as other humans as the image of God, then that the person participates in God. That is, a form of transformation occurs that leads him or her to be fully human as God intended, regardless of the explicit knowledge of the Gospel, and the person can reach the salvation of God.

The point of Tutu that claims for the ontological equality of human beings no matter what, owing to the truth that everyone is created in the image of God, is well received. However, there are some weaknesses to note. One comes from Reinhold Niebuhr; similar to Tutu, Niebuhr indicates that "the doctrine of 'image of God'" in Christianity is one of the ideas that "is sharply distinguished from all alternative views" in understanding humans.[517] Furthermore, he says that it means humans "may reveal elements of the image of God even in the lowliest aspects of his natural life."[518] Nonetheless, Niebuhr

511. Tutu, *God Is Not a Christian*, 8.
512. Tutu, *God Has a Dream*, 20.
513. Tutu, *God Has a Dream*, 24.
514. Tutu, *God Has a Dream*, 43.
515. Battle, *Reconciliation*, 62.
516. Battle, *Reconciliation*, 63.
517. Niebuhr, *Nature and Destiny of Man*, 150.
518. Niebuhr, *Nature and Destiny of Man*, 150.

does not ignore the problem of sin in the existence of humans and the utter necessity of redemption.[519] Rejecting romanticism or an idealistic view of humans, but advocating a morally (moderate) realistic perspective, Niebuhr contends that, "The high estimate of the human stature implied in the concept of 'image of God' stands in paradoxical juxtaposition to the low estimate of human virtue in Christian thought. Man is a sinner."[520]

As Niebuhr's words illustrate, Tutu's anthropology seems in a way to be similar to the naïve optimism on humans advocated by the liberal theologians in the nineteenth century such as Adolf von Harnack. As the first biblical narrative of human murder (i.e., Cain killing his brother Abel in Gen. 4) illustrates, the ultimate need for reconciliation is caused by the sinfulness of humans against God in the vertical dimension, which entails animosity against other humans in the horizontal dimension. Tutu's emphasis on human dignity through the claim that humans are *created* in the image of God should not to be separated from the other essential claim of Christianity (in both "Eastern" and "Western" traditions) that human sinners are to be *redeemed* through the salvific work of Christ.

It can be presumed that Tutu, as an Anglican bishop, would agree with the importance of both claims as essential in Christianity, yet it seems that, at least in his public appearances throughout his ministry and particularly obvious in the later phase, one claim has been underlined more than the other.[521]

This raises a significant concern in discussing reconciliation. In Christian doctrine, as the previous thinkers have presented, the scandal of division is caused by the sinfulness of humans. The issue of sin is not sufficiently dealt with, recalling the fact that humans are created in the image of God. The redemptive work of Jesus on the Cross should be proclaimed

---

519. Niebuhr, *Nature and Destiny of Man*, 178.

520. Niebuhr, *Nature and Destiny of Man*, 16.

521. As it is the case for many Christian thinkers, it may need to take account the development of Desmond Tutu's theology as one examines his theology of reconciliation. About quotes presented above from the books, *God Is Not a Christian*, and *God Has a Dream*, one can notice that those writings are from Tutu's later phase of ministry. One would not see words with similar extent of tones and nuances in either of his speeches or writings from 1980s. However, in this study, the discussion of development is not included because even though those exact phrases and nuances seem to be absent in earlier writings, the theological focus of Tutu (humans as the image of God) remains consistent throughout his ministry. One can assume that the focus has been there from the beginning, yet it further developed in a way as it appeared in later phase. In terms of evaluation, Tutu's unbalanced attitude toward creation over redemption can still be recognized.

and acknowledged because, as Barth said, the moral consciousness of fallen human-beings is erroneous and cannot be trusted.

Furthermore, the unsolved problems of injustice and the absence of repentance remain primarily between God and the individual, according to the Bible, prior to becoming an issue between one person to another. As Tutu rightly indicates, it is *blasphemous* behavior to treat fellow humans without showing dignity that they deserve as the image of God.[522]

In this sense, the following questions are legitimate. How can people really change their hearts and their blasphemous behavior? Where does the source and power of the change come from? Is it sufficient to know that their fellow humans are the image of God? Or, should one contemplate the entire vertical dimension of the relationship with God in investigating how one can be changed? The theological discourse and practice of reconciliation *in the social dimension after Tutu's steps* should seriously consider and reflect upon these questions, which have been answered, at least partially, by Barth, Volf, and Son.

However, it should be clearly stated that Tutu's contribution to the discourse and practice of reconciliation is still immense, especially the church's engagement with society as an agent of peace. He has established an exemplary case in the church's history of how the church can engage and impact the sociopolitical reality with its theological message. Perhaps, Tutu's statements should be interpreted in the context of his ministry taking place mainly *in the social sphere as a religious leader*, although it is questionable whether being biased in delivering the basic Christian doctrine between creation and redemption is legitimate.

Even though Tutu's messages have a tendency toward the "centrality of Jesus' victory over Evil"—a salvation approach in which he did not consider liberation "as an alternative to salvation"—it seems that the conclusive points of the approach tend to be the demand for change in the sociopolitical sphere.[523] Tutu's main ministry field is the sociopolitical arena of South Africa. One piece of evidence comes from a qualitative research study on Tutu's messages. In terms of key words and themes, Pieterse, Scheepers, and Wester report that Tutu "has given fairly equal attention to both religious (theological) themes (mentioned 292 times, i.e. 48%) and political themes (mentioned 303 times, i.e. 49%)."[524] Through a close examination, one can even observe that most of Tutu's theological themes are under the category of "liberation theology," rather than under

---

522. Tutu, *No Future Without Forgiveness*, 92–93.
523. Pieterse et al., "Structure of Thought," 49.
524. Pieterse et al., "Structure of Thought," 38, 51.

"general theology" as classified by Pieterse, Scheepers, and Wester.[525] This indicates that in both categories of themes, Tutu's main focus was on the social realities of his nation and people.

Furthermore, as the Kairos Document claims, when Tutu appeared in public, it was true that the issue of liberation from injustice, particularly apartheid, was clearly an urgent issue in the pursuit of reconciliation in the South African context.[526] In addition, the majority of South Africa's population are Christians, which has probably led him to easily assume that we are all God's children.

Nevertheless, to what extent Tutu's theology and ministry have demonstrated the comprehensive concept of reconciliation in Christian theology remains a valid concern. It seems there is much room for discussing and developing a robust and wholesome theology of reconciliation after the example that Tutu has shown.

---

525. Pieterse, *Desmond Tutu's Message*, 137.

526. Kairos Theologians (Group) et al., *Kairos Document*, 9–11.

5

An Evaluation of Robert Schreiter's Theology of Mission as Reconcliation and the Presentation of a Proposal

IN THE DISCUSSION OF mission as reconciliation, Robert Schreiter has been a pioneering theologian and an influential voice. To review the current academic discourse of mission as reconciliation in mission studies, in spite of its existing diversity of voices, the theology of Schreiter is assessed in this section as a representative case based on the theological discussions in previous chapters. Later in this chapter, a proposal for a wholesome and robust theology of mission as reconciliation is presented.

A Theological Evaluation of Robert Schreiter's Theology of Reconciliation

In assessing Schreiter's theology of reconciliation, three key aspects are concentrated on: (1) the relationship between the vertical and horizontal dimensions of reconciliation, (2) the issue of justice and liberation in reconciliation, and (3) the meaning of spirituality. These three areas are intersected in many ways and crucial for evaluating his theology for the research focus of this dissertation.

All these three aspects fall under the issue of the relationship between the vertical and horizontal reconciliation, engaging "how" question. Regarding the first aspect, Schreiter's writings and speeches have faced some disagreement from certain scholars on how the two dimensions are to be presented and practiced in the church's ministry of reconciliation, as explored in chapter 2. The first aspect concerns the questions of what, who, and why questions, for instance, what the Christian understanding of reconciliation is; who takes what roles in the ministry of reconciliation (the work of God and human agency); and why the church must pursue reconciliation. However, considering the relationship between the two dimensions more easily leads directly to a *how* question: How can horizontal reconciliation occur based on the vertical dimension? This how question is a central underlying question that this study seeks to answer. The second aspect, which is a significant theme in Schreiter's discussion of the process of reconciliation, is an answer from Schreiter to an aspect of the how question: How should it progress? Alternatively, what steps should the church take in its efforts to achieve reconciliation? Then, the third aspect offers more of a primary answer from Schreiter to a how question: How can reconciliation be achieved?

For these reasons, the three selected aspects are primarily reviewed for evaluating Schreiter's theology of reconciliation, particularly his view on the relationship between the vertical and horizontal dimensions of reconciliation.

The Relationship Between the Vertical and Horizontal Dimensions of Reconciliation

The chapter 2 of this dissertation discussed that after Tormod Engelsviken participated in Athens 2005 as an evangelical representative, he expressed "a certain disappointment" with a plenary speech by Schreiter.[1] His critique was that "no significant attention was devoted to 'vertical reconciliation,'" and the "ministry of reconciliation with God was simply assumed."[2] Engelsviken also reported that there were several participants, British missiologists, at Athens 2005 CWME who expressed their concerns that the vertical dimension of reconciliation was not being presented positively.[3] Scholars such as Craig Ott, Stephen Strauss, and Timothy Tennent have similarly indicated that the vertical dimension is "overlooked" in the current academic discourse of mission as reconciliation.[4]

To begin with, to examine his understanding of the two dimensions, Schreiter argues that "reconciliation is the work of God" and "not a human achievement."[5] It seems explicit in many of his writings that he considers vertical reconciliation as the foundation of horizontal reconciliation and God as

1. Engelsviken, "Come Holy Spirit," 191.
2. Engelsviken, "Come Holy Spirit," 191.
3. Engelsviken, "Come Holy Spirit," 191.
4. Ott et al., *Encountering Theology of Mission*, 97.
5. Schreiter, *Ministry of Reconciliation*, 14.

the initiator and author of all genuine reconciliation.[6] The problem, however, lies in what he means by the work of God, or the term *foundation*.

For Schreiter, it seems that vertical reconciliation is the foundation for horizontal reconciliation to the extent that it offers the core principle to follow or lessons to be learned in the pursuit of horizontal reconciliation, and furthermore, it lays the foundation on which the horizontal dimension becomes possible. That is to say, while he evidently argues that reconciliation belongs to God and the work of God, and horizontal reconciliation becomes possible by vertical reconciliation, Schreiter does not clearly present how horizontal reconciliation can be achieved *through*, *with*, or *in* the pursuit of vertical reconciliation. In other words, he does not present *how* the church should endeavor to establish vertical reconciliation, the foundation, to see the horizontal reconciliation.

Schreiter does offer some theological elaborations on this issue. For example, he mentions, "a spirituality of reconciliation can be deepened by a meditation on the stories of the women and the tomb."[7] Also, in describing how to forgive, Schreiter states, "The ability to decide to forgive comes from the restoration of humanity that is the grace of reconciliation. The restoration comes from the God who loves and who forgives . . . God's love is what both restores the victim and, in making of the victim a new creation, also makes forgives possible."[8] However, Schreiter does not sufficiently address how to strengthen the relationship with God (i.e., having a deeper understanding of God's forgiveness in Christ) concerning one's pursuit of horizontal reconciliation.

Instead, several implications that Schreiter suggests from his reflections on vertical reconciliation are "an attitude of listening and waiting," "attention and compassion," and "holding a post-exilic stance."[9] Additional factors he suggests are "accompaniment, hospitality, making connections and commissioning" from the stories after Jesus's resurrection.[10] Furthermore, the key steps of horizontal reconciliation suggested by Schreiter include the healing of victims, truth-telling, the pursuit of justice, and forgiveness.[11] They are all legitimate elements to be inferred from the biblical reflections on the vertical relationship with God in Christ. All of these steps

6. Schreiter, *Reconciliation*, 26; Schreiter, "Reconciliation as a New Paradigm," 2, 5; Schreiter, "Emergence of Reconciliation," 13, 15.

7. Schreiter, *Ministry of Reconciliation*, 39.

8. Schreiter, *Ministry of Reconciliation*, 61.

9. Schreiter, *Reconciliation*, 71–73.

10. Schreiter, *Ministry of Reconciliation*, 94.

11. Schreiter, *Ministry of Reconciliation*, 15; Schreiter, "Reconciliation as a New Paradigm," 3–4; Schreiter, "Emergence of Reconciliation," 18–20.

are certainly crucial and have their roots in the biblical narratives of reconciliation. It would be true to say that vertical reconciliation has enlightened these principles for horizontal reconciliation. However, these are still principles from the biblical reflections that can be applied to one's pursuit of horizontal reconciliation, rather than the explanations of how the vertical reconciliation enables horizontal reconciliation as the foundation and how God becomes the initiator and author of horizontal reconciliation. These are the more profound questions of the relationship between the vertical and horizontal dimensions of reconciliation.

Schreiter states such expressions as "the power of God's grace welling up in one's life" and "the mercy of God welling up in my own life" to illustrate that reconciliation is not something humans achieve but discover.[12] In the most recent article, Schreiter even notes the importance of evangelism and proclamation in relation to reconciliation as follows:

> Reconciliation encompasses the message of a call to conversion to Christ and situates it in a larger cosmic drama of all things being brought together in Christ . . . It reveals too the depth of sin and brokenness in human life and society from which humanity needs to be delivered and healed. So reconciliation does not replace or reduce the importance of preaching. Rather, it situates it in a larger frame—God's very intention for the world—and can lead usefully away from a purely conceptual concern about the nature of sin to the concreteness of life that needs to be engaged in if genuine reconciliation is to take place.[13]

However, even in the expressions of "welling up" and the explanation of the "co-existed" relationship between reconciliation and verbal proclamation, Schreiter does not concretely present how vertical reconciliation promotes and cultivates reconciliation with others in one's life.[14] It is still questionable how sufficiently Schreiter's elaborations address the issue of how the work of God in the vertical reconciliation affects horizontal reconciliation between humans as the inseparable foundation. It seems that Schreiter's writings primarily engage the horizontal dimension of reconciliation *separately* or *distinctively* from vertical reconciliation to a certain extent. How vertical reconciliation works in each step of the process in horizontal reconciliation is not discussed in-depth.

Although, Schreiter states that it is vertical reconciliation from which the horizontal dimension "continuously" "draws its life," he does

---

12. Schreiter, *Reconciliation*, 26, 43.
13. Schreiter, "Emergence of Reconciliation," 23–24.
14. Schreiter, "Emergence of Reconciliation," 23, 26, 43.

not present how it becomes the case, other than the implication that one can elicit essential insights or principles to follow in seeking horizontal reconciliation.[15] One may need to take account that his theology of reconciliation primarily concentrates on the issues of "social order," "structure," "suffering," and "violence" in the sociopolitical sphere, holding the frame of victims and oppressors, in discussing reconciliation.[16] Nevertheless, as he attempts to present a Christian understanding of reconciliation, Schreiter needs to present more clearly on how the vertical reconciliation becomes the foundation of the horizontal reconciliation; stated differently, how the reconciliation with God in the vertical dimension works in the horizontal dimension of reconciliation.[17]

Vertical reconciliation should be the *perpetual* foundation in every moment of horizontal reconciliation. This is because, as Karl Barth presented, inhumanity comes from humans' sinfulness, which often becomes a hindrance in every step that Schreiter suggests. The sinfulness and rebellious hearts of humans who resist reconciliation with fellow humans should be confronted and dealt with. It can be dealt with most profoundly only in light of the Gospel. As Miroslav Volf argued, the Gospel of Christ transforms and shapes one's identity as an embracing identity of others through the decentering and recentering process of the self which enables one to overcome the dominance of exclusion in sinful humanity. It is the work of the Holy Spirit.

In this sense, the success of horizontal reconciliation depends on the extent of one's *change of heart*. It is the case for both victims and perpetrators of Schreiter's categorization. It means one's inner being—the identity, the value system, desires, and motivations are changed. The change of heart is what the central message from the Bible targets on in discussing one's relationship with God. In numerous places in the Bible, sinfulness is often described as a *hardened heart,* illustrating arrogance and pride against the call for repentance from God (i.e., Exod 10:1; Ps 81:12; Isa 46:12; Jer 16:12; Ezek 3:7; 11:19; Eph 4:18; and Heb 3:8). Since horizontal reconciliation follows and reflects the fundamentals of vertical reconciliation as its central steps, the change of hearts of both victims and perpetrators are indispensable in the pursuit of reconciliation between them.

To synthesize what Karl Barth and Miroslav Volf have claimed, the power of the Gospel and the quickening power of the Holy Spirit *reveal*

15. Schreiter, "Emergence of Reconciliation," 13.

16. Schreiter, *Reconciliation*, 1–3, 17–18, 29–30, 51–52, 60–61. This is the case more explicitly in his first book, *Reconciliation*, yet a similar focus can be continuously observed in his subsequent writings.

17. Schreiter, *Reconciliation*, 41.

one's inhumanity and the sinful tendency of exclusion, and *transform* the self to imitate the fellow humanity of Christ and be able to embrace others. The message of the Gospel that God forgives and loves humanity melts down one's hardened heart and change it. From many passages in the Bible, it can be inferred that the motivation of horizontal reconciliation is through vertical reconciliation as a commandment (i.e., Matt 5:24; 5:43-48; 6:14-15; Phil 2:4-5; Col 3:12-14; 1 Tim 6:18; 1 John 3:14-24). In short, the change of heart that includes one's identity, value system, desires, and motivations—or in another expression, conversion—is needed for the horizontal reconciliation, and it comes from a genuine form of vertical reconciliation. In this sense, one should continuously revisit the core message of the vertical dimension of reconciliation to be empowered for the horizontal dimension of reconciliation.

Another way of explaining that the vertical reconciliation becomes the perpetual foundation of horizontal reconciliation is to understand it within the frame of sanctification. Vertical reconciliation includes the verbal proclamation of the Gospel as its crucial step (i.e., Rom 10:14-15), yet it does not end there; it continues. After conversion, one's vertical relationship with God should continuously be strengthened and grow, becoming a Christ-like character—this is sanctification (i.e., Phil 1:6-11, and 2 Pet 3:18).

Thus, horizontal reconciliation, which should reflect God's reconciling nature, can be best understood under the theme of sanctification. This is a point that has generally been demonstrated by Barth, Volf, Son, and Tutu in the previous chapters. The rationale is simple and clear: God is a reconciling God. The deeper the relationship one has with God, the more reconciliation one will see in one's life with fellow humans.

If horizontal reconciliation is a matter of sanctification, then one's perspective and practice of it should be continuously shaped and empowered in one's relationship with God. The fruit of the genuine humanity of Jesus can be born only when a person remains in Him (John 15:5). No one can accomplish holiness or make an advance even a single step of being sanctified in his or her spiritual formation unless endless guidance and help come from the Holy Spirit, or the *Parakletos*. In other words, again, the vertical dimension of reconciliation should be pursued *continuously* in every moment of the horizontal dimension reconciliation, and thereby the vertical reconciliation can be the perpetual foundation of the horizontal reconciliation. This is how the two dimensions are not separated. Therefore, the vertical dimension of reconciliation must be sought in the Christian ministry of reconciliation, and it includes both the starting point, verbal declaration of the Gospel, and the continuous effort, the pursuit of sanctification.

Schreiter reflects the church's history by writing that, "Much of the previous theological literature on reconciliation has been addressed to what might be called the 'vertical' reconciliation between God and sinful humanity."[18] Furthermore, "much of liturgical language of the churches focuses on this vertical dimension of reconciliation."[19]

In regretting this side of history, he rightly suggests a holistic language of reconciliation, saying that "It is within this framework of vertical, horizontal, and cosmic reconciliation that we are to see Christian mission."[20] This is a desirable suggestion for the church's understanding and ministry of reconciliation. Certainly, the mistake in the past that ignoring the biblical passages of horizontal reconciliation and considering vertical reconciliation only matters should not be repeated in any case. Unfortunately, it is true that inseparable dimensions of reconciliation have been separated in many occasions of the church's history.

However, a warning must also be given that the dimensions can conversely be separated when the church concentrates on horizontal reconciliation while overlooking the significance of the vertical dimension. Schreiter's reflection of the past is legitimate. However, there is a risk of repeating the same mistake again in reverse, separating the two dimensions once more, if he fails to consider the vertical reconciliation as the perpetual foundation (fails to pursue the horizontal reconciliation through promoting the vertical reconciliation), and tries to focus primarily on the horizontal reconciliation based on his reflections. In this case, reconciliation encompassing all dimensions would not be accomplished, and moreover, the genuine form of reconciliation would not be attained. This is because reconciliation truly belongs to God. Those who believe that they are called to be peacemakers by God in the broken society should remind themselves of this simple—but not necessarily easily-mastered—truth. Horizontal reconciliation should not be separated from its perpetual basis, vertical reconciliation, through which the whole process of reconciliation can be advanced and properly achieved.

In short, in Schreiter's theology of reconciliation, the attention on the vertical dimension of reconciliation should be reinforced as the perpetual foundation of reconciliation to construct a more wholesome theology of reconciliation in mission studies, as well as to achieve a more profound reconciliation in the church's engagement with the broken world. As previously mentioned, Barth rightly says that sanctification without justification

---

18. Schreiter, "Reconciliation and Healing," 79.
19. Schreiter, "Emergence of Reconciliation," 13.
20. Schreiter, "Reconciliation as a New Paradigm," 2.

is equivalent to "a favoured man who works in isolation, and therefore to an illusory activism."[21]

The Issue of Justice and Liberation in Reconciliation

Schreiter has argued that reconciliation without the pursuit of justice is false reconciliation.[22] To him, false reconciliation attempts to "deal with a history of violence by suppressing its memory."[23] Schreiter explicates this as follows:

> Not surprisingly, this kind of reconciliation is often called for by the very perpetrators of violence who, either having seen what they have done or having realized the potential consequences of their actions, want to get on to a new and different situation. They want the victims of violence to let bygones by bygones and exercise a Christian forgiveness. While reconciliation as a hasty peace bears a superficial resemblance to Christian reconciliation, it is actually quite far from it.[24]

In this respect, the issue of liberation has a significant place throughout his writings of reconciliation. Schreiter asserts that "liberation is not an alternative to reconciliation; it is the prerequisite for it. Thus, we do not call for reconciliation instead of liberation; we call for liberation in order to bring about reconciliation."[25]

In a more recent article, Schreiter discusses the concept of justice into three categories: punitive, restorative, and structural justice.[26] According to him, punitive justice engages with the wrongdoers: "the punishment of wrongdoers" and the statement that such behaviors will not be tolerated publicly in the future.[27] Restorative justice concerns the victims, involving their "restitution and reparation."[28] Lastly, structural justice deals with "changing social structures" that "promote and sustain injustice."[29] For liberation, he

---

21. Barth, *CD* IV/2:505.
22. Schreiter, *Reconciliation*, 18–21.
23. Schreiter, *Reconciliation*, 18.
24. Schreiter, *Reconciliation*, 19.
25. Schreiter, *Reconciliation*, 22.
26. The MMR presents identical categorization. Matthey, *Come Holy Spirit, Heal and Reconcile*, 79.
27. Schreiter, "Emergence of Reconciliation," 20.
28. Schreiter, "Emergence of Reconciliation," 20.
29. Schreiter, "Emergence of Reconciliation," 20.

states, "Reconciliation as a paradigm of mission goes beyond a liberation *from* oppression to a liberation *for* building the new creation."[30]

Although he continually underscores the importance of justice in reconciliation, Schreiter also warns that if one argues "there can be no reconciliation unless there is full justice," a fallacy could be fallen into of reducing "reconciliation to the pursuit of justice."[31] This can "paralyze or obviate other practices going into the process of reconciliation."[32] In an eschatological understanding, Schreiter reminds us that the fullness of justice and reconciliation can take place at the end in Christ.[33]

Schreiter's reflections of justice and liberation are well-taken. Those are the voices to be heard in the process of reconciliation from the church as well as society. However, two critical suggestions can be made based on the discussions of Schreiter and others thus far. First, in the Bible, justice is the first and foremost issue in the vertical reconciliation with God.

Schreiter's suggestion of a holistic understanding and language of reconciliation that include all dimensions in Christian mission is again necessary and appropriate for current needs in the contemporary context of the church.[34] As stated, the vertical dimension is the foundation for the others. Furthermore, he rightly indicates the issue of justice as a key element in navigating the often-complicated issues of reconciliation, because reconciliation itself is about revealing the truth, rectifying wrongdoings, and restoring the relationships between victims and perpetrators based on justice.

Based on these statements, one may envisage that justice is a salient issue in vertical reconciliation in this holistic concept of reconciliation based on biblical reflections. It is an essential Christian doctrine that humans' relationship with God has been broken and they have become the enemy of God through their sinfulness and wrongdoings before God (Col 1:21; Rom 5:10). The issue of justice is evident in the vertical reconciliation. For example, the epistle to Romans clearly testifies how the justice and righteousness of God can only be obtained through faith in Jesus Christ who was crucified and resurrected for humans (Rom 3:19–26; 4:23–25; 5:1). Having said that, Christian faith examines hatred, brokenness, and strife in today's world as being derived from the sinfulness of humanity, being apart from God. If anyone admits that genuine reconciliation belongs to God, that person should carefully examine whether the issue of justice has been

---

30. Schreiter, "Emergence of Reconciliation," 23.
31. Schreiter, "Emergence of Reconciliation," 20.
32. Schreiter, "Emergence of Reconciliation," 20.
33. Schreiter, "Emergence of Reconciliation," 20.
34. Schreiter, "Reconciliation as a New Paradigm," 2.

handled as God demands in the vertical dimension to discover the genuine form of reconciliation in other dimensions. It is also about the liberation in Christ from being enslaved by sinfulness.

Therefore, the problem of justice in the vertical dimension of reconciliation should not be overlooked. Rather, Christian traditions have consistently declared throughout history that it should be seriously dealt with. Because the vertical dimension is the foundation for the others, unless the problem of justice is solved in that dimension, it is difficult to anticipate that reconciliation in the other dimensions would occur. In Schreiter's theology of reconciliation, however, this issue does not seem to be clearly reflected. Thus, in Schreiter's discussion of justice, the issue of justice in vertical reconciliation must be addressed.

Second, pursuing justice merely as a step of reconciliation without actively and continuously promoting the work of God in the vertical dimension, which transforms one's heart, may result in only limited success. Here, the previous reflection on liberation theology by Miroslav Volf is relevant.

Similar to Schreiter, Volf highlights the predicaments of "first justice, then reconciliation" such as partiality, irreversibility, and ambiguity. Although any attempt at cheap reconciliation—reconciliation without justice—should not be considered an option but denounced (neither is it a suggestion by Volf), Volf properly asserts that when justice is sought before reconciliation, an "endless cycle of pursuit of justice will be launched by both parties."[35] Moreover, Volf describes how today's conflicts easily become "very messy" because every group considers themselves to be more victimized than the others.[36] Thus, he argues that the frame of liberation theology seems "ill-suited" to "the overarching schema by which to align our social engagement."[37] This is because as Volf explains, it provides "only limited help in this arduous task."[38]

In the same vein, Volf claims that "theologians should concentrate" on "fostering" "social agents" who are "capable of envisioning and creating just, truthful and peaceful societies," rather than "social arrangements" unless they become "helpmates" to other disciplines.[39] Then, he follows up with the themes of the Cross of Christ, and the center of one's self. As explored previously, in this view, he deals with the issue of self-centered

---

35. Volf, "Social Meaning of Reconciliation," 163.

36. Volf, "Exclusion and Embrace: Theological Reflections," 234; Volf, "Vision of Embrace," 200; Volf, *Exclusion and Embrace*, 103.

37. Volf, *Exclusion and Embrace*, 104; Volf, "Exclusion and Embrace," 235.

38. Volf, "Vision of Embrace," 201.

39. Volf, *Exclusion and Embrace*, 21.

identity in an individual in the light of the Gospel. This again leads our attention to the point of *the change of one's heart*, which happens in one's vertical relationship with God.

Justice is a significant prerequisite of reconciliation, yet it sometimes does not induce reconciliation. For example, suppose there is a criminal who was arrested for a terrible crime. If he or she was imprisoned as just punishment for the wrongdoings, would that criminal come to repent and have the heart to apologize to the victims? Not necessarily. The criminal could feel that he or she has been purged of sin entirely and owes nothing to anyone. Schreiter even notes a similar point, yet his conclusion does not address how the Gospel changes one's heart in the vertical dimension, which promotes reconciliation in the horizontal dimension as a result.[40] What engenders reconciliation is the change of heart from a hardened to a softened one before the light of justice. Reconciliation thus inevitably engages one's self-centered and sinful ego.

To concisely address Volf's thought again, it can be addressed as the process of decentering and recentering of the self by the Gospel of Jesus, which enables one to be transformed as embracing identity. Specifically, it includes obtaining a healthy tension of distance and belonging regarding one's culture, shaping a porous and catholic identity to other humans, and seeing through double vision in interpreting conflict situations. At the same time, the quickening power of the Holy Spirit is the main source of strength that enables one to overcome the dominance of exclusion in one's sinfulness and to imitate a Christlike character.

Reconciliation itself refers to the change from being an enemy to a friend. This is not possible without the transformation of heart that deals with one's motivation, desire, and identity. Furthermore, these are primary targets of the Gospel of Christ and the work of the Holy Spirit. All of these discussions again highlight a crucial point—that the vertical dimension of reconciliation enables a person to bear the fruit of horizontal reconciliation as a proper and necessary outcome. As Ott, Strauss, and Tennent correctly comment, "On the basis of vertical reconciliation, horizontal reconciliation becomes possible in the most profound way."[41]

In sum, after assessing the second aspect of Schreiter's theology, the following suggestions are presented. First, the concept of justice should not be merely applied to horizontal reconciliation but first and foremost to the vertical dimension of reconciliation. Thereby, justice can be found in *both*

---

40. Schreiter, *Reconciliation*, 46.
41. Ott et al., *Encountering Theology of Mission*, 97.

dimensions of reconciliation in the holistic frame. Also, a sound understanding of justice can come from God, who is a God of justice.

Second, while the pursuit of justice is an indispensable factor of the Christian understanding of reconciliation, it is extremely difficult and not particularly appropriate to seek justice *as a separate step* from vertical reconciliation. It must be executed under the theme of reconciliation, in particular within the pursuit of vertical reconciliation, which facilitates the change of one's heart.

Transforming one's heart and rebuilding one's moral consciousness would be observed to a very limited extent, if not to none, without explicit proclamation and acknowledging the Gospel of Christ and work of the Holy Spirit, as Barth rightly suggests.[42]

The Meaning of Spirituality

Schreiter has continually underlined the importance of spirituality in his writings of reconciliation. In his first book on this topic, *Reconciliation*, he argues that the process of reconciliation "cannot be reduced to a technical, problem-solving rationality," rather "a successful process of reconciliation is a spirituality, a view of the world that recognizes and responds to God's reconciling action in that world."[43] Later, in *The Ministry of Reconciliation*, based on the reflections on multiple biblical narratives, Schreiter claims that "the cultivation of a relationship with God" is significant for making reconciliation happen: "Reconciliation as a spirituality is absolutely essential."[44]

More recently, in *Mission as Ministry of Reconciliation*, which he edited, he elaborates as follows: "If God is indeed the author of all reconciliation, then we will be effective messengers and ministers of reconciliation only to the extent that we live lives that are in deep communion with God. We need to seek out spiritual disciplines that will facilitate and sustain such deep communion."[45]

Based on these statements, Schreiter's emphasis on spirituality of reconciliation can be considered his answer to the *how* question in reconciliation: how horizontal reconciliation can happen. This demonstrates a significant aspect in describing the relationship of the two dimensions.

Schreiter comments that reconciliation "becomes a way of life, not just set of discrete tasks to be performed and completed," as well as "The ministry

---

42. Barth, *CD* IV/3.1:371, 389; Busch, *Great Passion*, 201.
43. Schreiter, *Reconciliation*, 60.
44. Schreiter, *Ministry of Reconciliation*, 16.
45. Schreiter, "Emergence of Reconciliation," 15.

of reconciliation, then, is more of spirituality than a strategy."[46] It seems these statements are biblically grounded and theologically well-supported. From a theological examination of the Bible, one can conclude that the actualization of reconciliation between humans relies on the extent to which they know, reflect, and imitate the reconciling personality of the triune God.

However, as noted in the first aspect, what Schreiter really means in mentioning the importance of spirituality does not seem so clear nor sufficiently deliberated. Does spirituality in his terms deal with the issue of the sinfulness of human beings, which is the ultimate cause of horizontal brokenness according to the Bible? Or, does Schreiter's spirituality mainly imply adopting or imitating the principle of reconciliation revealed by God as the fundamental style of life into the attempt of horizontal reconciliation?[47] It seems the spirituality that Schreiter defines concerning reconciliation does not fully reflect nor address how the vertical relationship with God transforms and shapes one's horizontal relationship with other fellow humans. He instead presents principles that are inferred from the biblical stories and can be applied in the relationship with others, which are still valuable.[48] However, the most significant and concrete issue of spirituality concerning reconciliation is *how* the vertical reconciliation initiates, enables, and achieves one's horizontal reconciliation.

Schreiter explains that Protestants tend to underline "Christ's atoning death" and "justification by faith" in discussing reconciliation, and they perceive reconciliation as "in continuity with the saving acts of God."[49] On the contrary, he addresses, "the Catholic emphasis would be slightly different, focusing on the love of God poured out upon us as a result of the reconciliation God has effected in Christ. Here the emphasis is on the new creation"[50] Different Christian traditions may have different theological emphases, regarding the understanding of the reconciliation with God. They are, however, hardly excluded from each other.

The Christian understanding of spirituality can be and has been defined in multiple ways throughout history, yet if a potential consensus exists in those various views, it would be resembling God and becoming a Christ-like person. This presumes an intimate relationship with God.

46. Schreiter, *Reconciliation*, 60; Schreiter, "Emergence of Reconciliation," 15.

47. For this question, one can still ask to what extent does adopting the principle is possible or effective without having knowledge and relationship with God, the reconciler, as Barth suggested before (knowing the abstract notion of reconciliation vs. knowing reconciler personally).

48. Schreiter, *Ministry of Reconciliation*.

49. Schreiter, *Ministry of Reconciliation*, 14.

50. Schreiter, *Ministry of Reconciliation*, 14.

These are prerequisites for addressing any type of spirituality. There can be no Christian understanding of spirituality without knowing God and having a relationship with Him.

Dallas Willard,[51] a prominent scholar and writer on the issue of spirituality, says that "spiritual formation[52] for the Christian basically refers to the Spirit-driven process of forming the inner world of the human self in such a way that it becomes like the inner being of Christ himself." Therefore, he highlights how "Christian spiritual formation is focused entirely on Jesus."[53] Willard further states the following:

> The ideal of the spiritual life in the Christian understanding is one where all of the essential parts of the human self are effectively organized around God, as they are restored and sustained by him. Spiritual formation in Christ is the process leading to that ideal end, and its result is love of God with all of the heart, soul, mind, and strength, and of the neighbor as oneself. The human self is then fully integrated under God.[54]

Willard rightly clarifies that one's spirituality is fundamentally related to God in Christ, resulting in the fruits of love to God and to other humans. If spirituality is a key factor in promoting reconciliation in the broken world, as Schreiter claims, then how to initiate and cultivate spirituality should be clearly indicated in the church's ministry of reconciliation.

Stated differently, spirituality engages the issues of justification and sanctification; that is, there should be (1) an explicit declaration and message about how to be reconciled with God for starting one's spirituality, followed by (2) continuous teaching, training, and living examples presented for how to deepen one's spirituality. Only the ministry of reconciliation by the church that fully involves both of the two aspects can be considered a comprehensive theology and practice of spiritual formation that ultimately lead to reconciliation.

Regarding the former, one might defend Schreiter's view, saying that he rather focuses on the church's engagement as an agent of reconciliation in society, as was the case for Tutu; thus, only spirituality of the church

---

51. Willard, *Renovation of the Heart*, 22.

52. Even though Willard differentiates spiritual formation from spirituality which he views not necessarily Christian nor positive, but rather a natural and neutral concept, it is assumed that both Schreiter and Willard are discussing the same topic since the connotation on the term, spirituality, by Schreiter is similar to that for spiritual formation by Willard. Willard, *Renovation of the Heart*, 19; Schreiter, "Emergence of Reconciliation," 15.

53. Willard, *Renovation of the Heart*, 22.

54. Willard, *Renovation of the Heart*, 31.

itself is necessary to account for. It is understandable that some cases of the church's ministry of reconciliation are not allowed to declare the message, to be reconciled with God, to society in an explicit manner. In such cases, demonstrating the identity of the church itself, as the follower of Jesus Christ, is often the only way to deliver the Gospel message, through the virtuous actions that the Bible commands.

Nevertheless, the comprehensive message and picture of reconciliation that the church brings into the world *do* include a call for being reconciled with God. This is an intrinsic message that the church has, as Barth argued when discussing the witness of the church. It is based on its theology that (1) reconciliation with God is the foundation of all other dimensions of reconciliation, and (2) without being reconciled with God, reconciliation between humans can only be achieved to a highly limited degree. In this comprehensive message, the meaning of spirituality can be fully understood and properly practiced.

Regarding the latter, people should be reminded of how sanctification can occur. Sanctification can be demonstrated in various ways in different aspects of one's life; however, as justification, sanctification is primarily the calling and work of God in human beings (Heb 2:11; 1 Thess 4:7; and 2 Thess 2:13). Furthermore, as 1 Tim 4:5 says, one can be sanctified "by the word of God and prayer."

As Barth clarified in chapter 3, justification and sanctification are "in the *simul* of the one divine will and action," and they are also "the two moments and aspects" of the loving and saving act of Jesus Christ, which "is justifying and sanctifying grace."[55] Sanctification is an "aim" and "consequence" that happens upon the "basis" of justification, being reconciled with God.[56] Furthermore, Barth rightly claims that, "Our sanctification consists in our participation in His sanctification as grounded in the efficacy and revelation of the grace of Jesus Christ."[57] Furthermore, as Son Yang-Won's life and ministry show, it happens in those who are obediently willing to cooperate with the sanctifying work of the Holy Spirit.

Having considered these aspects of the spirituality of reconciliation, it can be concluded that vertical reconciliation is indispensable in the notion of Christian spirituality, and thus should be clearly placed as a central idea for addressing any type of Christian spirituality. Schreiter may have merely assumed that it has already been widely acknowledged; however, the risk can exist of distorting the ideas in understanding the relationship between

55. Barth, *CD* IV/2:508–9.
56. Barth, *CD* IV/2:508–9.
57. Barth, *CD* IV/2:517.

the vertical and horizontal dimensions of reconciliation, if one omits the foundational element when proposing a picture of how the church's ministry of reconciliation can and should happen.

As continually noted, vertical reconciliation[58] should be the perpetual foundation and continuously reminded and sought in the church's ministry of reconciliation, simply because true reconciliation can come only from God through the power of the Gospel and the Holy Spirit. The horizontal dimension of reconciliation can be properly sought and achieved *through* pursuing the vertical dimension, albeit within the framework of indivisibility of the two dimensions. As Volf rightly argues, in Christian faith, it is the case that "the cure" for violence is "not less religion" but "more religion."[59] In the words of Volf, "the more the Christian faith . . . the better off we will be."[60]

Son Yang-Won demonstrated an excellent example regarding these words of Volf. Son's deep commitment in his faith, sensitivity of heart not to sin in his sanctification steps, and a prayerful life to be obedient to the Lord all together were the main factors of the life of reconciliation that he lived. They strengthened his relationship with God, deepened the work of the Gospel and the Holy Spirit in him, and eventually enabled him to manifest reconciling love of God in his life, forgiving and adopting the person who murdered his two sons.

As Son's theology and life manifested, it is not so uncommon to see in the church's history or the ordinary life of Christians today that when their relationships with God are radically renewed, they become deeply motivated by the Gospel and the work of the Holy Spirit to reflect and follow the reconciling character of God in their relationships with fellow humans. Perhaps, the British missiologists and Tormod Engelsviken were expecting to hear a plenary speech that contained such contents when Schreiter spoke at the CWME in Athens 2005.

Summary

All three points for evaluating Schreiter's theology of reconciliation are interrelated and eventually accentuate one encompassing point together: in Schreiter's theological arguments on mission as reconciliation, the discussion of the vertical dimension should be reinforced and presented in a

---

58. It includes both evangelism and discipleship, in other words, justification and sanctification.

59. Volf, "Forgiveness, Reconciliation, and Justice," 862.

60. Volf, *Public Faith*, 40.

more in-depth manner, describing its work within the horizontal dimension of reconciliation. How horizontal reconciliation can be promoted and accomplished through seeking deeper and stronger vertical reconciliation, which embeds horizontal reconciliation in itself, must be more explicitly and deliberately presented.

Because the vertical dimension is the foundation of reconciliation in other dimensions, and as Schreiter argues, Christian mission should have a framework that includes all dimensions of reconciliation together, there should be some methods of promoting the vertical dimension of reconciliation in the holistic theology of reconciliation, which would eventually bear the fruit of reconciliation horizontally.[61]

The contribution from the pioneering thoughts of Robert Schreiter in the discussion of mission as reconciliation is immense and needs to be acknowledged. However, as some theologians have legitimately expressed, in the Christian discourse of reconciliation, vertical reconciliation cannot be simply assumed but should be pursued, because the horizontal dimension can possibly be seen as a fruit based on vertical reconciliation as well as through it.

Furthermore, separating the two dimensions is theologically fallacious and even unchristian, as Haddon Willmer argued. Two misleading traps should thus be avoided: (1) considering the vertical dimension only to be matter and rejecting the necessary outcome of the horizontal dimension, and (2) pursuing the horizontal dimension while forgetting the significance of the vertical dimension. Neither can find its place in the Christian theology of reconciliation: they are truly inseparable, and they should promote and be promoted by each other.

A Proposal

In this proposal, based on the entire discussion presented thus far, several theological statements are claimed in regard to the academic discourse of mission as reconciliation. This proposal suggests the framework of mutual promotion relationship in which one can understand the vertical and horizontal dimensions of reconciliation as truly inseparable and promoting each other. Furthermore, it presents an eschatological viewpoint in which both the *alpha* and *omega* of the Christian understanding of reconciliation are the vertical relationship between the triune God and humanity.

---

61. Schreiter, "Reconciliation as a New Paradigm," 2.

The Framework of Mutual Promotion Relationship

In examining biblical passages related to the both dimensions of reconciliation, one can draw the conclusion that the Bible describes the two dimensions as being placed in a so-called "positive correlation" relationship in terms of social science. This denotes that when one factor increases, the other also increases, and vice versa. The manner of promotion in each direction is different from each other (direct vs. indirect), yet it can still be said that they are in mutually promoting relationship.

The key verses in the discourse of mission as reconciliation have mostly been from the Pauline letters (Rom. 5, 2 Cor. 5, Col. 1, and Eph. 2) because of the explicit mentioning of the term "reconciliation" (*katallage*; reconciliation, *katallasso*; reconcile, and *apokatallasso*; reconcile), as introduced in chapter 2.[62] Considering the facts that reconciliation is an overarching theme, and the relevant biblical passages are prevalent in the Bible, the biblical references of reconciliation must be expanded. Leon Morris rightly claims that the theme of reconciliation should be considered "the general climate of New Testament thinking rather than upon specific references."[63] Among several related passages, to list only a few representative examples of each case, Matt. chapters 5 and 6, John chapters 13 and 15, and the 1 John chapters 3 and 4 are engaged. In these passages, the mutual promotion relationship (direct and indirect) within the two dimensions of reconciliation is demonstrated.

Vertical Reconciliation Directly Promotes Horizontal Reconciliation

As the first aspect of the mutual promotion relationship, vertical reconciliation directly promotes horizontal reconciliation. The following biblical passages imply the first aspect: Matt 5:43–48, John 13:34–35, John 15:1–12, and 1 John 4:7–8, 11, 19. It is a salient point that all four of these passages that require one to love others are given as *commandments* to either the disciples of Jesus or an early Christian community. Karl Barth's theology, explored in chapter 3, regards ethics as commandment and is recalled here.

In that chapter, Barth's argument was presented that ethics is not self-evident apart from God's commandment, rather "the ethical reflection" can be understood "in awareness of the absolute *givenness* of the command."[64] In other words, commanding God requires our obedient

---

62. Engelsviken, "Reconciliation with God," 83.
63. Morris, *Apostolic Preaching*, loc. 3569.
64. Barth, *Ethics*, 76.

actions: "dogmatics is ethics."[65] As Barth correctly understands, God's grace evokes humans' correspondence and their actions, and the gracious God is the commanding God.[66] In this sense, Webster notes that Barth views that the "divine grace" of God as being "not simply information, but action-eliciting divine activity."[67]

It was then inferred that vertical reconciliation necessarily leads to horizontal reconciliation. This is because vertical reconciliation initiates, enables, and achieves horizontal reconciliation. Horizontal reconciliation is a necessary outcome of having a genuinely reconciled relationship with the triune God, who is a relational God. The selected passages serve as biblical foundations for the argument and illustrate this aspect of the mutual promotion relationship. Furthermore, the passages commonly signify that the horizontal dimension of reconciliation is required and expected for those who are reconciled with God. Reconciliation with others is given as a commandment for them. Thus, vertical reconciliation directly promotes horizontal reconciliation.

In the first passage, Matt 5:43–48, Jesus gives a commandment to his disciples, calling for the change of one's attitude and action toward one's enemy.[68] This contains two presumptions: (1) who God is; and (2) the vertical relationship that the listeners—the disciples—have with God. First, the teaching of Jesus bases itself on the character of God: it is how God treats the evil and sinful ones, His enemy (cf. Col 1:21–22). Second, Jesus refers to God as Father God, not just for himself but for the disciples as well (v.45 and 48). Without these two presumptions, the commandment of loving one's enemy is untenable. The two presumptions are indeed what Karl Barth based his thought upon on the issue of fellow-humanity: the attributes of God (the immanent and economic Trinity and the humanity of God) and

---

65. Barth, *CD* I/2:793; Barth, *Christian Life*, 34.

66. Webster, *Barth's Ethics of Reconciliation*, 174; Barth, *Christian Life*, 30.

67. Webster, *Barth's Ethics of Reconciliation*, 7.

68. It may need to be noted here that as both R. T. France and Leon Morris note, "hate your enemy" does not directly come from the Old Testament. France, *Gospel According to Matthew*, 132; Morris, *Gospel According to Matthew*, 129. In addition, one may consider that the attitude toward the enemy in the Old Testament is "complex" from "a stern attitude" in "Exodus 34:12; Deuteronomy 7:2; 23:6" to being merciful "at least to the resident alien" in "Leviticus 19:34" or "even to the enemy" in "Exodus 23:4–5; Proverbs 25:21–22." Morris, *Gospel According to Matthew*, 129–130. Nevertheless, it is true that the teaching of Jesus holds a rather clear presentation of loving one's enemy compared with the complex attitude toward the enemy in the Old Testament. Jesus can be regarded to open up this new dimension of God's commandment, fulfilling the Law (Matt 5:17), expanding loving commandment even to one's enemy with a specific course of action (v. 38–42; 44; 47).

how the fellow-humanity of Jesus can be actualized in oneself through the Gospel and the Holy Spirit.

Not so evident in the passage is that whether it is their Jewish identity, or being disciples of Jesus, or something else that allows them to be considered as children of God by Jesus. Nonetheless, it is inevitable that on the basis of the vertical relationship with God, the commandment of loving one's enemy is given. To those who follow Christ and serve God as heavenly Father, Jesus connects their identity with a specific action of godly loving. Loving one's enemy is explicitly commanded and directly promoted by Jesus's own words for his disciples.

The second passage, John 13:34–35, enhances the Christological focus of the first aspect of the mutual promotion relationship. The new commandment given to the disciples by Jesus is to love one another. For this commandment, D. A. Carson comments, "the standard of comparison is Jesus's love" "exemplified in the footwashing" and eventually "to his death."[69] Carson states that "the *new* command is not 'new' because nothing like it had ever been said before," considering "the Mosaic covenant," which "had mandated two love commandments."[70] He continues, "Its newness is bound up not only with the new standard ('As I have loved you') but with the new order it both mandates and exemplifies"[71] Carson further elaborates that for this new order, "there is an indirect allusion to the new covenant that was inaugurated at the last supper ... that promised the transformation of heart and mind (Jer 31:29–34; Ezek 36:24–26)."[72] Having elaborated that, Carson claims that,

> Whether or not that allusion can be sustained, this commandment is presented as the marching order for the newly gathering messianic community, brought into existence by the redemption long purposed by God himself. It is not just that the standard is Christ and his love; more, it is a command designed to reflect the relationship of love that exists between the Father and the Son, designed to bring about amongst the members of the nascent messianic community the kind of unity that characterizes Jesus and his Father (John 17).[73]

Carson's statements regarding this passage confirm the point that the depth of the meaning of the new commandment, which applies to one's

69. Carson, *Gospel According to John*, 484.
70. Carson, *Gospel According to John*, 484.
71. Carson, *Gospel According to John*, 484.
72. Carson, *Gospel According to John*, 484.
73. Carson, *Gospel According to John*, 484–85.

horizontal dimension, can be fully comprehended only in light of the salvific activity of God through the Messiah Jesus. The commandment reflects and imitates God's love and forgiveness, which culminates in Christ's atonement. It thus leads one's attention to the Cross, the place of God's forgiveness for humanity. The Cross is the perfect illustration of Jesus's words, "as I have loved you." The atonement of Christ on the Cross has crucial significance and power for one's horizontal reconciliation with other humans—the power of the Gospel. Furthermore, it is the power of the Holy Spirit that actualizes and activates the work of the Gospel in a person.

In previous chapters, both Karl Barth and Miroslav Volf were shown to have identified these two factors—the power of the Gospel and the Holy Spirit— as the essential elements that actualize the humanity of Jesus and empower a person to overcome exclusion and to embrace (in Barth's and Volf's expressions respectively).[74]

In this respect, the Cross is the place that the vertical dimension of reconciliation, which has been started from God's heart, reaches those of humans and, consequently, it becomes the place that the horizontal dimension of reconciliation is initiated from the person's transformed heart. Therefore, the Cross is the place that being forgiven and being willing to forgive intersect in one's heart. As the previous passage describes, a person in Christ would be able to forgive and love ones' enemy as he or she was once the enemy of God,[75] but is forgiven and reconciled.[76] This was well exemplified in the life, ministry, and reconciliation of Son Yang-Won, who identified himself as a forgiven sinner and endeavored to experience the deep meaning of the Gospel and the power of the Holy Spirit in his effort toward sanctification.

Repeating the new commandment (John 15:12), the third passage, John 15:1-12, amplifies what the previous passage indicated. The new commandment of loving one another is portrayed in the motif of the vine. The vine imagery denotes that "the whole fullness of God," God's love, "can flow" into the disciples of Christ as "the mystery of love being enacted."[77] This illustrates the point that the disciples, who become already cleaned by the words of Jesus (v.3), can bear much fruit only when they abide in Christ.

Carson states the following: "No branch has life in itself; it is utterly dependent for life and fruitfulness on the vine to which it is attached. The

---

74. Barth, *CD* IV/2:747, 752; Volf, *Exclusion and Embrace*, 69-70, 92.

75. As Leon Morris argues, "The New Testament undoubtedly teaches that men are enemies of God," as represented in "Romans 5:10" and "Colossians 1:21." Morris, *Apostolic Preaching of the Cross*, loc. 3688.

76. Morris, *Apostolic Preaching of the Cross*, loc. 3688.

77. Haenchen, *John 2*, 131.

living branch is thus truly 'in' the vine; the life of the vine is truly 'in' the branch."[78] It again relates to "new covenant theology" "not far from the Old Testament new covenant texts, all of which promise a renewed heart or a right mind or the presence of the Spirit in the new covenant people, such that they will obey what God says."[79] This mutual abiding image between Jesus and the disciples reflects that between Jesus and Father God. It demonstrates that Jesus is the true mediator between God and humanity, who is the revelation of the true humanity of God.[80]

The last passage, 1 John 4:7–8, 11, 19, explicitly mentions the relationship between vertical love and horizontal love. Similar to the previous passages, John Stott asserts that the whole "argument for brotherly love" of this passage "is based on God's eternal nature," *"for love comes from God"* (v.7) and *"because God is love"* (v.8).[81] On the basis of the understanding of God and love, the commandment of loving each other is given. The author of 1 John seems to contemplate that loving one another is a *must-do* action for those who have realized the love of God. The call for horizontal loving is given and validated upon the fact that it is possible and required to love others because of what one earns: vertical reconciliation with God. As is the case for John 15 and others, 1 John 4 holds a tight connection in understanding the relationship between loving God and loving others. It entails not only "positive and inclusive" statements but also "negative and exclusive" "deduction" because *"whoever does not love does not know God"* (v.8).[82] This implies that true vertical reconciliation directly promotes true horizontal reconciliation.

Having discussed that, it can be concluded that the vertical dimension of reconciliation promotes the horizontal dimension in a direct manner. The underlying reason is that the horizontal dimension is embedded in the genuine form of vertical reconciliation. This statement has two explanations. First, vertical reconciliation indicates the standard for what is horizontal reconciliation is and when it is deficient or absent. God shines the light of truth into humans' hearts. The sinfulness of humans on the surface of their relationship is not just their hatred against other humans but also their unawareness and ignorance of to what extent they are broken and should be restored—the absence of the standard. In this regard, as Barth rightly claims, ethics can

---

78. Carson, *Gospel According to John*, 516.
79. Carson, *Gospel According to John*, 516.
80. Barth, *CD* III/2:218, 226.
81. Stott, *Letters of John*, 161.
82. Stott, *Letters of John*, 161.

be understood and should be shaped by dogmatics. Eberhard Busch, citing Barth's *Evangelium und Gesetz,* writes the following:

> It is not only uncertain and dangerous but perverse to want to understand the Law of God on the basis of any other things, of any other event which is different from the event in which the will of God, tearing in two the veil of our theories and interpretations, is visible in grace . . . Because this occurrence of the will of God, therefore the occurrence of his grace, becomes *manifest* to us, the *Law* becomes manifest to us."[83]

Busch continues,

> We know the *law* of God, therefore, only when we know *God.* We know God only in his *revelation,* and thus we know his *commandment* rightly only in connection with his *grace.*[84]

Volf's[85] argument that "the cure" of violence is "not less religion" but "more religion," it can be overcome by "thick faith," corresponds to what Barth argues. In a previous chapter, Volf has claimed,

> The more we reduce faith to vague religiosity that serves primarily to energize, heal, and give meaning to the business of life whose course is shaped by factors other than faith (such as national or economic interests), the worse off we will be. Inversely, the more the Christian faith matters to its adherents as faith that maps a way of life, the more they practice it as an ongoing tradition with strong ties to its origins and history, and with clear cognitive and moral content, the better off we will be.[86]

Second, as discussed in the section of the evaluation of Schreiter's theology and commented by D. A Carson, the change of one's heart is a prerequisite for reconciliation. Transforming relationships from enmity to friendship requires going beyond one's intellectual agreement or acknowledgment of the necessity—it involves the conversion of one's heart. Having awareness and experiences of being forgiven by God can become the main motivation to forgive other humans.

---

83. Karl Barth, *Evangelium und Gesetz,* 9; English translation from "Gospel and Law," in *Community, State, and Church,* 77–78. as quoted in Busch, *Great Passion,* 158–59.

84. Busch, *Great Passion,* 158–59.

85. Volf, "Forgiveness, Reconciliation, and Justice," 862; Volf, *Public Faith,* 19–20, 39–40.

86. Volf, *Public Faith,* 40.

As reminded in Volf's terms previously, the transformation of heart—the process of decentering and recentering which empower oneself to overcome exclusion and to perform embrace—is the work of God.[87] "The Spirit enters the citadel of the self, de-centers the self by fashioning it in the image of the self-giving Christ, and frees its will so it can resist the power of exclusion in the power of the Spirit of embrace."[88] In that respect, the vertical dimension of reconciliation, in its revelatory and redemptive ministry, makes an accurate diagnosis and proper restoration possible for the brokenness in the horizontal dimension.

Thus, vertical reconciliation should be sought in-depth in the church's ministry of mission as reconciliation. It must be sought within the framework of holistic reconciliation, with the implications in the horizontal dimension embedded in it. In specific, the church should declare the Gospel and pursue the renewal of its faith and commitment to God, attempting to obtain and deliver a deeper understanding of God's love in Christ.

Evangelism, therefore, is an indispensable step in the church's ministry of holistic reconciliation. The church should do evangelism because the witness and declaration of the Gospel are the intrinsic nature of every ministry that the church engages with, as Karl Barth has argued.[89] Also, it includes the steps of sanctification, and again, this process of sanctification can be driven by the Gospel and revitalized through the work of the Holy Spirit. It can be achieved when the church commits itself to the will of God and prayer, as Son's case demonstrates.

In every step, the church must be reminded that the horizontal dimension of reconciliation is not to be separated in its pursuit of spiritual renewal; instead, it is embedded in the vertical pursuit as a fundamental commandment from God. Tutu has correctly claimed that the many issues in the sociopolitical realm, the horizontal dimension, are spiritual issues by nature.[90] Therefore, under the framework of holistic reconciliation, when this teaching of embedded horizontal reconciliation goes along with the tireless effort of spiritual renewal, they would break the ground of false division between the two dimensions, and offer godly grief and convictions in one's heart, helping one to bear the fruit of repentance and transform in mind and action (2 Cor 7:10).

---

87. Volf, *Exclusion and Embrace*, 69–70.
88. Volf, *Exclusion and Embrace*, 92.
89. Barth, *CD* IV/2:812–13.
90. Tutu, "Nobel Peace Prize Lecture," 38; Tutu, *No Future Without Forgiveness*, 92–93.

In conclusion, the vertical dimension of reconciliation directly promotes the horizontal dimension of reconciliation in that horizontal reconciliation is given as commandments to obey for those who are reconciled with God in Christ. The victorious atonement on the Cross by Jesus is the culmination of the revelation of God's love for sinful humans, which concomitantly indicates the way of loving one another between humans as well as enables it (Eph 2:11–22). Furthermore, the vertical reconciliation enlightens the magnitude of horizontal brokenness and transforms one's heart, enabling one to forgive and love other human beings as God does. The vertical reconciliation is, therefore, both revelation and power for horizontal reconciliation; the former directly promotes the latter.

Christians' ministry of reconciliation is thus active participation in God's reconciliation in an intrinsically passive manner. It fundamentally imitates and reflects God's, which constitutes the primary motivation. In that respect, it is not surprising that the quality of horizontal reconciliation is determined by that of vertical reconciliation. Hence, vertical reconciliation should be pursued by the church with horizontal concentration embedded in the ministry of mission as reconciliation.

Horizontal Reconciliation Indirectly Promotes Vertical Reconciliation

As the second aspect of the mutual promotion relationship, horizontal reconciliation indirectly promotes vertical reconciliation. The following biblical passages illustrate this aspect: Matt 5:23–24 and 6:12 (and 14–15); Matt 5:44–45; 1 John 3:10, 14; and 4:12; and John 13:34–35 and 15:10–12. The second aspect of the relationship can be discussed in three main ways.

First, horizontal reconciliation pleases God: it is what God wants to see from His children (Matt 5:9). As God is a God of righteousness and peace, He is glad when one lives with his or her best efforts to be righteous and holy before Him, which involves one's righteous behaviors to others (Deut 14:29; Jas 1:27; Luke 19:8–10). In Matt 5:23–24 and 6:12 (and 14–15), it is illustrated how one's life in the horizontal dimension relates to the vertical dimension with God in this way. The first passage (Matt 5:23–24) indicates that worshipping God can be properly established upon restoring relationships with others. It does not mean, however, that being friendly with neighbors will automatically result in an appropriate relationship with God. Here, it must be recalled that the audience of the Sermon on the Mount were the disciples of Jesus (Matt 5:1). This denotes that God *delights* when His people come to Him with their effort for a righteous life and purified hands in their relationships with others. John

Nolland makes the following comments regarding this passage: "Worship that is acceptable to God cannot take place against the background of a damaged human relationship which is being ignored."[91] As Nolland states, this passage recalls the prophetic teaching of fasting in Isa 58:1–7, which shows what kind of fasting God pleases and chooses.[92]

The passage of the Lord's Prayer, Matt 6:12 (and 14–15), similarly indicates that when one appeals for forgiveness to God, forgiving others is a precondition. As Nolland clarifies, due to the shared linguistic root of both words debt and sin, it is "natural" "to use the imagery of debt in relation to sin" "in Aramaic."[93] It is thus about sin. Forgiving others' sins against oneself is then "a necessary" condition for being forgiven by God.[94] Nevertheless, it is not "a sufficient one."[95] As mentioned previously, reconciliation with others does not guarantee it with God. Leon Morris also states that "it is not that the act of forgiving merits an eternal reward, but rather it is evidence that the grace of God is at work in the forgiving person and that that same grace will bring him forgiveness in due course."[96]

That having peace with others becomes a necessary condition is based on the fact that God is a God who is gratified to see forgiving and loving among His people. The character of God lays the foundation for the argument that horizontal reconciliation indirectly promotes vertical reconciliation; it deepens one's communion with God.

Second, horizontal reconciliation offers an opportunity to evaluate one's relationship with God and rectify it if necessary. Horizontal reconciliation often serves as a sign of confirmation of reconciliation in the vertical dimension. One can recognize the extent of having communion with God (sanctification) and the genuineness of one's reconciliation with Him through examining horizontal reconciliation in one's life. In Matt 5:44–45, it seems that through horizontal love and kindness, a person is affirmed for the position of being associated with God. It sounds radical, yet again it should be understood in light of who God is. Ulrich Luz makes the following comments on Matt 5:44–45:

> That is related to Jesus' idea of God . . . His command to love one's enemy corresponds not to the world's harmony but to God's will. The extreme demand to love one's enemy corresponds to

---

91. Nolland, *Gospel of Matthew*, 233.
92. Nolland, *Gospel of Matthew*, 233.
93. Nolland, *Gospel of Matthew*, 290.
94. Nolland, *Gospel of Matthew*, 294.
95. Nolland, *Gospel of Matthew*, 294.
96. Morris, *Gospel According to Matthew*, 149.

God's extreme love toward sinners and outcasts in the inbreaking of his kingdom. That is why Jesus links his demand with an eschatological promise: you will be sons of God.[97]

As is the case for the previous passage, loving others serves as evidence of being loved by God. For this passage, Morris comments that "to be God's children means to love. Love and membership in God's family go together."[98] That the horizontal reconciliation becomes a sign of confirmation or evidence of the vertical reconciliation makes a serious claim to oneself to evaluate one's relationship with God through this lens. Horizontal reconciliation thus indirectly promotes vertical reconciliation in this sense. Moreover, this point can be similarly observed in the next selected passages, namely 1 John 3:10, 14; and 4:12, and John 13:34–35; and John 15:10–12.

In 1 John 3:10, 14; and 4:12, loving others is considered a verification of one's belonging to God. It is again based on the core understanding of the nature of God, "God is love" (4:16). Therefore, as Colin Kruse says, the brotherly love "is the sign that God lives in" a person.[99] These verses lead a person to reflect upon the soundness of one's faith and connection with God. It offers an opportunity to scrutinize one's allegiance to God, as well as enhance it (2 Cor 13:5).

In the same vein, what Jesus commands in John 13:34–35; and 15:10–12 clarifies that by keeping the commandment of loving one another, the identity of being disciples of Jesus will be certified, and also the relationship with Jesus will be maintained. Horizontal love demonstrates one's faith and belonging to Christ before God and to other people. It is because the same kind of love, *agape*, of God, revealed in Christ, can be obtained in oneself only through the living relationship with Him. This *agape* love of God in oneself will be and should be manifested in one's horizontal dimension. It again makes a person examine his or her belonging to Christ.

A helpful reference can be noted here. In *Transforming Mission*, David Bosch discusses the theme of liberation, and defends the importance of the theme as follows: "Once we recognize the identification of Jesus with the poor, we cannot any longer consider our own relation to the poor as a social ethics question; it is a gospel question."[100] He continues, "Jesus will not be our Savior if we persistently reject him as Lord of our total life."[101] Based on the biblical passages examined thus far, in the same principle, the theme

---

97. Luz, *Matthew 1–7*, 286–88.
98. Morris, *Gospel According to Matthew*, 131.
99. Kruse, *Letters of John*, 161.
100. Bosch, *Transforming Mission*, 437.
101. Bosch, *Transforming Mission*, 438.

of reconciliation can function as a self-assessment of one's faith in God as Bosch argued for the theme of liberation.

Third, horizontal reconciliation itself testifies the truthfulness of vertical reconciliation with God to the world—it witnesses who God is and what the Gospel is. It witnesses God's love. All the biblical passages that urge one to confirm one's identity in Christ also describe, at least partially, this third point, in particular, John 13:34–35. It is because the visible love for neighbors inherently reflects and witness the invisible love for God (1 John 4:20), and this love to God is a returning love from a human, responding to the love of God toward humanity, which is the first (1 John 4:9–11; 19). Therefore, horizontal love among Christians testifies the vertical love of God for humanity to the world.

In John 17:21, Jesus prays that as the disciples become one in Christ, resembling the mutual interiority between the Father and the Son, the world will acknowledge this witness of *agape*-driven unity among the disciples, and may believe that Jesus is the Lord and the Savior sent by God. The following two verses (22–23) confirm this. Jesus depicts how the oneness of the disciples itself will be a witness of God's love revealed in Christ to the world.

Lesslie Newbigin has constantly underlined this aspect of reconciliation and unity among Christians and its possible concomitant fruits in their mission to the world. In *The Household of God* (1953), he claims,

> When the Church faces out towards the world it knows that it only exists as the first fruits and the instrument of that reconciling work of Christ, and that division within its own life is a violent contradiction of its own fundamental nature. His reconciling work is one, and we cannot be His ambassadors reconciling the world to God, if we have not ourselves been willing to be reconciled to one another.[102]

In *A Faith for this One World* (1961), Newbigin further states,

> [. . .] how can those who are not reconciled to one another be the instruments of God's reconciling action? How can he use us to draw all men to himself if we do not let him draw us to one another? How can the world believe our witness to Christ's love if we ourselves have found that love too weak to overcome our natural differences? Our divisions are a public denial of the sufficiency of Christ.[103]

102. Newbigin, *Household of God*, 17–18.
103. Newbigin, *A Faith for this One World*. as cited in Weston, *Lesslie Newbigin*, loc. 872–74.

In this respect, he considers the immoderate denominationalism in the "Western" church, which he observes, as a form of division in the body of Christ. In *Reunion of the Church* (1979), he criticizes that "it [this denominationalism] would be the public denial of the Gospel, which we preach, the good news of Him, who, being lifted up, will draw all men to Himself."[104]

The point that Newbigin makes corresponds to the prayer of Jesus in John 17. The horizontal love, the same kind of love in Christ, among Christians who have reconciled with God through Christ, transforms into a public witness of the Gospel when it encounters those who do not know God's love. As a faithful witness, the visible horizontal love performed by Christians promotes the potential vertical reconciliation between the invisible God and the non-Christians of the world. Horizontal reconciliation thus promotes vertical reconciliation in a way that it testifies the Gospel of Christ through accepting which one can turn one's relationship with God from enemy to a child. Thus, in this sense, horizontal reconciliation *indirectly* promotes vertical reconciliation.

Related to this, Karl Barth explained the nature of the church's ministry and its various form as follows:

> The ministry and therefore the witness of the community is also essentially and in all forms and circumstances (3) evangelical address, i.e., proclamation and explication in the form of application. For this reason it cannot achieve its declaration and explanation in a vacuum. For it does not itself live in a vacuum. In every age and situation it stands in definite relations to the world around, i.e., non-Christians, who like its own members are above all living men who have in some way gone astray and are therefore under assault.[105]

Mission as reconciliation is an imperative and legitimate mode of the church's mission and ministry today. Through this mode, the church engages with the issues around it. In this step, however, the mode of the ministry never loses its intrinsic constitution, the declaration of the Gospel to the world. Therefore, it is both appropriate and necessary that horizontal reconciliation eventually promotes vertical reconciliation.

In conclusion, based on the selected biblical passages and theological elaborations, it has been proposed that the two dimensions of reconciliation (vertical and horizontal) are placed in a mutual-promotion relationship (direct and indirect, respectively). They promote and are promoted by each other. In this "positive correlation" relationship, they should increase

---

104. Newbigin, *Reunion of the Church*, 21.
105. Barth, *CD* IV/3.2:850.

and decrease together. If one is noticed to increase while the other decreases, it can be assumed that a flawed or unsound understanding of reconciliation exists in that theology or practice. The Christian understanding of reconciliation is like a double-edged sword in this respect. It contains and delivers two inseparable messages simultaneously: (1) Do you want to see true reconciliation? This is not possible apart from God who is the author of reconciliation; and (2) Are you being reconciled with fellow humans? If not, you need to examine your relationship with God. When either side of the sword engages, the other side always goes together. They are truly inseparable in this way. One of the strongest pieces of evidence for the inseparableness of the two dimensions is the mutual-promotion relationship that they hold toward each other.

Having discussed this, one may ponder the meaning or nature of the horizontal reconciliation observed in our societies when it seems that no—at least explicit—vertical reconciliation exists. As reviewed in the previous section on Desmond Tutu, although the creation of God must be comprehended with the redemption of God to be a wholesome understanding of reconciliation, it is still a valid point to view humans solely through the lens of *imago Dei*. This means that somehow as the part of the divine image remains that was not obliterated in humans after the Fall, those who are not Christians still do relate to each other in ways that reflect the divine nature given by God. Regardless of their religious commitment, all humans prefer being reconciled with people around them to the alternative.

Furthermore, based on the mutual promotion framework, it must be clarified that Christians' efforts in the ministry of reconciliation can engage the horizontal dimension of reconciliation even before the evangelistic ministry, even though they will never be perfect nor fulfilled without the basis of vertical reconciliation. Stated differently, churches do not have to wait until the point that evangelism is completed to begin the works of horizontal reconciliation. Churches should engage with the issues of the horizontal dimension even if they may not have an opportunity to explicitly witness their faith.

This is affirmed by the teaching of Jesus in the Sermon on the Mount, when as Matt 5:9 states, "Blessed are the peacemakers, for they shall be called sons of God." In this passage, Jesus implies that peacemaking is what God's people do—it mirrors their new identity and character, belonging to the God of reconciliation. Nevertheless, again, to what extent reconciliation can be observed in one's life often depends on the aspect of sanctification of that person, which underscores the significance of the vertical relationship with God. In addition, as argued, it will indirectly promote vertical reconciliation eventually as it becomes the declaration of the Gospel.

Moreover, in terms of how one can view and understand the church's ministry of reconciliation in the horizontal dimension, it is helpful to view the ministry as churches' prayer to God. As in the Lord's Prayer, the church prays "Thy kingdom come, thy will be done on earth as it is in heaven." The ministry of reconciliation in this broken world is thus churches' living out prayer as they hope to see God's kingdom come and His will be done. The prayer will be finally and completely answered when Jesus returns and renews the whole world. Until that Day, the church's prayer and ministry of reconciliation should continue. This point naturally leads to the *alpha* and *omega* of reconciliation in the following section, which contains the eschatological understanding of reconciliation.

The *Alpha* and *Omega* of Reconciliation

The entire story of the Bible, from Genesis to Revelation, can be understood as a grand narrative of reconciliation between God and humanity. Within this framework, the theme of reconciliation can be comprehended with its full extent of meaningfulness and contribution to in the church's understanding of God's mission. The story tells that God's plan of reconciliation was instantly revealed as soon as the fall of humans took place in the beginning (Gen 3:15). At the same time, this narrative lens reminds us that there will be an end to this whole story.

The last two chapters (21 and 22) of the Book of Revelation, present a narrative of the New Heaven and the New Earth. These chapters close the entire story of reconciliation. They claim not only that reconciliation starts from God but also ends by God.[106] Theologians, in the discourse of mission as reconciliation, have agreed that God is the initiator of reconciliation, which implies that the vertical dimension of reconciliation becomes the foundation for the other dimensions. Notably, God is also the finisher of reconciliation—he accomplishes the final reconciliation. The horizontal and cosmic dimensions of reconciliation come back to the place before God where reconciliation started, and complete themselves in the vertical dimension as they become present before Him.

In the opening story of the Genesis, as humans became fallen and turned away from God, brokenness in the horizontal dimension emerged among them (the story of Cain and Abel in Gen. 4). Consequently, humans

---

106. No matter one's view of interpretation on the book of Revelation, from literal-apocalyptic to symbolic (already happened in the first century), it can still be claimed that the same theological message about finality of reconciliation can be inferred from the chapters.

lost their peace in both dimensions—with God and with fellow humans. God started to execute His redemptive plan through the Messiah to engage the vertical dimension of humans. As humans have been reconciled with God in Christ, the situation in the horizontal dimension changed. Therefore, vertical reconciliation as the final step of reconciliation does contain the accomplished horizontality.

In *Surprised by Hope*, N. T. Wright illustrates the final chapters of Revelation as the redeemed community having a vertical encounter with God with horizontality involved:

> And when they [all the children of heaven] finally come together, that will be cause for rejoicing in the same way that a wedding is: a creational sign that God's project is going forward; that opposite poles within creation are made for union, not competition; that love and not hate have the last word in the universe; that fruitfulness and not sterility is God's will for creation . . . This doesn't mean, as I have stressed throughout, that God will wipe the slate clean and start again. If that were so, there would be no celebration, no conquest of death, no long preparation now at last complete . . . As in Romans and 1 Corinthians, the living God will dwell with and among his people, filling the city with his life and love and pouring out grace and healing in the river of life that flows from the city out to the nations. There is a sign here of the future project that awaits the redeemed in God's eventual new world. So far from sitting on clouds playing harps, as people often imagine, the redeemed people of God in the new world will be the agents of his love going out in new ways, to accomplish new creative tasks, to celebrate and extend the glory of his love.[107]

In this final picture, humans regain both dimensions which they had lost. However, as Wright correctly highlight, it is not starting over again. The final reconciliation is where humanity has never been before—a new creation. Robert Schreiter similarly notes that reconciliation itself is a new creation.

> Reconciliation makes of both victim and oppressor a new creation. Reconciliation is about more than righting wrongs and repenting of evildoing. These are surely included, but the understanding of reconciliation in the Christian Scripture sees that we are indeed taken to a new place, a new creation.

---

107. Wright, *Surprised by Hope*, 105–6.

> Reconciliation is not just restoration. It brings us to a place where we have not been before.[108]

Hence, reconciliation, which is a form of new creation, is redemptive and eschatological by its nature, as Miroslav Volf notes. It implies an obvious end to the story. The whole story of the reconciliation of human beings, which was started by God, will be finished in its vertical dimension with God fulfilling the ultimate level of justice and love simultaneously and gloriously. It is thus ultimately about the glory of God.

Without its *omega*, God of reconciliation, where would reconciliation finish its long journey? It will certainly be lost. The only finale is in the presence of God, the author of reconciliation. The whole story of reconciliation finishes itself with the proclamation of God's presence with His people, which they have lost and gained back.

Correspondingly, in Karl Barth's thought, reconciliation is "the fulfillment of the covenant between God and man" in Christ.[109] It is "a fulfilment of the saying: 'I will be your God, and ye shall be my people.'"[110] Reconciliation as the fulfillment of the covenant places the atonement of Jesus Christ at the center of the story.

Therefore, Barth argues, "In our own development we have started with the person and work of Jesus Christ, for to say reconciliation is necessarily to name at once this name in which it is accomplished."[111] Barth's words dovetail with the illustration in the Revelation, which depicts the heavenly worship centered around "the Lamb who was slain" (Rev 5:12), and portrays the New Jerusalem as "the Bride, the wife of the Lamb" (Rev 21:9). In this sense, the final reconciliation is all about redemption and recreation of humanity in Jesus Christ, our Lord and Savior.

In sum, it has been proposed that the *alpha* and *omega* of reconciliation are ultimately the vertical dimension of reconciliation, with horizontality within. As discussed, in the *alpha* of reconciliation, horizontality is embedded from the beginning; therefore, vertical reconciliation initiates and enables horizontal reconciliation. Vertical reconciliation is the *alpha*, in that as Chung Sung-Wook notes, "the vertical always precedes the horizontal."[112] In the *omega* of reconciliation, the accomplished horizontality will be included in the final form of vertical reconciliation. According to the book of Revelation, the final manifestation of reconciliation in human history will be the

108. Schreiter, *Reconciliation*, 60.
109. Barth, *CD* IV/1:22.
110. Barth, *CD* IV/3.1:6.
111. Barth, *CD* IV/3.1:6.
112. Chung, "Salvation as Reconciliation," 144.

redeemed humanity becoming ultimately reconciled with God, the *omega*, embedding its horizontality with fellow brothers and sisters.

6

The Divided Contexts of the Korean Peninsula

A Brief History of National Division in Korea From Liberation to the Korean War

AFTER THE BRIEF JOYFUL moment of national liberation from Japanese forceful occupation on August 15, 1945, the Korean peninsula soon became entangled in nationwide "political and ideological division" under the Cold War's influence.[1]

As Japan was defeated in the Pacific War by the Allied forces, the Union of Soviet Socialist Republics (USSR) and the United States (US) began an ideological contest on the Korean peninsula, each of whom were concerned that Korea might be ideologically taken by the other party.[2]

Bruce Cumings discusses this as follows:

> There was no historical justification for Korea's division: if any East Asian country should have been divided it was Japan (like Germany, an aggressor). Instead Korea, China, and Vietnam were all divided in the aftermath of World War II. There was no internal pretext for dividing Korea, either: the thirty-eighth parallel was a line never noticed by the people of, say, Kaesŏng, the Koryŏ capital, which the parallel cut in half. And then it became the only line that mattered to Koreans, a boundary to be removed by any means necessary. The political and ideological divisions that we associate with the Cold War were the reasons for Korea's division; they came early to Korea, before the onset of the global Cold War, and today they outlast the end of the Cold War everywhere else.[3]

---

1. Cumings, *Korea's Place in the Sun*, 185.

2. Kang, *Korean Contemporary History Rewritten*, 264; Eckert et al., *Korea, Old and New*, 337.

3. Cumings, *Korea's Place in the Sun*, 186.

The Foreign Affair ministers of the US, the United Kingdom, and the USSR met from December 16 to 26, 1945 to discuss the issue of Korea. They decided to support Koreans' own provisional government, yet also operate a trusteeship on the Korean peninsula for up to 5 years "under four-power trusteeship (US, Britain, China, USSR)."[4] Regardless of political orientation, a national struggle rose against the decision because Koreans had suffered enough from losing self-government under Japanese occupation.[5] Suddenly, from early in 1946, the Communist Party of Korea began to support trusteeship.[6] The Joint Commission of the US and USSR eventually failed to reach an agreement.[7]

There were constant efforts to establish a unified government of North and South. For example, Yŏ Un-Hyŏng (or Lyuh Woon-Hyung), who was "a tireless advocate of coalescing the left and right . . . and eliminating North-South division," led the Korean Establishment Preparation Board to build a unified government,[8] but it failed. Under the occupation of the US, which suppressed the communist party, both left and right wings became extreme.[9]

The issue of Korea was handed over to United Nations (UN) at the suggestion of the US. The UN General Assembly "passed a resolution" to have a South–North general election. However, this did not occur because of the USSR's opposition, which claimed the issue should remain between the US and USSR, not the UN.[10] Meanwhile, Kim Il-Sung of northern Korea "pushed fundamental reforms that restructured northern society and, more than any other action in 1946, served to separate the north from the south."[11] Cumings claims that "after these reforms, unification of the peninsula could only occur in two ways: through a similar revolution in the south, or through a war."[12]

---

4. Seo, *Contemporary History of South Korea*, 35–37; Kang, *Korean Contemporary History Rewritten*, 266; Yi, *New History of Korea*, 376.

5. Seo, *Contemporary History of South Korea*, 36; Yi, *New History of Korea*, 376.

6. Seo, *Contemporary History of South Korea*, 36; Kang, *Korean Contemporary History Rewritten*, 267; Yi, *New History of Korea*, 377.

7. Seo, *Contemporary History of South Korea*, 40; Kang, *Korean Contemporary History Rewritten*, 268–71.

8. Cumings, *Korea's Place in the Sun*, 191.

9. Seo, *Study in Contemporary National Movement*, 212, 216.

10. Kang, *Korean Contemporary History Rewritten*, 272; Seo, *Contemporary History of South Korea*, 40–41.

11. Cumings, *Origins of the Korean War*, 1:414.

12. Cumings, *Origins of the Korean War*, 1:414.

After all, there was only an election for the Constitutional Assembly in the South.[13] The South Korean moderate party, including some center-rightists and nationalist leaders such as Kim Koo, declined the decision and "attempted to make an autonomous move" to remain undivided.[14] This was because Kim Koo believed that "the movement of united government establishment is the extension of the independence movement."[15] They met the leaders of the North and negotiated to form a united government; however, it fell a step behind.

Consequently, two ideologically different regimes were established separately by the 38th Parallel: the Demographic People's Republic of Korea (DPRK) in the north and the Republic of Korea (ROK) in the south. In their constitutions, "each government claimed exclusive legitimacy, and condemned the other as a puppet regime" of either the US or USSR.[16] The two Korean regimes believed there ought to be only one regime on the peninsula and were willing to endure even military conflict to "liberate" each other—liberating the North from communism and liberating the South from American imperialism.[17]

Kang Man-Gil identifies external reasons for national division: "the geographical location of Korea, the Japanese colonization, the proposal of division by the US to stop the USSR's occupation of entire Korea and the USSR's acceptance of it, stratagem of the US in passing the issue of Korea to the UN, and the intensified tension of the global Cold War."[18] For internal reasons, Kang further mentions "some naïve national sentiment to accept nothing but instant independence rejecting any type of grace period suggested by powerful nations, people's oblivion that Korea was a colony of a defeated nation, not a victorious nation, and instigation of some opportunist politicians who attempted to rule the separated government and their supporters."[19]

Two years after the establishment, when both the USSR and US armies had evacuated, the Korean War was launched by the DPRK[20] who

13. Seo, *Contemporary History of South Korea*, 41; Yi, *New History of Korea*, 378.

14. Seo, *Contemporary History of South Korea*, 42; Kang, *Historical Perception*, 146, 150–52.

15. Kang, *Historical Perception*, 152.

16. Seo, *Contemporary History of South Korea*, 45.

17. Kim, *History of North Korea 1*, 140.

18. Kang, *Korean Contemporary History Rewritten*, 265.

19. Kang, *Korean Contemporary History Rewritten*, 265.

20. Some would disagree with this statement. It is the issue of "Who started the Korean war?" Bruce Cummings argues it "cannot be answered" and is "the wrong question." Cumings, *Origins of the Korean War*, 2:619. The entire chapter of Cumings's book

had prepared a war mainly with the USSR's support,[21] whereas "South Korea's military was poorly equipped."[22] Due to the war, the South Korean government was driven to build an anticommunist nation. However, one unresolved national issue was the public demand for the elimination of pro-Japanese collaborators. Similar to the case for the DPRK, the regime of the first president of the ROK, Rhee Syngman, failed to adequately punish former Japanese collaborators in a sense.[23] The former collaborators were still appointed in different places of the regime because Rhee considered North Korea to be more of an imminent threat at the time and wished to avoid national chaos.

The unresolved demand of the people against the collaborators provided a reason to oppose the succeeding rightist regimes. The rightists, however, have polemicized that there are pro-North people among their opponents; that is, leftists. This political conflict—between anti-communism and anti pro-Japanese groups—has offered a profound reason for South–South strife until the present day, and still affects people's views toward North Korea.

As a result, the ideological war between the Communist World versus the Free World on the Korean peninsula lasted over 3 years, killing more than a million soldiers and civilians on both sides, before a cease-fire agreement was reached.[24] The consequences of the war were immense. Seo Joong-Seok discusses the post-war era of the Korean peninsula as follows:

> The war contributed to the rule of rigid single party systems that alienated or eliminated any diversity of pluralism in the politics, society, and culture of both North and South Koreas. Cold War ideology prevailed in the South where no criticism of

examines this question. Cumings, *Origins of the Korean War*, 2:568–621. John Merrill notes it was a multilayered incident, having "both local and international factors." Merrill, *Korea*, 189. As all historical events are, the Korean War had probably multiple aspects and factors that provoked it, however, several explicit evidences that North Korea intentionally prepared the war were discovered after the collapse of USSR. Some, including Merrill and Keum Jooseop, still argue that the question cannot be clearly answered because there previously were multiple armed conflicts initiated by both sides before the war. Keum, "Korean War," 103–6.

21. Bruce Cumings considers this statement is prevalent; yet "heavily biased by the cold war". He thinks the weapons were prepared through China, USSR, and DPRK's own capability to produce weapons from the Japanese former arsenals in the northern Korea. Cumings, *Origins of the Korean War*, 2:445–48. He argues, "Koreans were by no means dependent only on Moscow for supplies" (2:448).

22. Yi, *New History of Korea*, 379.

23. It is a controversial issue whether DPRK had successfully punished Japanese collaborators compared to ROK. Yi, *New History of Korea*, 381–82.

24. Yi, *New History of Korea*, 380–81.

anticommunism was permitted, while no political force other than Kim Il Sung's group was allowed to exist in the North. North Korea was reborn as the land of the Juche Ideology of self-reliance in the 1970s, under a system oriented exclusively around the "Supreme Leader."[25]

The South–South Conflict: Division in Views Toward the North in the South

The term, *nam-nam-gal-deung* (the South–South conflict)—in contrast to the *nam-buk-gal-deung* (the South–North conflict)—means the ideological or social conflict *within* South Korea associated with the issue of North Korea.[26][27] The term has been widely used since the first South–North Korea Summit Talks on June 15, 2000 by Kim Dae-Jung's administration, which caused an infuriated response from opponents.[28][29]

The concept of South–South conflict itself, however, did not emerge in the 2000s.[30] Son Ho-Chul states that "it is not an exaggeration to say that the contemporary history of Korea since liberation has been a history of South-South Conflict."[31] Cumings similarly argues, "Nothing about the politics of contemporary Korea can be understood without

---

25. Seo, *Contemporary History of South Korea*, 60.

26. Another issue deeply interrelated with this is how one views the United States. Kim, "South-South Conflict in Korea," 31, 37. As Korean history demonstrates, anticommunism has been associated with pro-Americanism (38). Thus, one aspect of South-South conflict is about the perception of the US and US Forces Korea. Baek, "Reshuffle of Korea-US Alliance and South-South Conflict."

27. Son, "Origin of South South Conflict," 13; Han and Jang, "Study on the Ideological Debates," 64; Kim, "South-South Conflict in Korea," 35; Kang, "Empirical Investigation on Ideological Features," 56; Kwon, "Study on the Phenomenon of South-South Conflict," 52, 57.

28. One possible explanation of why South-South conflict rose increasingly in Kim Dae-Jung's regime is presented by Kim Gab-Sik referring Choi Wan-gyu. Citing W. Choi, Kim claims that it was the time that dominant position of power was moved from conservatives to progressives in Kim's regime and it made conservatives to solidarize and protest. Choi, "Reflective Approach to Policy of Reconciliation," 20; Kim, "South-South Conflict in Korea," 41.

29. Son, "Origin of South South Conflict,"14; Kim, "South-South Conflict in Korea,"35, 39; Kwon, "Study on the Phenomenon of South-South Conflict," 58; Han and Jang, "Study on the Ideological Debates," 64.

30. Son, "Origin of South South Conflict,"14; Kwon, "Study on the Phenomenon of South-South Conflict," 58.

31. Son, "Origin of South South Conflict," 14.

comprehending the events of this decade [from 1943 to 1953]," which was "the period of national division."[32]

Both Kim Gab-Sik and Kwon Sook-Do also acknowledge that "South-South conflict is where all sorts of conflict of our society are condensed."[33] Kim adds that "polarization can be more easily seen in the issue of North Korea, national security, and unification" compared with other societal issues.[34] Kang Won-Taek also identifies how "ideological and political polarization has been advanced" in South Korea in relation to South–South conflict.[35]

Furthermore, South–South conflict has become more visible because, since the late twentieth century, South Korea has been "in a transitional period from the legacy of Cold War (animosity and exclusion) to post-Cold War era (embrace and recognition)."[36] It is also based on unavoidable realities that South Korea has an ambivalent attitude toward the North: the brother country, which simultaneously is an enemy.[37]

In this sense, anti-communism has been a significant factor in comprehending the conflict, which imposes a cautious attitude toward North Korea.[38] South–South conflict is largely related to the extent of one's sympathy to anti-communism.[39]

Son Ho-Chul schematizes the types of South–South conflict as follows:[40]

---

32. Cumings, *Korea's Place in the Sun*, 185.

33. Kim, "South-South Conflict in Korea," 34–35; Kwon, "Study on the Phenomenon of South-South Conflict," 51–52.

34. Kim, "South-South Conflict in Korea," 34–35.

35. Kang, "Empirical Investigation on Ideological Features," 70.

36. Kim, "South-South Conflict in Korea," 39; Kwon, "Study on the Phenomenon of South-South Conflict," 60.

37. Kim, "South-South Conflict in Korea," 40; Kwon, "Study on the Phenomenon of South-South Conflict," 60.

38. Kim, "South-South Conflict in Korea," 35.

39. Kang, "Empirical Investigation on Ideological Features," 77; Kwon, "Study on the Phenomenon of South-South Conflict," 60.

40. Son, "Origin of South South Conflict," 15, figure 1.

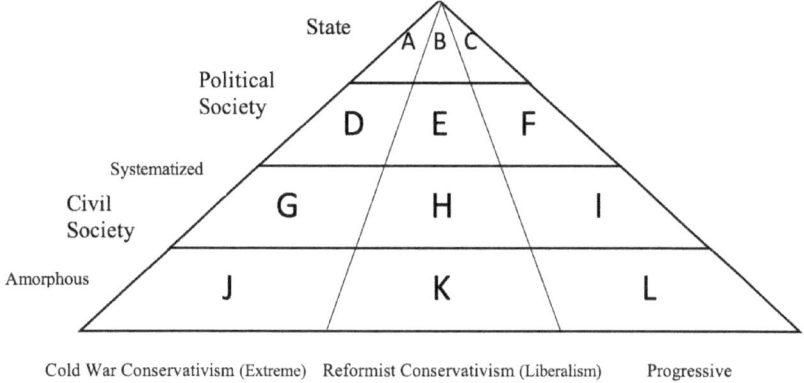

Figure 1. A category of political groups in South Korean society.

In his examination of South–South conflict, Son presents three time periods. The first period was 8 years after liberation (1945–1953); the second period was the autocratic regime characterized by anti-communism (1953–1987); and the third period was after democratization (since 1987), which includes an extended period of anti-communism (1987–1992), a transitional period (1993–1997), and the post-Cold War period (1998–).[41]

The first period (1945–1953) was filled with South–South conflicts, such as the issue of trusteeship, a conflict between the supporters of a separated and unified government, and armed resistance by leftists before the war.[42] According to the illustration, it was A+D+G+J versus F+I+E.[43] Some features of this period were (1) the middle ground—reformist conservativism was weak in general, and (2) "North Korea directly and fully engaged South-South conflict as the Korean War demonstrates."[44]

In general, the second period "did not really have South-South conflict" compared with the previous period.[45] The progressive group was almost eliminated from political society and even reformists were largely committed to anti-communism because of the memory of the Korean War and the influence of the Cold War.[46] After 1961, when Park Chung-Hee took the regime in the May 16 military coup, most progressive groups, both political and civil,

41. Son, "Origin of South South Conflict," 18.
42. Son, "Origin of South South Conflict," 19.
43. Son, "Origin of South South Conflict," 20.
44. Son, "Origin of South South Conflict," 20.
45. Son, "Origin of South South Conflict," 20.
46. Son, "Origin of South South Conflict," 21.

were destroyed and went underground: A versus F.[47] Some progressive movement returned to systematized civil society after the Gwangju Democratization Movement of 1980: A versus I.[48] Son describes this period as follows: "in every dimension of society—state, political society, and civil society, the influence of the Cold War was enormous."[49]

The third period exhibits different opinions toward North Korea, which had been suppressed under military regimes. In the extended period, progressive politicians and civilians visited North Korea, advocating peace on the peninsula and trying to move beyond anti-communism: A versus E, and A versus I.[50] As a response, conservative civil society began to be systematized and reacted to this progressive movement.[51]

Meanwhile, a conflict emerged within progressive civil society, the National Liberator (NL) group versus the People's Democratic (PD) group, which could be distinguished by one's affinity to Kim Il-Sung's *juche* ideology:[52] I versus I.[53] In the transitional period, under Kim Young-Sam's administration, a new type of conflict appeared: B versus G.[54] Son notes that "the emergence of conservative media is noteworthy; they began to engage in South-South conflict as one of the main players since this period."[55]

In the post-Cold War period, under Kim Dae-Jung's regime, the conflict was enhanced. It became B+(E+II+I) versus G+D.[56] Since the end of 2000, after Kim Dae-Jung met Kim Jung-Il in North Korea, approximately 40 conservative civil societies united to speak against Kim Dae-Jung's so-called Sunshine Policy (promoting economic support to alleviate the hostile atmosphere).[57] It was during this period that the systematized civil society of both progressives and conservatives began to collide, exhibiting

47. Son, "Origin of South South Conflict," 24–25.
48. Son, "Origin of South South Conflict," 26.
49. Son, "Origin of South South Conflict," 21.
50. Son, "Origin of South South Conflict," 27–28.
51. Son, "Origin of South South Conflict," 28.
52. It is the ideological and philosophical idea that the government of DPRK officially advocates for its socialism revolution and national development. It literally means being self-reliant and denotes that men should become "the master" of their destiny. For the society and the nation of DPRK, this idea leads to continue the socialism revolution "in their one way," and to increase their military power against the "imperialism" of the world powers.
53. Son, "Origin of South South Conflict," 28.
54. Son, "Origin of South South Conflict," 29.
55. Son, "Origin of South South Conflict," 29.
56. Son, "Origin of South South Conflict," 30.
57. Son, "Origin of South South Conflict," 31.

an aspect of full-scale war: I(+H) versus G. This can be observed today on national holidays every year in the central square of Seoul, Gwanghwmum Plaza, South Korea.[58]

Since then, no matter which administration has been elected, conflicts in the civil society dimension—I(+H) versus G—have appeared continually as well as intensified.[59] The conflict in civil society is based not only in a classical ideology contest, such as anti-communism and traditionally "embedded" regionalism (*honam* vs. *youngnam*),[60] but also "newly arising generational conflict" (20–30 year olds vs. 50–60 year olds).[61]

In both civil and political society, the conflict has become a fight characterized by hatred: associating each other with *chin-il* ("political" descendants of the pro-Japanese group) or *chin-buk* or *jong-buk* (pro-North or following North group). It is unfortunate that the two tragedies in the modern history of Korea, Japanese colonialism and the Korean War, have still exerted significant influences on people's emotions and understanding of how to view the current realities on the Korean peninsula.

Different Views and Missional Activities by South Korean Churches Toward Mission for North Korea

The South–South conflict has affected South Korean churches' views of North Korea. South Korean churches' mission for North Korea has been influenced by politics, and thus North Korea mission should be approached "from both missionary and political viewpoints."[62] There have been different views and missional approaches in South Korean churches toward North Korea. First, there have been anti-communist Christians. A majority of South Korean churches have generally advocated anti-communism, being perceived as "one of the most conservative groups."[63] This is because the majority of Korean Christians were in the northern area before independence and came south after being oppressed under the communist

---

58. Son, "Origin of South South Conflict," 31–32.

59. Son, "Origin of South South Conflict," 34.

60. There has been a regional conflict between south-west and south-east areas of South Korea in the sociopolitical context. The political view of the two areas have been contrasted to each other until today. People in honam (south-west) region have strongly supported the progressive political party while those in youngnam (south-east) region have enthusiastically endorsed the conservative political party.

61. Son, "Origin of South South Conflict," 40–41; Kim, "South-South Conflict in Korea,"34, 49; Kang, "Empirical Investigation on Ideological Features," 73–76.

62. Ahn, "North Korea Mission in Historical Perspective," 117.

63. Yoon, *Korean Church and North Korean Human Rights Movement*, 11.

movement in the north from 1945 to 1950.[64] Those who did not escape "hid themselves underground."[65] The Christianity in the northern area was "suppressed completely and vanished under the communist regime" after the Korean War, that is, until it "officially" reappeared in 1972 in a form that was seriously affected by the *juche* idea.[66]

As a result, many South Korean Christians have understood Christianity and communism to be incompatible. Since Rhee Syngman's anti-communist regime, "the agenda of reunification came to be seen as dangerous and even antigovernmental," "Korean Christians, in general, took a progovernmental stance."[67] Moreover, Rhee Syngman himself was a Christian who supported pro-Christian policy—"'Christian' national reconstruction plan"—which attracted many Korean Christians at that moment.[68] In that sense, "many South Korean Christians even supported voluntarily or involuntarily military [dictatorship] governments," which succeeded Rhee's regime (from the 1960s to the 1980s), providing an excuse for the autocratic regimes to advocate anti-communism, which they associated with pro-Christianity.[69]

Second, another group of Korean Christians were actively involved in democratization under the dictatorships.[70] This group pursued a unification movement toward the northern partner, exhibiting no anti-communism or to a lesser degree,[71] but having a "more sympathetic" attitude for their "blood relations."[72] However, until the détente period,

---

64. The Society of the History of Christianity in Korea, 31–32, 153; Ahn, "North Korea Mission in Historical Perspective," 118; Kim and Kim, *History of Korean Christianity*, 161–62; Park, "Approach Method of North Korea Mission," 198. Ahn Kyo Seong further explains that those who escaped from the north during this period, the first wave of North Korean refugees (*Wolnammin* in Korean), could not talk about reunification with the north, but cautiously align themselves with anti-communism for their own settlement in the south. Ahn, "North Korea Mission in Historical Perspective," 117.

65. Kim, "Towards Peace and Reconciliation," 131.

66. Kim, "Towards Peace and Reconciliation," 131.

67. Ahn, "North Korea Mission in Historical Perspective," 118.

68. The Society of the History of Christianity in Korea, 28–31; Lew, *Youthful Time of Syngman Rhee*, 60–65.

69. Yi, "Seventy years of Division," 13.

70. Park, "Approach Method of North Korea Mission," 204.

71. Kang In-Chul says "many progressive Christians had agreed with anti-communism in the early period, but later they evidently and officially separated themselves from the conservative Christians by 1988"; Kang, *Korean Protestant and Anti-Communism* as cited by Y. W. Park. Park, "Approach Method of North Korea Mission," 201–2.

72. Kim, "Reconciliation Possible?" 160.

the reunification movement (and North Korea mission) by South Korean churches was "in reality deactivated" because Rhee and the following military regimes "equated the unauthorized reunification movement with pro-Communist activities."[73] This group of Christians became more visible during the 1980s as the atmosphere of democratization was elevated. They believed "democratization could not be completed without reunification," and this belief served as "a breakthrough" for the reunification movement inside and outside of Korean peninsula.[74]

In the 1980s, this group made several attempts, often represented as the National Council of Churches in Korea (NCCK), to meet North Korean Christian representatives to talk about peaceful reunification. The first successful meeting was held in Glion (Switzerland; 1986) arranged by the Committee of International Relations of the WCC.[75] The second meeting was also in Glion (1988) in which they announced together the "Declaration of the Korean Church for the Reunification and Peace."[76] The declaration contained statements of confessing "sins of mutual hatred," "justifying the division of Korea," and "accepting each ideology as absolute, which is contrary to God's absolute authority."[77]

However, this statement resulted in a heated debate between conservative and progressive Christian leaders.[78] The conservative section rejected endorsing the declaration, expressing "deep concern" because of its naïve views toward the DPRK and its support for some politically sensitive issues such as "American military retreat" from the Korean peninsula, which was constantly argued by the DPRK government and agreed with by progressive Koreans.[79] They claimed that the NCCK was not the "representative of the South church," but represented only progressive Christians.[80]

Thus, between these two groups of Korean Christians, there has been a political conflict, as can be seen in secular Korean society.[81] The Society of the History of Christianity in Korea (SHCK) states, "The Korean War

---

73. Ahn, "North Korea Mission in Historical Perspective," 119.
74. Ahn, "North Korea Mission in Historical Perspective," 5.
75. Kim, "Towards Peace and Reconciliation," 132.
76. Kim, "Towards Peace and Reconciliation," 134.
77. Kim, "Reconciliation Possible?" 161.
78. Kim, "Towards Peace and Reconciliation," 134.
79. Kim, "Towards Peace and Reconciliation," 134; Kim, "Reconciliation Possible?" 162.
80. Kim, "Towards Peace and Reconciliation," 134.
81. The Society of the History of Christianity in Korea, 209–13.

eventually split not only the country and nation but also the churches according to socio-political ideologies."[82]

Another controversial issue of Christians' South–South conflict is how to acknowledge the Joseon Christian Fellowship of North Korea (Chogeerion), which reappeared during the détente period (1972–89). A heated debate remains unquenched today on whether it is a "genuine" form of Christianity or "a part of the Communist Party," and based on such views, "cooperation" with it has been supported or rejected.[83]

Consequently, the political conflict within South Korean Christianity has influenced the "methodologies of the North [Korea] missions."[84] In other words, the various views and missional activities of South Korean churches have been shaped according to the perceptions of the North Korean government.[85] Conservative Christians with anti-communist views have more likely protested openly against human rights issues in North Korea, which would threaten the regime, as well as have tried to support "the underground church" by any means. On the other hand, progressive Christians have more likely attempted to communicate with both the North Korean government and the "official" Christian association (Joseon Christian Fellowship) as an effort for the unification movement rather than confronting human right issues inside the DPRK.[86]

Chris Rice proposes "four identities regarding North Korea and reunification": (1) "Enemy Nation," (2) "Another Country," (3) "Disadvantaged Sibling," and (4) "Ruptured Family."[87] All can be all observed in the views of South Korean Christians.[88] Rice comments that "Tragically, the churches in South Korea are fully and emotionally caught up in the hostile climate of disunity."[89]

---

82. The Society of the History of Christianity in Korea, 230.

83. Ahn, "North Korea Mission in Historical Perspective," 5; Kim, "Reconciliation Possible?" 162.

84. Kim, "Towards Peace and Reconciliation," 136.

85. Park, "Approach Method of North Korea Mission," 193.

86 For not lifting loud voices for human right issues of DPRK, they often justify their position saying that a long-term and ultimate resolution for human right issue is reunification and thus they try to minimize provoke DPRK government.

87. Rice discusses "they also have fluidity; the multiple identities can be held together in paradoxical tension, much like a kind of 'love-hate' association with North Korea. (For example, resist the North Korean government, but provide humanitarian support for ordinary North Korean people.)" Rice, "Contested South Korean Identities," 134–36.

88. Rice, "Contested South Korean Identities," 134–36.

89. Rice, "Contested South Korean Identities," 136.

Since the 1990s, when North Korea suffered from famine, these divided views and activities have been alleviated in a sense or even complicated: the two groups began to overlap with each other's area as the majority of churches responded to the urgent needs of North Korean people.[90] For example, the Christian Council of Korea (Hangeechong; a conservative Christian organization) started the "Love Rice Sending" movement, sending 800,000 kilograms of rice to the north.[91] In December 1992, Christians from both conservative and progressive groups agreed to establish the "Movement of Sharing between the South and the North for Peaceful Reunification."[92]

In short, according to Sebastian Kim, South Korean Christians' missional efforts can be categorized into three types according to their political orientation: (1) reunification "as part of an anti-communist campaign and mission agenda (conservative Christians)"; (2) "promoting dialogue between two nations (liberal Christians)"; and (3) "involvement in a supportive and sharing humanitarian campaign (both conservative and liberal Christians)."[93] Thus, as Ahn claims, both political and missional perspectives should be examined in understanding South Korean churches' engagement in North Korea mission.[94]

Yoon Eunju presents a helpful frame of South Korean churches' engagement in North Korea.[95] Similar to Ahn, Yoon explains the various forms of engagement of South Korean churches' missional activities in the DPRK can be understood according to two factors: "missional paradigms" and the "perception of NK."[96]

---

90. Yoon, *Korean Church and North Korean Human Rights Movement*, 11; Park, "Approach Method of North Korea Mission," 209.
91. Kim, "Towards Peace and Reconciliation," 135.
92. Kim, "Towards Peace and Reconciliation," 135.
93. Kim, "Reconciliation Possible?" 160.
94. Ahn, "North Korea Mission in Historical Perspective," 121.
95. Yoon, *Korean Church and North Korean Human Rights Movement*, 243, figure 4.1.
96. Yoon, *Korean Church and North Korean Human Rights Movement*, 10.

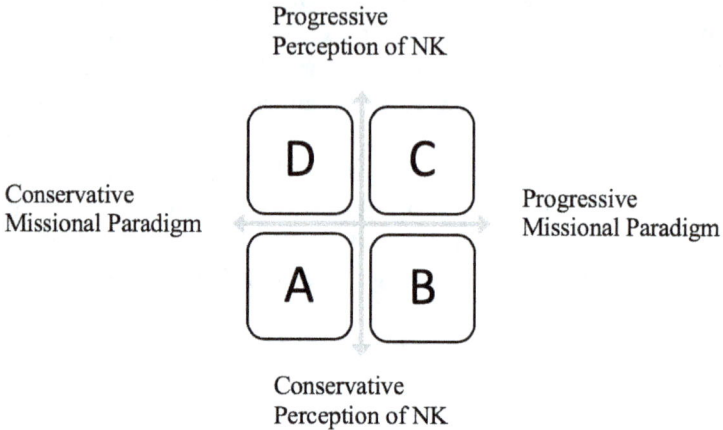

Figure 2. The types of NK human rights movements in South Korean churches by missional paradigms and perception of NK.

To illustrate each type:

Type A: "Based on the conservative missional paradigm and conservative perception of NK, it pursues mission for NK mainly through church planting."

Type B: "Based on the progressive missional paradigm and conservative perception of NK, it seeks human rights movements focusing on the rights of freedom."

Type C: "Based on the progressive missional paradigm and progressive perception of NK, it aims at a human rights movement of the right to live in the context of existing human rights movements and unification movement."

Type D: "Based on the conservative missional paradigm and progressive perception of NK, it seeks a human rights movement of the right to live."[97]

Due to the influence of the progressive mission paradigm, the post-Cold War atmosphere on the peninsula, and the contacts with the North through humanitarian assistance, Yoon[98] argues that South Korean churches have engaged in North Korea mission according to the following trends: A˚B˚C and A˚D. Yoon discusses how they resulted from the

97. Yoon, *Korean Church and North Korean Human Rights Movement*, 211–243.
98. Yoon, *Korean Church and North Korean Human Rights Movement*, 244–48.

increased chances of "mutual exchange" between the North and South through humanitarian aid; for example, nongovernmental organizations based on conservative Christian denominations and associations.[99] These actions might have positively impressed the multitudes of DPRK who considered Christians to be "the agents of imperialism" of Western nations, particularly the United States.[100] However, at the same time, many (including quite a few North Korean refugees) have raised voices of concern about the efficiency and legitimacy of the humanitarian aid from the Korean church to the DPRK, questioning issues such as (1) whether those in severe need are within the coverage of the aid which is still distributed by the DPRK government; and (2) whether the aid unintentionally and mistakenly has supported the Kim regime, which largely neglects the people, focusing only on nuclear development for itself.

The Issue of North Korean Refugees in South Korea Today

During the tragic famine in North Korea that followed Kim Il-Sung's death in 1994, as well as a disastrous flood in 1995, countless North Koreans escaped the country to survive.[101] Several studies in various academic disciplines have examined the issue of North Korean refugees in South Korean society, and among them, a consensus exists that the refugees have faced multiple problems in social adjustment. A majority of North Korean refugees "have difficulties in socioeconomic and psychological adjustment, for example, economic hardship, reconstruction of their social network, and adaptation in a different value system."[102]

The main concern in the socioeconomic adjustment of refugees is for them to find a stable job, which only relatively few achieve.[103] The high technology of South Korean society is an extra hindrance.[104] Furthermore, the children of refugees have difficulty adjusting to the competitive education system of South Korea.[105] As a result, many belong to the lower class in South Korean society because of maladjustment to society, as well as

99. Yoon, *Korean Church and North Korean Human Rights Movement*, 249–51.
100. Kim, "Reflections on North Korea," 25.
101. Yoon, "Social Adjustments of North Korean Migrants," 107.
102. Chung and Seo, "Study on Posttraumatic Stress Disorder," 366.
103. Yoon, "Who is NK Defectors to us?" 226–27.
104. Lankov, "Bitter Taste of Paradise," 122.
105. Lankov, "Bitter Taste of Paradise," 122.

prejudice and discrimination by South Koreans who treat them as "others" or "outsiders."[106]

Moreover, the psychological struggles of North Korean refugees include "identity crisis," "feelings of guilt" for the family members left behind in the DPRK, and "traumatic events" in their escape from the North and subsequent journey to the South.[107] Chung and Seo problematize that "in spite of these problems, [psychological trauma] the government policy for supporting refugees' settlement process has centered on material and institutional support, and has been essentially confined to the level of simply monetary compensation."[108]

Yoon In-Jin argues that, "A considerable number of North Korean refugees feel that they are treated as aliens, second class people, or troublesome beings by the government and South Koreans."[109] This impression was even "enhanced for those who stayed in South Korea longer."[110] Similarly, Sarah Son argues that the identities of North Korean refugees are not considered sufficiently with careful treatment of their distinctive background under the DPRK's oppressive regime; however, under the frame of "shared ethnic identity," they are treated by South Koreas who often hold "hierarchical, moral superiority."[111] Lee Woo-Young also acknowledges that "misunderstanding and prejudice are significant obstacles for refugees' social adjustment."[112]

Caused by such experiences, it is reported that North Korean refugees have held an ambivalent attitude toward South Korean society: "they admit the South is more affluent, yet is under the law of the jungle, not caring for the weak, and even inhumane"; by contrast, "North Korea is poorer, but has more attachment to each other."[113] Many refugees suffer from "loneliness," resulting in a "high suicide rate" that is "three times more than" that of South Koreans.[114]

In sum, the two greatest concerns related to the issue of North Korean refugees are the "lack of social community or network" and "economic instability"; thus, a social safety net for refugees as well as employment support

---

106. Yoon, "Social Adjustments of North Korean Migrants," 108–9.
107. Chung and Seo, "A Study on Posttraumatic Stress Disorder," 366.
108. Chung and Seo, "A Study on Posttraumatic Stress Disorder," 366.
109. Yoon, "Who is NK Defectors to us?" 229.
110. Yoon, "Who is NK Defectors to us?" 229.
111. Son, "Identity and Social Reconciliation," 145–46.
112. Lee, "Settlement of Local Communities," 59.
113. Yoon, "Social Adjustments of North Korean Migrants," 117.
114. Chung, "Understanding of North Korean Defectors," 240.

are necessary.[115] Also crucial is "to raise social awareness" and "overcome discrimination and prejudice by South Koreans."[116]

South Korean Churches' Ministry for North Korean Refugees

Since the mid-1990s when the "mass exodus" occurred, the ministry for North Korean refugees has received significant attention from South Korean churches, because mission for North Korea was highly limited otherwise.[117] Ahn claims that, "This phenomenon gave us a new perspective of mission and reunification: mission and reunification by North Korean defectors, and mission for North Korean defectors."[118] Many North Korean refugees admit that Korean churches have played a significant role for Christian refugees' resettlement.[119] North Korean Christian refugees identify the following positive aspects of belonging to South Korean churches: "psychological comforts," "healing trauma," messages of hope such as "financial blessing" and being "born again as a new start."[120]

On the other hand, much room for improvement has consistently been identified in the church's ministry toward refugees. North Korean refugees have reported experiencing problems with South Korean Christians, such as they look down on them because of their social class or North Korean background, they are overly didactic, and they perceiving them as mere objects of evangelization.[121]

As introduced previously, based on his qualitative research on 20 North Korean refugees with experience of South Korean churches, Song Young-Sub found that these refugees experience multiple "social barriers" such as "alienation" and "separation" in their "social relationships" within South Korean churches, which lead them to feel "detachment" from South Korean Christians.[122] Song identifies that "loving encouragement," "hospitality," and "prayer" by South Korean Christians have hugely and positively

---

115. Park, "Study on Settlement of Defector," 16–17; Chung, "Understanding of North Korean Defectors," 239–42.

116. Yoon, "Social Adaptation of North Korean Migrants," 57–58.

117. Ahn, "North Korea Mission in Historical Perspective," 122.

118. Ahn, "North Korea Mission in Historical Perspective," 122.

119. Jeon and Cho, "Religious Experiences of North Korean Defectors," 106.

120. Han, "Ethnographic Study on North Korean Defectors," 141–43.

121. Chung, "Understanding of North Korean Defectors," 243–45.

122. Song, "Socio-Cultural Factors," 163–64.

impacted North Korean refugees' lives.[123] However, he also finds that quite a few of his interviewees have experienced the "inconsistency" of South Korean churches, which has manifested as "separation," "discrimination," and "prejudice."[124]

Moreover, some problems have been raised related to the prevalent practice by Korean churches of supporting refugee members financially. The side effects of material-centered support, often without a profound accepting attitude toward them, are identified in many ways.[125] These issues indicate that Korean churches have many areas for improvement related to their understanding of, communicating with, and embracing of refugee members.[126] For many reasons including these, North Korean refugees are constantly leaving South Korean churches.[127]

Thus, voices in South Korean Christianity have asserted that the mission of hospitality, "participating in the hospitality of the triune God," must be advanced and demonstrated by South Korean churches.[128] Furthermore, an attitude of "interdependent mutuality" between North Korean refugee Christians and South Korean Christians should be acknowledged and acquired, rather than the refuges being treated as socially inferior or second-class citizens.[129]

---

123. Song, "Socio-Cultural Factors," 199–200.

124. Song, "Socio-Cultural Factors," 202–6.

125. Han, "Ethnographic Study on North Korean Defectors," 145–49; Chung, "Understanding of North Korean Defectors," 245.

126. Han, "Ethnographic Study on North Korean Defectors," 145–47.

127. Chung, "Understanding of North Korean Defectors," 243.

128. Kim, "Toward a Mission of Hospitality," 163–69.

129. Chung, "Understanding of North Korean Defectors," 247.

7

Summary and Conclusion: Reconciliation for Missiology in the Korean Context

RECONCILIATION IS ONE OF the most relevant missiological themes in the Korean context today. The national division over seventy years, the concomitant tragedy of the Korean War, and the subsequent sociopolitical conflicts within South Korea all demonstrate the significance of the theme in this context. For South Korean churches, the theme of reconciliation urges them to reflect upon their theological and missiological adequacy. Furthermore, this theme leads the church to equip itself to be prepared for the ministry for North Korean refugees who reside next to the church as neighbors, and eventually North Korean people in the forthcoming reunification period.

In this chapter, several categories and core ideas that have repeatedly emerged in the previous chapters are highlighted for the missiological implications in the Korean context. The previously described multilayered issue of division in the Korean context is interrelatedly but separately engaged in this chapter, focused on the role of the church (North–South, South–South, and North Korean refugees). The following discussion of implications is thus categorized into three main focuses: (1) the issue of justice and liberation of North Korean people in the Korean context (engaging the North–South relationship); (2) the ministry of reconciliation of South Korean churches for North Korean refugees as well as in relation to the South–South conflict; and lastly, reflecting upon the previous discussions on spirituality, (3) the need for renewed spirituality in South Korean Christianity.

The Issue of Justice and Liberation in the Korean Context

The first missiological implication shines attention on the issues of justice and liberation. As previously discussed, any genuine form of reconciliation should never ignore justice. Justice must be understood in the broader frame of reconciliation, pursuing restorative justice, because of its predicaments that appear when it is pursued separately, as Tutu and Volf have noted. However, as most theologians correctly acknowledge, justice is still placed in the central discourse of reconciliation.

Volf rightly asserts that the paradigm of liberation fits into political struggles rather than ethnic or social conflicts. The human rights issues of the North Korean people under their current political situation properly suits that aspect. The miserable conditions of the majority of North Korean people, observed and testified on multiple occasions, including the testimonies of North Korean refugees, must not be neglected in any case in the discussion of reconciliation on the Korean peninsula. The ministry and message of Desmond Tutu may offer an exemplary reference for this matter, because he has invested much effort into becoming a voice of the voiceless. As discussed, Tutu supported to put pressure on the regime which abused human dignity, for example, calling for the economic sanctions against the government and telling the truth to the international community.

Therefore, in their pursuit of reconciliation, South Korean churches should engage with the issues of justice and liberation for people in the DPRK to be a voice on behalf of them. However, thus far in the academic discourse of reconciliation in South Korean Christianity, one seldomly hears this type of voice. For example, in his article "Mission as Reconciliation in the Korean Peninsula," Hwang Hong-Eyoul criticizes how innocent civilians were "falsely accused" and "murdered" in "injustice and violence" under "the military regimes" of South Korea and "the ideologies of conflicts and hatred" were dominant in the past.[1] Hwang argues that justice and peace go together and "Jesus is a liberator."[2] His point which advocates for those who were wrongfully victimized during South Korean military dictatorships and ideological contests between South and North Korean regimes is well-taken. However, when one applies the principle of justice and peace in the Korean context, if the application only suggests reflecting on the deaths of "innocent civilians" (who stood accused of being communists) in South Korean history, to overcome "cold-war perspectives" as well as to establish a "peace system" through "rebuilding North Korean industry" and "economic cooperation and aid to North Korea," without problematizing the current situation of human rights violations in the DPRK, it can be considered as biased and critically disputed.[3] Hwang does

1. Hwang, "Mission as Reconciliation in the Korean Peninsula," 375–76.
2. Hwang, "Mission as Reconciliation in the Korean Peninsula," 377–78.
3. Hwang, "Mission as Reconciliation in the Korean Peninsula," 429–33.

not mention the violation of human rights in North Korea. Similarly, in a recent article, Hwang argues for "justice" and "human dignity" in the process of reconciliation, yet his main points instead focus on criticizing how conservative South Korean governments have enacted anti-peace policies, and suggesting economic exchange.[4] Again, the human rights issues of people in the DPRK go unaddressed.

Similar patterns are observed in the theological discussions of reconciliation among conciliar theologians in the Korean context.[5] For the core argument, they all suggest overcoming the ideology of anticommunism in South Korean society as well as in South Korean churches, and changing an exclusive and hate-filled attitude against the DPRK into a forgiving, cooperative, and reconciliatory one.[6] Moreover, Lee Sang-Eun asserts that "it is not helpful to treat the church in the DPRK with unconditional enmity and doubt" and "it is possible that God even works through the Choseon Christian Fellowship under the will of *missio Dei*."[7]

An exclusive and hate-driven attitude rooted in anti-communism definitely has no place in any South Korean Christian theology of reconciliation. However, this does not mean that South Korean churches should imprudently accept whatever the current situation is under which North Koreans may suffer and incautiously cooperate with the regime and the "official" Christian fellowship. As Volf identifies, the will to embrace is indiscriminate and what South Korean Christians should equip for the ministry of reconciliation, yet the will to embrace and embrace itself can still be distinguished.[8] The issue of justice cannot be overlooked under any circumstance. Moreover, this distinction can be more explicit as the conflict appears to be a political one that legitimatizes the frame of liberation, as Volf and Tutu previously demonstrated.

In this respect, some inevitable questions that arise from reviewing these writings are as follows: What is the basis for not differentiating the downtrodden North Korean people—many of whom are not being treated with human dignity—from the North Korean regime? Furthermore, what

---

4. Hwang, "Tasks of Peace Mission," 329, 332, 352.

5. Chung, *History of Unification Movements*; Lee, *Reunification Based on the Doctrine of Reconciliation*; Kim, *Theology of Peace for the Divided Korea*; Lee, *Theological Discourse of Reunification in Korean Peninsula*.

6. Chung, *History of Unification Movements*, 382, 383–84, 386; Lee, *Reunification Based on the Doctrine of Reconciliation*, 224–25; Kim, *Theology of Peace for the Divided Korea*, 166, 194–95, 218–22; Lee, *Theological Discourse of Reunification in Korean Peninsula*, 34–35, 58, 127, 140, 231.

7. Lee, *Reunification Based on the Doctrine of Reconciliation*, 224–25.

8. Volf, "Final Reconciliation," 103.

is the basis for instead indiscriminately merging them to objectifying the dialogue and process of reconciliation? Moreover, on what evidence can they consider the DPRK regime to have sufficiently reflected the will of the North Korean people and the Choseon Christian Fellowship as a justifiable conversation partner, while overlooking the "underground" Christians who have allegedly been persecuted by the regime? Unfortunately, it seems that the cases of the abuse of North Korean people's human rights and dignity are not included in South Korean churches' primary considerations. In the effort for reconciliation, Desmond Tutu's theological reflection on *imago Dei* and his strenuous efforts to make a change in his sociopolitical sphere should be referred to, not only in South Korean territory but on the entire Korean peninsula in the effort for reconciliation.

When the 10th Assembly of the WCC in Busan, South Korea, adopted its "Statement on Peace and Reunification of the Korean Peninsula," even though the assembly focused on such issues as justice, peace, and reconciliation, it did not speak up about the human rights issues in the DPRK.[9] The core intent of the statement as to reject war, promote peace, and stop competitive arms races. It denied the necessity of economic sanctions against the DRPK. For these goals, the statement demanded that South Korean churches take the initiative in a peace-building movement and talk with North Korean Christian groups.

This perspective views the division itself as suffering and evil. In the Declaration of Korean Churches for National Unification of the Korean People and Peace in the Korean Peninsula in 1988, which have continually been mentioned as significant reference points in the dialogue of theology of reconciliation until today, the primary aim is to confess the sin of the divisive structure, hatred, anger, and ideological exclusion.[10] It is correct but partially correct in the Korean context. As true reconciliation should reject "cheap reconciliation," if the voices of the oppressed are significantly

9. https://www.oikoumene.org/en/resources/documents/assembly/2013-busan/adopted-documents-statements/peace-and-reunification-of-the-korean-peninsula.

10. This document *does* mention the issue of human rights violation in both North and South Korea in their competitive ideological contest. It is true that under both regimes, violations of human dignity happened, and mostly by the leading effort of progressive citizens and Christians, South Korean political society has become democratized, at least sooner. This should be appreciated. Nevertheless, as the South becomes changed, the North's change should be demanded by the theologians who base themselves upon the declaration of 1988. It should also be noted that the statement was written in 1988, right after Jeon Du-hwan's strong military regime was replaced by Noh's transitional one in 1987. It was the time that South Korean society still shares the vivid memory of oppression of human rights, in particular to the pro-democracy movement. Full document can be accessed through: https://www.presbyterianmission.org/resource/declaration-of-the-churches-of-korea-on-national-reunification-and-peace/.

ignored (either in ROK or DPRK), the direction of the ministry of reconciliation must be reconsidered.[11]

Sebastian Kim, arguing that *han* as a significant theological theme of Korea, says "The cross of division" of the Korean people is their "cross of *han*."[12] The Korean version of liberation theology, *minjung theology*, which had flourished and been widely remarked upon under the suppressive military regimes from the 1970s, is something that North Korean people desperately need today. However, it seems the contemporary theologians of Korean *minjung theology*, which deals with the suffering of people theologically, have primarily considered the suffering of South Korean *minjung*, not that of the North Korean people in spite of their efforts to reunification movement.

Again, it seems that assumptions underlie this approach: (1) the current DPRK regime reflects the will of the people, and (2) the Joseon Christian Fellowship in the DPRK is a legitimate Christian body. These assumptions can be controversial. However, it cannot be easily disregarded that these assumptions would be questioned by many, and even contradicted by the testimonies of a number of North Korean refugees, and the report from minute observations by multiple human rights organizations.

Morse Tan, in his comprehensive legal research on the human rights issue in DPRK entitled *North Korea, International Law and the Dual Crises: Narrative and Constructive Engagement*, maintains that "North Korea has an atrocious human rights record."[13] Tan explains that "In North Korea, the government has not only failed to protect its people from human rights abuses that include torture, mass imprisonment, and denial of rights such as free speech, but the government itself has intentionally perpetrated these mass human rights abuses."[14] Tan adds, "Hundreds of thousands of citizens have found themselves enslaved in one of the many concentration camps."[15]

One of the main reasons for being sent to these concentration or political camps is having a religion. Without permitting religious freedom in reality, "the government regards people found engaged in Christianity as political criminals and sends them to these camps."[16] In short, Tan describes it as "gross" and "systematic" "violations of human rights" that North Korean

---

11. Kairos Theologians (Group), *Kairos Document*, sec. 3.1.
12. Kim, "Reconciliation Possible?" 167.
13. Tan, *North Korea, International Law*, 132.
14. Tan, *North Korea, International Law*, 255.
15. Tan, *North Korea, International Law*, 37.
16. Tan, *North Korea, International Law*, 71–74.

people are experiencing in DPRK.[17] Tan's analysis corresponds to the reports from the UN Security Council[18] as well as Human Rights Watch.[19] The case of Kim Jong-un's violations of human right has been submitted to the International Criminal Court (ICC). The extent of the multi-layered suffering that North Korean people have faced had already reached the limit long before, and it has been expressed by their numerous illegal escapes at the risk of their own and their families' lives since the 1990s.

Still, it can be appreciated that South Korean conciliar theologians have tried to overcome the existing structure of hatred and exclusion, and continually spoken about reconciliation and reunification from a relatively early period within the international ecumenical circle, as the Tozanso Consultation in 1984 demonstrated. It is also understandable that they have made statements against South Korean conservative regimes, especially military dictatorships throughout history, of which the sociopolitical influence has yet to diminish. It can be considered a reasonable suspicion that the military dictatorships have made political profits as they advanced the propaganda of anti-communism as well as national division, and branded the DPRK an evil country. This unfortunate history should surely be dealt with through justice in our steps toward reconciliation. Furthermore, some might say that the DPRK regime, as a unique and impossible state of the current time, requires a delicate and cautious approach due to the complexity of the internal and external issues that face the nation.

However, when people tend to overlook the seriousness of the oppressive and systematic violations of human rights by the DPRK regime and its hereditary dictatorship, this still seems naïve and biased. No matter how complicated the problems are that the regime faces, this issue of justice and liberation for North Korean people should be dealt with and addressed by any means in the pursuit of reconciliation. Undoubtedly, achieving the two goals of justice and peace together is not an easy task. However, as Nicholas Wolterstorff claims, "both together are necessary" because God's shalom "incorporates" each, yet "goes beyond."[20] As he insightfully argues, based on an examination of the theologies of neo-Calvinists and liberation theologians, Christianity has been a "world-formative religion," which targets on the "re-formation" of the "general structure" of the "social world."[21] Thus, in their pursuit of reconciliation,

17. Tan, *North Korea, International Law*, 96, 254.
18. https://www.un.org/securitycouncil/sanctions/1718.
19. https://www.hrw.org/news/2018/06/05/human-rights-north-korea#.
20. Wolterstorff, *Until Justice and Peace Embrace*, 72.
21. Wolterstorff, *Until Justice and Peace Embrace*, 9–10.

South Korean Christians should make constant efforts to improve human rights and liberate the oppressed in the DPRK.

Conservative Christians tend to address human rights abuses in North Korea, yet stay silent about those in South Korean history. By contrast, progressive Christians tend to highlight the issue of violence and injustice under South Korean conservative regimes, but not the violations of human rights against North Korean people. It is certainly not an either-or issue. For a comprehensive examination and proposal for theology of reconciliation on the Korean peninsula, justice should be addressed in both cases. Moreover, it seems reasonable to highlight the suffering of those who have less opportunity to lift voices for themselves, with more priority given to the matter of justice.

Suffering has become a major issue in theologies of Asian Christianity.[22] Theological reflections by theologians such as Kosuke Koyama, C. S. Song, Kazoh Kitamori, and Suh Nam-Dong (*minjung* theology) all center around the suffering of Asian people. According to their theologies, the solidarity of Christ with the suffering of people (or the pain of God in Kitamori's terms) is a central theological concept in the Asian context.[23]

As Miroslav Volf notes, "In the Scriptures, suffering was the basic lot of prophets." Jesus, as *the* prophet of God who had been prophesized in the Old Testament, comes into humans' suffering, ultimately death, and liberates them from it.[24] Therefore, acknowledging Jesus, who suffers with people, in a sense concerns the theology of liberation from the world "filled with injustice, oppression, and hatred" and hope "for both temporal and eternal life" "with justice, freedom, and love."[25] Suh Nam-Dong similarly argues that *han* (which can be roughly translated as deep grief or resentment) "can be cured only when the total structure of the oppressed society and culture is changed."[26]

Accordingly, when discussing reconciliation in the Korean context, the issue of suffering caused by oppressive and unjust social structures remains a central issue. How to deal with suffering is a key question in the journey of reconciliation. Based on the abovementioned Asian theologians, the vertical dimension of reconciliation can in a way be understood as Christ's solidarity with suffering people. They claim that Jesus came to us not only to

---

22. Sunquist, *Explorations in Asian Christianity*, 86.

23. Koyama, *Water Buffalo Theology*, 17; Song, *Jesus*, 11; Chin, *Perception of Christianity*, 20.

24. Volf, *Exclusion and Embrace*, 236.

25. Song, *Third-Eye Theology*, 137.

26. Suh, "Toward a Theology of Han," 28.

give eternal life *after* one's death but to suffer together *now*. The horizontal dimension of reconciliation is about giving best efforts and a continuous voice to transform the sociopolitical structures that enhance the suffering of people. In this respect, the two dimensions are not to be separated. If South Korean churches neglect the suffering of North Korean people and only focus on that of themselves in South Korea, they will have to explain their silence later with great regret before the North Korean people when reunification comes, and eventually before Christ who stands in solidarity with the suffering of the North Korean people.

The Ministry of Reconciliation by South Korean Churches

The second missiological implication concerns the ministry of reconciliation for North Korean refugees, and eventually North Korean people (and conditionally to the North Korean government).[27] It is also about South–South conflict, which has been a visible issue in South Korean society and also influenced South Korean churches. First, it calls for hospitality for North Korean refugees. The current struggle between North Korean refugees and South Korean people corresponds to many characteristics of social and cultural conflict. It is sometimes the case within the church as well.

In the previous chapter, Song Young-Sub was quoted as saying that North Korean refugees experience different "social barriers" within South Korean churches.[28] Furthermore "hospitality" from South Korean Christians has significantly contributed to the settlement of North Korean refugees in their new homes.[29] Similarly, through research involving in-depth interviews with eighteen North Korean refugees, Kim Eui-Hyuck found out that many refugees have faced cultural differences and thus difficulties in building relationship with South Koreans.[30] After explaining that "hospitality is ultimately based on the triune God," who embraced humanity, Kim

---

27. As previously argued, the issue of justice and liberation should be considered in regard to South Korean churches' ministry of reconciliation. The steps of embrace and reconciliation should go together with justice and liberation. Therefore, under the condition of improvement of human rights situation of North Korean people, the churches may support South Korean government continues to have dialogue with the DPRK regime and continue the humanitarian aid for the people as the cases of East and Wester Germany demonstrated.

28. Song, "Socio-Cultural Factors," 163–64.

29. Song, "Socio-Cultural Factors," 199–200.

30. Kim, "Toward a Mission of Hospitality," 157–59.

suggests that South Korean churches "participate in God's hospitality" in their relationships with North Korean refugees.[31]

As previously introduced, Sarah Son asserts that the social barriers faced by North Korean refugees are partially due to South Koreans' attitude of superiority over them.[32] Unfortunately, in spite of their continuous effort to welcome them, South Korean churches are not that different in many ways.

> This approach [hierarchical and moral superiority of South to North] pays little heed to North Korean agency and identity as a distinct community, let alone their needs in terms of recovery from decades of oppression. North Korean defectors in South Korea have experienced this hierarchical disparity firsthand, reporting discrimination in many aspects of life in the South, resulting in a sense that their place there is merely that of second-class citizens. The South Korean church has been found to be complicit in perpetuating this hierarchy by virtue of seeking to "share the Gospel from a position of cultural and economic power," rather than from that of vulnerability and humility.[33]

In this regard, multiple research articles have argued for a profound change of attitude by South Korean churches toward hospitality.[34] As Son recognizes, realizing that North Koreans have shaped a unique ethnic identity that differs from that of South Koreans seems crucial, against the intense communist background, although they both share a Korean ethnic identity.[35] Both South and North Koreans place their "Koreanness" at the core of their shared identity, rooted in their 5000-years history of Korean ancestry on the peninsula, which will not easily fade in the future. However, the differences in their social, political, and cultural identity formed in modern disparate history will require generations to recede into the background. Therefore, based on an acknowledgement of distinctiveness in their shared identity, they may be able to understand and embrace each other better.

In the same vein, Ha Chung-Yoube asserts that the two groups of Koreans are already heterogenized and thus it is necessary to build *tong-i*[36]

---

31. Kim, "Toward a Mission of Hospitality," 165.
32. Son, "Identity and Social Reconciliation," 145–46.
33. Son, "Identity and Social Reconciliation," 146.
34. Ko, "Cultural Integration in South–North," 161; Baik, "Application of a Trinitarian Theology," 144, 157.
35. Son, "Identity and Social Reconciliation," 145.
36. It literally means "two in combined" compared to, *tong-il*, which means "combined as oneness." The latter term is a Korean word for reunification or unification. Il

community first to establish *tong-il* community between South and North Koreans, which can be possible based on "interaction" and "making space" for each other.[37]

All of these points are well-taken. South Korean Christians are required to follow and imitate God's hospitality for humanity. The entire theological discussion of reconciliation regarding the two dimensions thus far can be applied in this respect. Vertical reconciliation with God should be revealed in and promote one's horizontal reconciliation with others. On this point, a feeling of superiority, discriminative attitude, and prejudice against the other have no place. The message of mutual promotion and holistic reconciliation (vertical reconciliation with embedded horizontality) should be declared in the churches of South Korea. It inevitably deals with one's relationship with God; in other words, the issue of sanctification, calling for resembling Christ and living an obedient lifestyle according to God's commandments.

To elaborate, South Korean Christians should imitate the sacrificial hospitality that Christ has shown on the Cross for humanity when they relate to North Korean refugees. South Korean churches' relationship with North Korean refugees is the point where the entire discussions of the fellow-humanity of Barth, the embrace of Volf, and the reconciliatory life and ministry of Son should be applied.

As the Cross demonstrates, the love of the triune God invites and welcomes humans into the perichoretic fellowship through the sacrificial atonement of Christ. The otherness, social stigma, or prejudices derived from the distinctively shared identity between North and South Koreans can be overcome through the divine hospitality that God has shown, and the church should follow.

Cho Yo-Sep, an expert on the North Korean refugee ministry, states that it is not easy for South Koreans "to form a bond of sympathy" with North Korean refugees who have been "socialized" in an extremely "closed society."[38] South Korean churches should "equip themselves" as if the ministry is "for the people from other cultures," or they "may fail."[39] That is, when South Korean Christians embrace North Korean refugees, one should expect that it will be an arduous job, this sacrificial hospitality.

Therefore, in the South Korean churches' steps of hospitality, much effort and perseverance will be required to overcome the disparity formed

---

means one, and I [pronounce as "ee"] means two.

37. Ha, "Migration Old and New," 245, 287; Ha, "Tong-i Community," 174–76.
38. Cho, *Priming Water of North Korea Mission*, 37, 83.
39. Cho, *Priming Water of North Korea Mission*, 83.

under different ideological, social, and cultural backgrounds over seventy years. Furthermore, it will take time for many North Korean refugees who need to be healed from the suffering experienced in the DPRK or in their escape from the nation and adaptation to the new social system of the ROK, where one relates others differently.

This implies that South Korean churches' hospitality should be proactive and enduring. The elements of Christian hospitality can be found in how God came to humanity. South Korean churches' hospitality toward North Korean refugees is an outcome of God's hospitality. As Joshua Jipp claims, "the God of the Christian Scriptures is a God of hospitality, a God who extends hospitality to his people and who requires that his people embody hospitality to others."[40] God's hospitality toward humanity has been proactive and enduring. It did not wait for nor is it triggered by humans' attitude of repentance or asking forgiveness. The salvific activity of God had already started before humans were aware of it, and the Incarnate God, the Messiah Jesus came to the world when it "did not know him" nor "receive him" (John 1:10–11). Leon Morris similarly comments that "the New Testament view is that reconciliation was wrought on the cross before there was anything in man's heart to correspond."[41]

Furthermore, as Jipp argues, "The recipients of divine hospitality in Luke-Acts are some of society's most stigmatized and marginalized people: sinners, tax collectors, the poor and hungry, a sinful woman, Samaritans, the physically disabled, non-Jews, eunuchs, and barbarians."[42] Considering the current struggle of North Korean refugees in South Korean society, the hospitality that God calls for the South Korean churches to embody would place North Korean refugees at the center of their ministry of reconciliation.

Correspondingly, South Korean churches, as recipients of God's hospitality, should be proactive in demonstrating their hospitality toward North Korean refugees. South Korean churches must actively invite, visit, and make a space for them. As the loving relationship between the triune God and the church indicates, mutuality should be placed at the center of South Korean churches' hospitality. This mutuality can be established upon equal treatment with dignity for each other. North Korean refugees should not be treated as second class citizens nor an inferior group of people who cannot sustain themselves without the churches' aid.

Furthermore, perseverance is a critical element in the ministry of reconciliation. As God has been patient to His people (2 Pet 3:8–9), His church in

---

40. Jipp, *Saved by Faith and Hospitality*, 2.
41. Morris, *Apostolic Preaching of the Cross*, loc. 3774.
42. Jipp, *Saved by Faith and Hospitality*, 38–39.

South Korea should also be patient in delivering His love and showing their hospitality. Perseverance will maintain the sacrificial hospitality in South Korean churches, preventing them from growing weary of doing good, whereas impatience will hinder the fruit from being produced (Gal 6:9).

Moreover, for some South Koreans, especially older ones, the traumatic memory of the Korean War and the subsequent suffering in rebuilding the nation must be healed in order to embrace North Korean refugees. Even for the South Korean younger generations, it seems that hostility, contempt, or indifference toward North Korean refugees have remained to be enacted. Unfortunately, South Korean churches seem to more or less share these attitudes. If the attitudes of bitterness, hostility, and indifference remain, they will consciously or unconsciously emerge at some point in South Korean churches' horizontal relationship with North Korean refugees. This will continue to be the case unless they are put down before the Cross and treated by the truth of the Gospel.

Therefore, to execute the sacrificial hospitality, therefore, the Cross of Christ, the place where the divine sacrificial hospitality was fully demonstrated, should be acknowledged in-depth to the extent that South Korean Christians renew their sense of their sinfulness and God's forgiveness in light of Christ.[43] The unending love of God revealed in and flowing through the Cross can melt down one's heart and transform it. The moment of healing can occur at this point. It is the power of the Holy Spirit that enables a person to make room for others and welcome them into one's territory, even when the very act of hospitality would cause the person to pay the price. The examination of the theologies of Karl Barth, Miroslav Volf, and Son Yang-Won has demonstrated this point. It is how the vertical dimension of reconciliation relates to the horizontal dimension of reconciliation. God's divine hospitality leads for the church to embody "Jesus' hospitality practices."[44] In other words, the Cross of Christ let the church take up its cross of sacrificial hospitality and follow Christ (Luke 9:23).

In addition, there should be moments of confession and forgiveness within South Korean churches. As both Volf and Tutu note, confession and forgiveness are significant milestones of the journey of reconciliation. First, the act of confession can be fully fruitful in light of Christ and through the power of the Holy Spirit. Confession out of the hardened heart going into another would not be fruitful. Both those who confess and those who hear the confession should be inspired by the love of God, which makes the confession truly work among them. This is the power of

---

43. Barth, *CD* IV/3.1:371, 389.
44. Jipp, *Saved by Faith and Hospitality*, 61.

transformation in the Gospel and the Holy Spirit. The confessing words that faithfully reflect the Gospel may become a manifestation of the power of God. Therefore, South Korean churches should be faithful in their confession before God and before North Korean refugees, and they should also pray for God's divine interventions during their confession. As argued previously, because vertical reconciliation is the perpetual foundation, the confession by the South Korean churches should continuously be guided by the principles of the Gospel as well as the work of the Holy Spirit in its all steps of the ministry of reconciliation. The God-inspired confession may touch the hearts of North Korean refugees and lead their confession as well, achieving the mutuality of confession.

Along with confession, South Korean churches should demonstrate forgiveness even before the thawing moment of hostility, or repentance. Regarding the tragic Korean War and the local military conflicts thereafter, the message of forgiveness and asking for forgiveness should be delivered by South Korean churches to North Korean refugees (and eventually North Korean people) regardless of how friendly and reciprocally they would respond to the church for that matters. This is how God has loved the fallen humanity (1 John 4:19). No one can truly love others first without God amid ongoing hostility and bitterness. Only God can initiate to forgive and love truly; that is, only those who are in Christ and become new creation can imitate God's forgiveness because the fellow-humanity is restored and actualized in them through Christ.

Forgiveness, as a crucial step of reconciliation, is thus an evidence for restored fellow-humanity. It implies that the self-identity as a relational being is reconstructed and become enacted again. It is the restoration of *imago Dei* in oneself. One forgives and asks for forgiveness because he or she wills to be with the others. South Korean churches, as a restored image of God, should echo the forgiveness of God in their relationship with people from North Korea, which reflects God's divine will to dwell with humans. These steps of Cross-centered hospitality, confession, and forgiveness are the applied forms of reconciliation that South Korean churches should equip and demonstrate in the Korean context.

South Korean Christians often identify with terms such as prayer or spirituality. In fact, they have been known according to those terms by the rest of the body of world Christianity. It may be time for South Korean churches to reflect on their spirituality and relationship with God, as well as renew their commitment to Him once again. This issue of spirituality is further discussed in the following section.

Second, South Korean churches should demonstrate an embracing perspective and attitude in the midst of South–South conflict. South–South conflict has become a serious social issue, not only in the secular society but in the church as well. As proposed by Miroslav Volf, constructing double vision and embracing identity is pertinent here. Volf explains that double vision "is the epistemological side of the will to embrace."[45] It is based on the fact that unlike God who is "all-knowing," humans "are finite beings" and only "know in part."[46] Volf rejects both modern (there is "truth of fact") and post-modern (revealing the "manifestations of power behind the truth") ways of approach, which are respectively impossible and "enthrones violence."[47] Instead, Volf argues that the "human way of seeing corresponds to God's seeing 'from everywhere'" is "seeing both 'from here' and 'from there.'"[48] It entails steps such as stepping outside ourselves, entering into the world of the other, taking the other into our own world, and repeating the process.[49]

As discussed, South–South conflict is rooted in one's perception of the DPRK and its legitimacy, and is largely shaped by one's historical perspective, especially after independence when both the South and North administrations were established in the midst of national chaos. How one discerns the merits and demerits as well as the legitimacy of the ROK and DPRK governments play key roles in one's attitudes to both regimes. In this sense, South Korean theologians and scholars have previously identified that the influence of anti-communism was significant in the inner conflict of South Korean society. Moreover, as has been indicated, it seems that conservative and progressive Christians in South Korea tend to concentrate on different issues of justice and human rights, and even have conflicting interpretations of the same historical event, underscoring the different aspects. This can be regarded as a typical conflict of viewpoints on a social and historical issue.

As Volf claims, one should be "interested in finding" the truth to achieve double vision.[50] If a person insists on not listening to others' perspective, being biased is difficult to avoid. It becomes the issue of one's heart, one's readiness to listen and embrace others' voices. In this respect, Volf says, "The will to truth cannot be sustained without the *will to obey* the

---

45. Volf, *Exclusion and Embrace*, 216.
46. Volf, *Exclusion and Embrace*, 243.
47. Volf, *Exclusion and Embrace*, 250.
48. Volf, *Exclusion and Embrace*, 251.
49. Volf, *Exclusion and Embrace*, 251–52.
50. Volf, *Exclusion and Embrace*, 254.

truth."[51] He also adds, "the will to truth must be accompanied by the *will to embrace the other, by the will to community.*"[52]

Therefore, in discussing reconciliation in the Korean context, South Korean churches must demonstrate accommodating views and attitudes, based on the comprehensive concept of justice and historical interpretations, and listen to each other's perspectives. It is about speaking the "narrative" as "witness" and as "revealing the truth" for establishing a shared "identity."[53] This is certainly not an easy process because people in church are often overwhelmed, as are those outside, by political ideologies and agendas more than Christians' shared convictions in the Gospel of Christ and the principles of His Kingdom.

However, as Ahn Kyo Seong argues, the missional activities of South Korean Christianity for North Korea, represented by North Korea mission by conservatives and the reunification movement by progressives, can be "implemented by the synergic effort of" the two parties when they attempt to understand each other's view point under the overarching hope of reconciliation, in which God's will will be done on the peninsula.[54]

The Need for Renewed Spirituality in Korean Christianity

The third missiological implication engages the spirituality of Korean Christianity. As discussed, reconciliation inherently depends on one's spirituality. In relation to the missiology of reconciliation, South Korean Christianity must examine itself spiritually. Different types of moral scandal within the churches, which have endangered their social trust severely in recent years, also urgently demand honest spiritual reflection in multiple aspects.

Karl Barth's frame of shaping-ethics-as-dogmatics should be heard in South Korean churches. The concept of the divine commandment of God and the fear of God should also be restored in them. As Kim Seyoon rightly diagnoses, the moral failures observed in South Korean churches are at least partially due to the unbiblical separation of justification and sanctification, bias toward justification, and the failure to recognize the significance of sanctification.[55] If one deals with justification genuinely and seriously, one will treat sanctification in the same manner.

---

51. Volf, *Exclusion and Embrace*, 255.
52. Volf, *Exclusion and Embrace*, 257.
53. Schreiter, "Establishing a Shared Identity," 8–9, 13.
54. Ahn, "North Korea Mission in Historical Perspective," 124.
55. Kim, *Justification and Sanctification*, 81, 190–192, 268.

In 2007, Rev. Oak Han-Heum, one of the most esteemed pastors in South Korea, honestly and openly confessed that he tried to avoid such themes as "sin, repentance, obedience, or holiness" in his sermons because he could sense the audience did not like them.[56] Mentioning that it is not what Jesus likes, and it is distorting the Gospel, Oak asserts that South Korean Christians should obey God's commandments with divine fear. This is a truly prophetic voice for South Korean churches today.

Having said that, the teaching of holistic reconciliation, which emphasizes horizontal reconciliation and is often evidence of one's vertical reconciliation, should be taught from the church pulpits. The understandings of mutual promotion as well as the indivisible connection between the two dimensions are to be widely perceived by South Korean Christians. As reconciliation becomes a spiritual issue, it provides a criterion by which one can ponder the extent of one's Christ-like character, focusing on one's fellow-humanity to others.

All concerns that emerge out of one's honest investigation of reconciliation with others can be expressed through prayer to God. As demonstrated in Son Yang-Won's life and spirituality, the role of prayer is central in one's journey of sanctification. Spiritual renewal can occur through the total commitment to prayer.

Although South Korean churches have committed themselves to prayer, the direction and focus of it, or in other words the underlying motivation of prayer, must be examined. Praying for God's providence for one's needs, for resolution in troubled situations, and even for spiritual formation or gifts, which can easily be observed from South Korean Christians, may be considered as biblically grounded and legitimate prayer contents. However, they should be reminded that the ultimate motivation of prayer, as Jesus shows in his prayer of Gethsemane, is to attune oneself to the will of God. Son maintained this as a clear focus in his prayer life. This contains one's inner struggle to obey God's commandments, to be faithful before God, and to overcome suffering, hindrances, and temptations in following our journey to Christ.

All three aforementioned aspects are interrelated and often occur simultaneously. The researcher suggests that South Korean churches organize and conduct prayer meetings, having these ideas as the core agenda, to liberate those in suffering and be faithful agents in the ministry of reconciliation. In such meetings, spiritual awakening should be pursued along with clear

---

56. In sermon in the united worship meeting for "Again 1907 Revival" in South Korean churches remembering the 100th anniversary of the historical revival movement. Full sermon transcript is available at: http://johnoak.sarang.org/data/sub_6.asp?db_idx=1461&page=4&search=&searchstring=&hid_button=.

biblical and theological presentations of (1) the fear of God who is righteous: "righteousness and justice are the foundation of his throne" (Ps 97:2); (2) the relationship between faith and obedience (justification and sanctification), which leads oneself to reflect on one's relationship with God; (3) the holistic notion of reconciliation; and (4) the fundamental direction and motivation of our prayer—to attune ourselves to the will of God.

Concluding Thoughts

Reconciliation is profoundly powerful. The truth of God's reconciliation with humanity in Christ has been so powerful that it has melted countless people's hearts around the world from generation to generation and transformed their lives dramatically. This is because humans are created as beings who yearn to be connected in genuine love, the self-giving love, in the image of the triune God who exists in the mutual interiority with perfect and glorious love in the everlasting. In this sense, the horizontal dimension of reconciliation, loving one another, is not only an obligation for Christian but also a huge privilege given from God. The call to love one another is an outcome of God's love for us in the full extent.

If God loved His children *moderately*, He would not tell them to love as He does. What God is and what God does are the most glorious positions that anyone can dream of. He is a loving God. In a "moderate" love, God would allow us to stay and satisfy in place of "being loved," which would still be graceful. However, because God loves us *fully*, and He wants to truly share His own glory with His children in that love, God commands them to love one another, resembling the love of God revealed in Christ. Becoming a person who loves as God does is the most glorious and privileged calling that anyone can receive from God. It is about coming to resemble their Father in Heaven.

Therefore, it can be argued that the horizontal dimension of reconciliation is planned, imposed, and embedded in the nature of the vertical dimension of reconciliation by God on purpose. It is an entitled opportunity to participate in the love of God and to become like God by His grace. Thus, genuine horizontal reconciliation can only be achieved through vertical reconciliation, which motivates one to pursue it with a transformed and grateful heart.

Suggestions for Future Research

First, identifying the specific factors based on qualitative research that hinder the inseparable connections between the vertical and horizontal dimensions of reconciliation may contribute to improving the church's awareness and ministry of reconciliation. As questioned in chapter 2, it is appropriate to be concerned about why the dimensions are far from each other in the real world, as if they are totally unrelated, as well as being concerned about what kinds of understanding (theological, social, or historical) in the church have promoted or hindered the separation of the dimensions. As mentioned, this study attempted to offer some theological resources with missiological intent for these questions. These questions must still be answered in various perspectives and contexts. Along with continuous theological inquiries on this issue, historical and social studies focusing on identifying specific factors that influence the separateness of the two dimensions may contribute to the church advancing its understanding of potential dangers and being better equipped for the ministry of reconciliation.

Second, future research could include studies on local examples and expressions of how the two dimensions of reconciliation can be combined and work together in a mutual-promotion relationship. Local stories of holistic reconciliation would enrich the academic discourse of mission as reconciliation. Furthermore, practical manuals for mission as reconciliation that focus on how the two dimensions promote each other in applying to specific local contexts must also be researched and presented.

Third, case studies examining the missiological implications claimed in this dissertation may be required. The groups of such case studies could be categorized as follows: South Koreans' churches, North Korean refugees' churches, and churches with both groups as their primary members. These case studies, which could investigate how the holistic and mutual-promotion perspectives are applied and reflected in their congregations and missional activities for reconciliation, may present some helpful advice for the forthcoming unification era.

Bibliography

Ahn, Kyo Seong. "North Korea Mission in Historical Perspective." *International Bulletin of Mission Research* 42 (2018) 116–24.
Ahn, Yong Choon. 사랑의 원자탄 *[An Atomic Bomb of Love]*. Rev. ed. Seoul: 성광문화사 [Seong Gwang Munwhasa], 2009.
———. *A Seed Must Die*. London: InterVarsity, 1965.
———. *Triumph of Pastor Son from Korea: A True Story of Faith under Persecution*. Translated by Phyllis Thompson. London: InterVarsity, 1973.
Allen, John. *Rabble-Rouser for Peace: The Authorized Biography of Desmond Tutu*. London: Rider, 2006.
Arendt, Hannah. *The Human Condition*. Chicago: University of Chicago Press, 1959.
Atzvi, Kyrika. "Ecumenism as Reconciliation." In *Mission as Ministry of Reconciliation*, edited by Robert Schreiter and Knud Jorgensen, 30–36. Regnum Edinburgh Centenary Series 16. Eugene, OR: Wipf & Stock, 2015.
Baek, Hak-Soon. "제 2부: 한미동맹재편과 남남갈등 [Chapter 2: The Reshuffle of Korea-US Alliance and South-South Conflict]." In 남남갈등진단 및 해소방안 *[Diagnosis of South-South Conflict and Way to Solution]*, 227–83. Seoul: The Institute for Far Eastern Studies of Gyungnam University, 2004.
Baik, Chung-Hyun. "삼위일체적 평화통일신학의 적용: 북한이탈주민들과 한국사회와의 상호이해와 포용을 중심으로 [An Application of a Trinitarian Theology for Peaceful Reunification: Focusing on Mutual Understanding and Embrace between North Korean Refugees and South Koreans]." 한국개혁신학 *[Korean Reformed Theology]* 49 (2016) 132–62.
Barth, Fredrik. *Ethnic Groups and Boundaries: The Social Organization of Culture Difference*. Waveland, 1998.
Barth, Karl. *Church Dogmatics*. Repr. Vol. I/1. Edinburgh: T. & T. Clark, 2006.
———. *Church Dogmatics*. Repr. Vol. I/2. Edinburgh: T. & T. Clark, 1956.
———. *Church Dogmatics*. Vol. II/1. Edinburgh: T. & T. Clark, 1957.
———. *Church Dogmatics*. Vol. II/2. Edinburgh: T. & T. Clark, 1957.
———. *Church Dogmatics*. Vol. III/1. Edinburgh: T. & T. Clark, 1958.
———. *Church Dogmatics*. Vol. III/2. Edinburgh: T. & T. Clark, 1960.
———. *Church Dogmatics*. Vol. III/3. Edinburgh: T. & T. Clark, 1960.
———. *Church Dogmatics*. Vol. IV/1. Edinburgh: T. & T. Clark, 1956.
———. *Church Dogmatics*. Vol. IV/2. Edinburgh: T. & T. Clark, 1958.
———. *Church Dogmatics*. Vol. IV/3.1. Edinburgh: T. & T. Clark, 1961.
———. *Church Dogmatics*. Vol. IV/3.2. Edinburgh: T. & T. Clark, 1962.
———. *Church Dogmatics*. Vol. IV/4. Edinburgh: T. & T. Clark, 1969.

———. *Community, State, and Church: Three Essays by Karl Barth with a New Introduction by David Haddorff*. Eugene, OR: Wipf and Stock, 2004.

———. *Ethics*. New York: Seabury, 1981.

———. *Evangelium und Gesetz*. Theologische Existenz heute! 32. Munich, 1935.

———. *God, Grace and Gospel*. Edinburgh: Oliver and Boyd, 1959.

———. *The Christian Life: Church Dogmatics IV, 4: Lecture Fragments*. Grand Rapids: Eerdmans, 1981.

———. *The Epistle to the Romans*. Translated by Edwyn C. Hoskyns. 6th ed. New York: Oxford University Press, 1968.

———. *The Humanity of God*. Richmond: John Knox, 1960.

———. *The Theology of John Calvin*. Translated by Geoffery W. Bromiley. Grand Rapids: Eerdmans, 1995.

Battle, Michael. *Reconciliation: The Ubuntu Theology of Desmond Tutu*. Cleveland, OH: Pilgrim, 1997.

———. *Ubuntu: I in You and You in Me*. New York: Seabury, 2009.

Bebbington, David. *Evangelicalism in Modern Britain: A History from the 1730s to the 1980s*. London: Routledge, 1989.

Bevans, Stephen. "Mission of the Spirit." *International Review of Mission Apr 2014*, April 1, 2014.

Bevans, Stephen, and Roger Schroeder. *Constants in Context: A Theology of Mission for Today*. Maryknoll, NY: Orbis, 2004.

Beyerhaus, Peter. "Mission and Humanization." *International Review of Mission Jan 1971* (January 1, 1971).

Blocher, Henri A. G. "Karl Barth's Anthropology." In *Karl Barth and Evangelical Theology: Convergences and Divergences*, edited by Sung Wook Chung, 96–135. Grand Rapids: Baker Academic, 2006.

Boer, Harry R. *Pentecost and Missions*. 5th ed. Grand Rapids: Eerdmans, 1979.

Bosch, David J. *Transforming Mission: Paradigm Shifts in Theology of Mission*. Maryknoll, NY: Orbis, 1991.

———. *Witness to the World: The Christian Mission in Theological Perspective*. Atlanta: John Knox, 1980.

Brown, G. Thompson. *Mission to Korea*. Board of World Missions, Presbyterian Church USA, 1962.

Brunner, Emil. *Man in Revolt: A Christian Anthropology*. Philadelphia: Westminster, 1947.

Buber, Martin. *I and Thou*. Hong Kong: Hesperides, 2011. Kindle.

Busch, Eberhard. *The Great Passion: An Introduction to Karl Barth's Theology*. Cambridge: Eerdmans, 2004.

Campbell, Arch. *The Christ of the Korean Heart*. Columbus, OH: Falco, 1954.

"The Cape Town Commitment." The Lausanne Movement, January 25, 2011. https://www.lausanne.org/content/ctc/ctcommitment.

Carson, D. A. *The Gospel According to John*. Grand Rapids: Eerdmans, 1991.

Cha, Chong-Soon. *Aeyangwon and Martyr of Love, Rev. Son Yang-Won*. Translated by Jae-Kon Son. Seoul: KIATS, 2008.

Chin, Clive S. *The Perception of Christianity as a Rational Religion in Singapore: A Missiological Analysis of Christian Conversion*. Eugene, OR: Pickwick, 2017.

Cho, Yo-Sep. 북한선교의 마중물 탈북자 *[Priming Water of North Korea Mission, North Korean Defectors]*. Goyang, Gyunggi: 두날개 [Two Wings], 2013.

Choi, Byung-Taek. "손양원과 구라선교-애양원 활동을 중심으로 [Son Yang-Won and Leprosy Relief Activities Centered around the Aeyangwon Church]." 한국기독교와역사 *[Christianity and History in Korea]* 34 (2011) 191–215.

Choi, Wan-Gyu. "대북화해협력 정책의 성찰적 접근 [Reflective Approach to the Policy of Reconciliation and Cooperation toward the North]." In 남북한관계의 회고의 전망 *[Remembrance and Prospect of South and North Relationship]*. Seoul: 한국정치학회 [The Korean Political Science Association], 2002.

Chung, Paul S. *Karl Barth: God's Word in Action*. Eugene, OR: Wipf & Stock, 2008.

Chung, Shung Han. 한국기독교 통일운동사 *[A History of Unification Movements in Korean Churches]*. Seoul: 그리심 (Grishim), 2003.

Chung, Soondool, and Ju-Yun Seo. "A Study on Posttraumatic Stress Disorder Among North Korean Defectors and Their Social Adjustment in South Korea." *Journal of Loss and Trauma* 12 (2007) 365–82.

Chung, Sung Wook. "Salvation as Reconciliation: Toward a Theology of Reconciliation in the Division of the Korean Peninsula." In *So Great a Salvation: Soteriology in the Majority World*, edited by Gene L. Green et al., 138–58. Grand Rapids: Eerdmans, 2017.

Chung, Won Bum. "탈북자 이해와 한국교회 탈북자선교의 과제 [Understanding of North Korean Defectors and Tasks of Korean Church for North Korean Defectors]." 선교와 신학 *[Mission and Theology]* 38 (2016) 231–65.

Cioran, E. M. *A Short History of Decay*. Translated by Richard Howard. London: Quartet, 1990.

Cooley, Charles Horton. *Human Nature and the Social Order*. New York: Scribner, 1902.

Cumings, Bruce. *Korea's Place in the Sun: A Modern History*. New York: W. W. Norton, 2005.

———. *The Origins of the Korean War*. 2 vols. 3rd ed. Princeton: Princeton University Press, 1989–1990.

Jacques Derrida. *The Other Heading: Reflections on Today's Europe*. Translated by Pascale-Anne Brault and Michael B. Naas. Bloomington, IN: Indiana University Press, 1992.

Dowsett, Rose. "Reconciliation as Reconstruction of a Wounded and Unjust Society." In *Mission as Ministry of Reconciliation*, edited by Robert Schreiter and Knud Jorgensen, 101–11. Regnum Edinburgh Centenary Series 16. Eugene, OR: Wipf & Stock, 2015.

Du Boulay, Shirley. *Tutu: Voice of the Voiceless*. Grand Rapids: Eerdmans, 1988.

Eckert, Carter J., et al. *Korea, Old and New: A History*. Cambridge, MA: Published for the Korea Institute, Harvard University by Ilchokak; Distributed by Harvard University Press, 1990.

Engelsviken, Tormod. "'Come Holy Spirit, Heal and Reconcile': An Evangelical Evaluation of the CWME Mission Conference in Athens, May 9–16, 2005." *International Bulletin of Missionary Research* 29 (2005) 190–92.

———. "Missio Dei: The Understanding and Misunderstanding of a Theological Concept in European Churches and Missiology." *International Review of Mission* 92 (2003) 481–97.

———. "Reconciliation with God—Its Meaning and Its Significance for Mission." In *Mission as Ministry of Reconciliation*, edited by Robert Schreiter and Knud Jorgensen, 79–89. Regnum Edinburgh Centenary Series 16. Eugene, OR: Wipf & Stock, 2015.

Feenstra, Ronald. "Trinity." In *The Cambridge Companion to Christian Philosophical Theology*, edited by Charles Taliaferro and Chad Meister, 3–14. Cambridge: Cambridge University Press, 2010.

Flett, John G. *The Witness of God: The Trinity, Missio Dei, Karl Barth, and the Nature of Christian Community*. Grand Rapids: Eerdmans, 2010. Kindle.

Frame, John M. *A History of Western Philosophy and Theology*. Phillipsburg, NJ: P. & R., 2015.

France, R. T. "The Gospel According to Matthew: An Introduction and Commentary." Downers Grove, IL: InterVarsity, 1985.

Gish, Steven. *Desmond Tutu: A Biography*. Westport, CT: Greenwood, 2004.

Glasser, Arthur F. "The Evolution of Evangelical Mission Theology since World War II." *International Bulletin of Missionary Research* 9 (1985) 9–13.

Gunton, Colin E., ed. *The Theology of Reconciliation*. London: T. & T. Clark, 2003.

Gutiérrez, Gustavo. *A Theology of Liberation: History, Politics, and Salvation*. Rev. ed. Maryknoll, NY: Orbis, 1988.

Ha, Chung Yoube. "이질화된 두 공동체간에 형성되는 통이 공동체 [Tong-i Community Formed between the Two Heterogenized Communities]." 교회사학 *[Studies on Church History]* 11 (2012) 163–79.

———. "Migration Old and New: Accepting Diversity in Creating a Catholic Community in Youngnak Presbyterian Church." Thesis, University of Edinburgh, 2009.

Haenchen, Ernst. *John 2: A Commentary on the Gospel of John, Chapters 7–21*. Philadelphia: Fortress, 1984.

Han, Jeong-Woo. "북한이탈주민의 기독교와의 만남에 관한 질적연구 [An Ethnographic Study on North Korean Defectors' Experiences of Christianity]." 다문화와 평화 *[Multiple Cultures and Peace]* 10 (2016) 134–54.

Han, Kwansoo, and Yoonsoo Jang. "한국의 보수와 진보의 대북관에 대한 연구 [A Study on the Ideological Debates over North Korea with the Progressive and Conservative in South Korea]." 한국 정치학회보 *[Korean Political Science Review]* 46 (2012) 63–88.

Hill, Johnny Bernard. *The Theology of Martin Luther King, Jr. and Desmond Mpilo Tutu*. New York: Palgrave Macmillan, 2007.

Hoekendijk, Johannes Christiaan. "The Call to Evangelism." *International Review of Mission* 39 (1950) 162–75.

Hogg, Michael A., et al. "A Tale of Two Theories: A Critical Comparison of Identity Theory with Social Identity Theory." *Social Psychology Quarterly* 58 (1995) 255–69.

Hwang, Hong-Eyoul. "한반도에서 화해로서의 선교 [Mission as Reconciliation in the Korean Peninsula]." 장신논단 *[Korea Presbyterian Journal of Theology]* 27 (2006) 369–440.

———. "한반도에서 남북의 화해와 평화통일을 위한 한국교회의 평화선교 과제 [Tasks of Peace Mission of the Korean Church for Reconciliation of South Korea and North Korea and Peace Reunification of Korea in the Korean Peninsula]." 선교신학 *[Theology of Mission]* 32 (2013) 321–57.

Jenson, Matt. *The Gravity of Sin: Augustine, Luther, and Barth on Homo Incurvatus in Se*. London: T. & T. Clark, 2006.

Jeon, Woo Taek, and Young A Cho. "탈북자들의 신앙경험과 교회의 통일준비 [Religious Experiences of North Korean Defectors in South Korea and the Role of Churches for the Korean Unification]." 통일연구 *[Unification Research]* 7 (2003) 105–28.

Jipp, Joshua W. *Saved by Faith and Hospitality*. Grand Rapids: Eerdmans, 2017.
Kairos Theologians (Group), ed. *The Kairos Document: A Theological Comment on the Political Crisis in South Africa*. Rev. ed. Third World Theology. London: Catholic Institute for International Relations: British Council of Churches, 1986.
Kang, In-Chul. 한국의 개신교와 반공주의: 보수적 개신교의 정치적 행동주의 탐구 *[Korean Protestant and Anti-Communism: Investigation on Political Activism of Conservative Protestants]*. Seoul: 중심 [Center], 2007.
Kang, Man-Gil. 고쳐쓴 한국현대사 *[Korean Contemporary History Rewritten]*. Paju, Gyunggi-do: 창비 [Changbi], 2006.
⸻. 통일운동시대의 역사인식 *[Historical Perception in the Era of Unification Movement]*. Paju, Gyunggi-do: 서해문집 [Seohae Collection of Literary Writings], 2008.
Kang, Won-Taek. "남남갈등의 이념적 특성에 대한 경험적 분석 [The Empirical Investigation on Ideological Features of South-South Conflict]." In남남갈등 진단 및 해소방안 *[Diagnosis of South-South Conflict and Way to Solution]*. Seoul: 극동문제연구소 [The Institute for Far Eastern Studies of Gyungnam University], 2004.
Kapic, Kelly M. "Anthropology." In *Mapping Modern Theology: A Thematic and Historical Introduction*, edited by Kelly M. Kapic and Bruce L. McCormack, 121–48. Grand Rapids: Baker Academic, 2012.
Keshishean, Aram. *Conciliar Fellowship: A Common Goal*. Geneva: WCC, 1992.
Keum, Jooseop. "Korean War: The Origin of the Axis of Evil in the Korean Peninsula." In *Peace and Reconciliation: In Search of Shared Identity*, edited by Sebastian C. H. Kim et al., 103–26. New York: Routledge, 2016.
Kim, Eui-Hyuck. "북한이주주민을 향한 환대의 선교 [Toward a Mission of Hospitality for North Korean Migrants]." 선교신학 *[Theology of Mission* 47] (2017) 146–73.
Kim, Gab-Sik. "한국사회 남남갈등: 기원, 전개과정 그리고 특성 [The South-South Conflict in Korea: Origin, Development and Characteristics]." 한국과 국제정치 *[Korea and International Politics]* 23 (2007) 31–59.
Kim, Hyun Sik. "Reflections on North Korea: The Psychological Foundation of the North Korean Regime and Its Governing Philosophy." *International Bulletin of Missionary Research* 32 (2008) 22–26.
Kim, In Soo. "Towards Peace and Reconciliation between South and North Korean Churches: Contextual Analysis of the Two Churches." In *Peace and Reconciliation: In Search of Shared Identity*, edited by Sebastian C. H. Kim et al., 127–40. New York: Routledge, 2016.
Kim, Jung-Hyung. 탈냉전시대 분단한국을 위한 평화의 신학 *[Theology of Peace for the Divided Korea in the Era of Post-Cold War]*. Institute of Shalom Theology for South and North Korea 7. Seoul: 나눔사 [Nanumsa], 2017.
Kim, Sebastian C. H. "Reconciliation Possible? The Churches' Efforts Toward the Peace and Reunification of North and South Korea." In *Peace and Reconciliation: In Search of Shared Identity*, edited by Sebastian C. H. Kim et al., 155–72. New York: Routledge, 2016.
Kim, Sebastian C. H., and Kirsteen Kim. *A History of Korean Christianity*. New York: Cambridge University Press, 2014.

Kim, Seung-Tae. "손양원의 초기목회활동과 신사참배 거부항쟁 [Son Yang-Won's Resistance to the Shinto Shrine Worship]." 한국기독교와 역사 [*Christianity and History in Korea*] 34 (2011) 217–48.

Kim, Seyoon. 칭의와 성화 [*Justification and Sanctification*]. Seoul: 두란노 [Duranno], 2013.

———. "Reconciliation." In *The Oxford Encyclopedia of the Bible and Theology*, 2:219–22. Oxford: Oxford University Press, 2015.

Kim, Simone Sung Hae. "Rev. Son Yang-Won (1902–1950), A Martyr of Love—Pastoral Theology and Care for Those Left Behind." 한국기독교 신학논총 [*Korean Journal of Christian Studies*] 78 (2011) 277–94.

Kim, Sung-Bo. 북한의 역사 1 [*The History of North Korea 1*]. 1st ed. Seoul: 역사비평사 [The Society of History Criticism], 2014.

Kinnamon, Michael. "Report on the World Mission Conference Athens 2005." *International Review of Mission* 94 (2005) 387–93.

Ko, Jye-Gil. "남북한의 문화통합과 한국교회의 과제 [Cultural Integration in South—North of Korea and Tasks of Korean Churches]." 신학과 선교 [*Theology and Mission*] 51 (2017) 159–93.

Koyama, Kosuke. *Water Buffalo Theology*. Maryknoll, NY: Orbis, 1999.

Kruse, Colin G. *The Letters of John*. Grand Rapids: Eerdmans, 2000.

Kwak, In-Sub. "개혁주의 생명신학과 손양원목사의 십자가신앙-손양원목사의 내면세계와 영적생활연구 [Reformed Life Theology and Rev. Son Yang-Won's Faith of the Cross—A Research on Rev. Son Yang-Won's Inner World and Spiritual Life]." 생명과 말씀 [*Life and Words*] 12 (2015) 39–74.

Kwon, Sook-Do. "구성주의적 관점에서 본 남남갈등의 이해 [A Study on the Phenomenon of South-South Conflict from Constructive Perspective]." 사회과학연구 [*Social Science Research Review*] 28 (2012) 51–69.

Langmead, Ross Oliver. "Transformed Relationships: Reconciliation as the Central Model for Mission." *Mission Studies* 25 (2008) 5–20.

Lankov, Andrei. "Bitter Taste of Paradise: North Korean Refugees in South Korea." *Journal of East Asian Studies* 6 (2006) 105–37.

Lee, Chi-Man. "손양원목사의 신학사상-역사적맥락을 중심으로 [Theological Thoughts of Rev. Son Yang-Won-Centering on the Historical Context]." 한국기독교와역사 [*Christianity and History in Korea*] 38 (2013) 155–76.

Lee, Dong-Chun. 한반도 통일논의의 신학담론, 정치신학에서 화해신학으로 [*Theological Discourse of Reunification in Korean Peninsula, from Political Theology to Reconciliation Theology*]. Institute of Shalom Theology for South and North Korea 10. Seoul: 나눔사 [Nanumsa], 2017.

Lee, Sang-Eun. 화해론에 기반한 통일 [*Reunification Based on the Doctrine of Reconciliation*]. Institute of Shalom Theology for South and North Korea 11. Seoul: 나눔사 [Nanumsa], 2017.

Lee, Sang-Gyoo. "해방이후 손양원의 생애와 활동 [Son Yang-Won's Life and Work in the Post-Liberation Era(1945–1950)]." 한국기독교와 역사 [*Christianity and History in Korea*] 35 (2011) 219–50.

Lee, Woo-Young. "북한이탈주민의 지역사회정착 [Settlement of Local Communities of North Korean Defectors]." 통일연구원 [*Center for Unification Research*] (2003) 1–74.

Lew, Young Ick. 젊은날의 이승만: 한성감옥생활 *(1899-1904)* 과 옥중잡기연구 *(Youthful Time of Syngman Rhee: Studies of Imprisonment in Hansong Jail and Writings in Jail)*. Seoul: Yonsei University Press, 2002.

Lim, Hee-Kuk, et al., eds. 손양원목사의 옥중서신 *(The Letters in Prison by Rev. Son Yang-Won)*. Seoul: 대한기독교서회 [The Christian Literature Society of Korea], 2017.

LOP No. 51. "Lausanne Occasional Paper No. 51." Pattaya, Thailand: 2004 Forum for World Evangelization, 2004. https://www.lausanne.org/content/lop/lop-51.

Luz, Ulrich. *Matthew 1-7: A Commentary*. Minneapolis: Fortress, 2007.

Matthey, Jacques. "Athens 2005: Reconciliation and Healing as an Imperative for Mission." In *Mission as Ministry of Reconciliation*, edited by Robert Schreiter and Knud Jorgensen, 37-51. Regnum Edinburgh Centenary Series 16. Eugene, OR: Wipf & Stock, 2015.

———, ed. *Come Holy Spirit, Heal and Reconcile! Called in Christ to Be Reconciling and Healing Communities: Report of the WCC Conference on World Mission and Evangelism, Athens, Greece, May 9-16, 2005*. Geneva: WCC, 2008.

———, ed. *"You Are the Light of the World": Statements on Mission by the World Council of Churches, 1980-2005*. Geneva: WCC, 2005.

Mbiti, John S. "African Views American Black Theology." *Worldview* 17 (1974) 41-44.

Mead, George Herbert. *Mind, Self, and Society: from the Standpoint of a Social Behaviorist*. Chicago: University of Chicago Press, 1967.

Merrill, John. *Korea: The Peninsular Origins of the War*. Newark: University of Delaware Press, 1989.

Molnar, Paul D. *Divine Freedom and the Doctrine of the Immanent Trinity: In Dialogue with Karl Barth and Contemporary Theology*. 2nd ed. London: T. & T. Clark, 2017.

Moltmann, Jürgen. *The Spirit of Life: A Universal Affirmation*. 1st ed. Minneapolis: Fortress, 1992.

———. *The Trinity and the Kingdom: The Doctrine of God*. 1st ed. New York: Harper & Row, 1981.

Morris, Leon. *Apostolic Preaching of the Cross*. 3rd ed. Grand Rapids: Eerdmans, 2010. Kindle.

———. *The Gospel According to Matthew*. Leicester, UK: Eerdmans, 1992.

Newbigin, Lesslie. *The Household of God: Lectures on the Nature of Church*. SCM, 1953.

———. *The Reunion of the Church: A Defence of the South India Scheme*. Rev. ed. Wipf & Stock, 2011.

Newbigin, Lesslie. *A Faith for This One World?* SCM Press, 1961.

Niebuhr, Reinhold. *The Nature and Destiny of Man: A Christian Interpretation, Volume 1*. 1st ed. Louisville: John Knox, 1996.

Nietzsche, Friedrich Wilhelm. *Human, All Too Human: A Book for Free Spirits*. Translated by Marion Faber. Lincoln, NE: University of Nebraska Press, 1996.

Nolland, John. *The Gospel of Matthew: A Commentary on the Greek Text*. Grand Rapids: Eerdmans, 2005.

Oakes, Kenneth. *Karl Barth on Theology and Philosophy*. Oxford: Oxford University Press, 2012.

Ott, Craig. *The Church on Mission*. Grand Rapids: Baker Academic, 2019.

Ott, Craig, et al. *Encountering Theology of Mission: Biblical Foundations, Historical Developments, and Contemporary Issues*. Grand Rapids: Baker Academic, 2010.

Pachuau, Lalsangkima. "Athens 2005: A Missiological Reflection." *International Review of Mission* 94 (2005) 414–24.
Pannenberg, Wolfhart. *Systematic Theology*. Translated by Geoffrey W. Bromiley. 2 vols. Grand Rapids: Eerdmans, 1994.
———. *Theology and the Philosophy of Science*. Darton, Longman & Todd, 1976.
———. *What Is Man? Contemporary Anthropology in Theological Perspective*. Philadelphia: Fortress, 1970.
Park, Isuk. "북한이탈주민 남한사회적응과정에 관한 연구 [A Study on Process of South Korean Society Settlement of Defector]." 정책과학연구 *[Research of Policy Science]* 25 (2016) 1–21.
Park, Yong Kyu. "위대한사랑의 사도 산돌 손양원목사 [Rev. Sohn Yang-Won, 'Living Stone.' (Sandol) A Great Apostle of Love]." 신학지남 *[Presbyterian Theological Quaterly]* (2018) 113–57.
Park, Young Whan. "기독교 진, 보수세력의 북한이해를 통한 북한선교의 접근 방법론의 유형 [Pattern of Approach Method of North Korea Mission through Understanding of North Korea in Radical and Conservative Christian]." 복음과 선교 *[Gospel and Mission]* 19 (2012) 191–228.
Pieterse, Hendrik J. C. "South African Liberation Theology." In *Desmond Tutu's Message: A Qualitative Analysis*, edited by Hendrik R. Pieterse, 26–36. Empirical Studies in Theology 5. Leiden, Netherland: Brill, 2001.
Pieterse, Hendrik J. C., et al. "Structure of Thought." In *Desmond Tutu's Message: A Qualitative Analysis*, edited by Hendrik R. Pieterse, 37–55. Empirical Studies in Theology 5. Leiden, Netherland: Brill, 2001.
Price, Daniel J. *Karl Barth's Anthropology in Light of Modern Thought*. Grand Rapids: Eerdmans, 2002.
"Report of the Inter-Orthodox Preparatory Consultation for the 2005 World Mission Conference." *The Greek Orthodox Theological Review* 51 (2006) 189–207.
Rhie, Deok-Joo. "백색순교에서 적색순교로-손양원목사의 순교와 신학적 의미 [From 'White Martyrdom' to 'Red Martyrdom': The Ministry and Theology of Son Yang-Won]." 한국기독교와 역사 *[Christianity and History in Korea]* 40 (2014) 147–90.
Rice, Chris. "Cape Town 2010: Reconciliation and Discipleship." In *Mission as Ministry of Reconciliation*, edited by Robert Schreiter and Knud Jorgensen. Regnum Edinburgh Centenary Series 16. Eugene, OR: Wipf & Stock, 2015.
———. "Contested South Korean Identities of Reunification and Christian Paradigms of Reconciliation." *International Bulletin of Mission Research* 42 (2018) 133–42.
Sampson, Anthony. *Mandela: The Authorized Biography*. New York: Vintage, 2000.
Schreiter, Robert J. "The Emergence of Reconciliation as a Paradigm of Mission: Dimensions, Levels and Characteristics." In *Mission as Ministry of Reconciliation*, edited by Robert J. Schreiter and Knud Jorgensen, 9–29. Repr. Regnum Edinburgh Centenary Series 16. Eugene, OR: Wipf & Stock, 2015.
———. "Establishing a Shared Identity: The Role of the Healing of Memories and of Narrative." In *Peace and Reconciliation: In Search of Shared Identity*, edited by Sebastian C. H. Kim et al., 1–14. New York: Routledge, 2016.
———. *The Ministry of Reconciliation: Spirituality & Strategies*. Orbis, 1998.
———. "Reconciliation and Healing as a Paradigm for Mission." *International Review of Mission* 94 (2005) 74–83.

———. "Reconciliation as a New Paradigm of Mission," 1–5. Plenary Speech. Athens: CWME, 2005.

———. *Reconciliation: Mission and Ministry in a Changing Social Order*. Maryknoll, NY: Orbis, 1992.

Schreiter, Robert, and Knud Jorgensen, eds. *Mission as Ministry of Reconciliation*. Reprint ed. Wipf & Stock, 2015.

Seo, Joong-Seok. *Contemporary History of South Korea - 60 Years*. Translated by Jung In Sohn. 1st ed. Korea Democracy Foundation, 2007.

———. 한국 현대 민족운동 연구 *[A Study in Contemporary National Movement of South Korea]*. 2nd ed. Seoul: 역사비평사 [The Society of History Criticism], 1992.

Shenk, Wilbert R. "Christian Mission and the Coming 'Clash of Civilizations.'" *Missiology* 28 (2000) 291–304.

Shults, F. LeRon. *Reforming Theological Anthropology: After the Philosophical Turn to Relationality*. Grand Rapids: Eerdmans, 2003.

Skreslet, Stanley H. *Comprehending Mission: The Questions Methods, Themes, Problems, and Prospects of Mission*. Edited by American Society of Missiology Series. Maryknoll, NY: Orbis, 2012.

The Society of the History of Christianity in Korea, ed. *A History of Christianity in Korea since 1945*. Translated by Jeong-Il Moon. Seoul: 한국기독교역사연구소 [The Institute of the History of Christianity in Korea], 2017.

Son, Dong-Hee. 나의아버지 손양원목사 *[Rev. Son Yang-Won, My Father]*. 3rd ed. Seoul: 아가페북스 [Agape], 2016.

Son, Ho-Chul. "제 1부: 남남갈등의 기원과 전개과정 [Chapter 1: The Origin of South South Conflict and Progress]." In 남남갈등진단 및 해소방안*[Diagnosis of South-South Conflict and Way to Solution]*, 11–53. 극동문제연구소 [The Institute for Far Eastern Studies of Gyungnam University], 2004.

Son, Sarah A. "Identity and Social Reconciliation in a Postconflict Korea: What Role for the Church?" *International Bulletin of Mission Research* 42 (2018) 143–51.

Song, Choan-Seng. *Jesus: The Crucified People*. Chestnut Ridge, NY: Crossroad, 1990.

———. *Third-Eye Theology: Theology in Formation in Asian Settings*. Eugene, OR: Wipf & Stock, 2002.

Song, Young Sub. "Socio-Cultural Factors Influencing the Conversion to Christianity among North Korean Refugees in South Korea." Thesis, Trinity Evangelical Divinity School, 2011.

Sparks, Allister Haddon, and Mpho Tutu. *Tutu: Authorized*. 1st ed. New York: HarperOne, 2011.

Stott, John R. W. *The Letters of John: An Introduction and Commentary*. Downers Grove, IL: InterVarsity, 1988.

Suh, Nam-Dong. "Toward a Theology of Han." In *Minjung Theology: People as the Subjects of History*, edited by Yong Bock Kim, 51–68. Singapore: Commission on Theological Concerns, CCA, 1981.

Sunquist, Scott W. *Explorations in Asian Christianity: History, Theology, and Mission*. Downers Grove, IL: IVP Academic, 2017.

Tan, Morse. *North Korea, International Law and the Dual Crises: Narrative and Constructive Engagement*. 1st ed. New York: Routledge, 2015.

Thomas, M M. "Salvation and Humanization: A Crucial Issue in the Theology of Mission for India." *International Review of Mission* 60 (1971) 25–38.

Thomas, Norman E. "Athens 2005: 'Come Holy Spirit—Heal and Reconcile.'" *Missiology* 33 (2005) 451–60.

Tiénou, Tite, and Paul G. Hiebert. "Missional Theology." *Missiology* 34 (2006) 219–38.

Tutu, Desmond. *Crying in the Wilderness: The Struggle for Justice in South Africa*. Edited by John Webster. Rev. ed. London: Mowbray, 1986.

———. *God Has a Dream: A Vision of Hope for Our Time*. 1st ed. New York: Doubleday, 2004.

———. *God Is Not a Christian: And Other Provocations*. 1st ed. New York: HarperOne, 2011.

———. *In God's Hands*. New York: Bloomsbury, 2015.

———. "My Credo." In *Living Philosophies: The Reflections of Some Eminent Men and Women of Our Time*, edited by Clifton Fadiman. Doubleday, 1990.

———. *No Future Without Forgiveness*. New York: Image, 2000.

———. "The Nobel Peace Prize Lecture: Desmond M. Tutu." Occasional Papers of the Phelps-Stokes Fund. New York: Anson Phelps Stokes Institute for African, Afro-American, and American Indian Affairs, 1986.

———. *The Rainbow People of God: The Making of a Peaceful Revolution*. Edited by John Allen. New York: Doubleday, 1994.

———. *The Words of Desmond Tutu*. 1st ed. New York: Newmarket, 1996.

Vanhoozer, Kevin J. "Atonement." In *Mapping Modern Theology: A Thematic and Historical Introduction*, edited by Kelly M. Kapic and Bruce L McCormack, 175–202. Grand Rapids: Baker Academic, 2012.

Vassiliadis, Petros. "Reconciliation as a Pneumatological Mission Paradigm: Some Preliminary Reflections by an Orthodox." *International Review of Mission* 94 (2005) 30–42.

Ven, Johannes A. van der. "The Moral and Religious Self as a Process." In *Desmond Tutu's Message: A Qualitative Analysis*, edited by Pieterse, Hendrik R., 74–95. Empirical Studies in Theology 5. Leiden, Netherland: Brill, 2001.

Volf, Miroslav. *After Our Likeness: The Church as the Image of the Trinity*. Grand Rapids: Eerdmans, 1998.

———. *The End of Memory: Remembering Rightly in a Violent World*. Grand Rapids: Eerdmans, 2006. Kindle.

———. *Exclusion and Embrace: A Theological Exploration of Identity, Otherness, and Reconciliation*. Nashville: Abingdon, 1996.

———. "Exclusion and Embrace: Theological Reflections in the Wake of 'Ethnic Cleansing.'" *Journal of Ecumenical Studies* 29 (1992) 230–48.

———. "The Final Reconciliation: Reflections on a Social Dimension of the Eschatological Transition." *Modern Theology* 16 (2000) 91–113.

———. "Forgiveness, Reconciliation, and Justice: A Theological Contribution to a More Peaceful Social Environment." *Millennium* 29 (2000) 861–77.

———. *Free of Charge*. Grand Rapids: Zondervan, 2005.

———. "God's Forgiveness and Ours: Memory of Interrogations, Interrogation of Memory." *Anglican Theological Review* 89 (2007) 213–25.

———. *A Public Faith*. Grand Rapids: Brazos, 2011.

———. "Soft Difference: Theological Reflections on the Relation Between Church and Culture in 1 Peter." *Ex Auditu* 10 (1994) 15–30.

———. "The Social Meaning of Reconciliation." *Interpretation* 54 (2000) 158–72.

———. "'The Trinity Is Our Social Program': The Doctrine of the Trinity and the Shape of Social Engagement." *Modern Theology* 14 (July 1998) 403–23.

———. "A Vision of Embrace: Theological Perspectives on Cultural Identity and Conflict." *The Ecumenical Review* 47 (1995) 195–205.

Volf, Miroslav, and Thomas R. Yoder Neufeld. "Conversations with Miroslav Volf on His Book Exclusion and Embrace: A Theological Exploration of Identity, Otherness, and Reconciliation (1996) Part 1." *The Conrad Grebel Review* 18 (2000) 71–82.

Waal, Alex de. "The Genocidal State: Hutu Extremism and the Origins of the 'Final Solution' in Rwanda." *Times Literary Supplement*, July 1, 1994.

Walls, Andrew F. *The Missionary Movement in Christian History: Studies in the Transmission of Faith*. 1st ed. Maryknoll, NY: Orbis, 1996.

Walshe, Peter. "The Evolution of Liberation Theology in South Africa." *Journal of Law and Religion* 5 (1987) 299–311.

Webster, John. *Barth's Ethics of Reconciliation*. Cambridge: Cambridge University Press, 1995.

———. *Barth's Moral Theology: Human Action in Barth's Thought*. 1st ed. Grand Rapids: Eerdmans, 1998.

Weston, Paul. *Lesslie Newbigin: Missionary Theologian: A Reader*. Eerdmans, 2006.

Willard, Dallas. *Renovation of the Heart: Putting On the Character of Christ*. Colorado Springs: The Navigators, 2002. Kindle.

Willmer, Haddon. "'Vertical' and 'Horizontal' in Paul's Theology of Reconciliation in the Letter to the Romans." *Transformation* 24 (2007) 151–60.

Wolterstorff, Nicholas. *Until Justice and Peace Embrace: The Kuyper Lectures for 1981 Delivered at the Free University of Amsterdam*. Grand Rapids: Eerdmans, 1983.

World Council of Churches, ed. "Mission as Ministry of Reconciliation." In *"You Are the Light of the World": Statements on Mission by the World Council of Churches 1980–2005*. Geneva: WCC, 2005.

Wright, N. T. *Surprised by Hope: Rethinking Heaven, the Resurrection, and the Mission of the Church*. Repr. HarperOne, 2009.

Yang, Nak-Heong. "손양원목사의 설교분석 [An Analysis of the Sermons of Rev. Son Yang-Won]." 한국기독교와 역사 [*Christianity and History in Korea*] 38 (2013) 127–53.

Yi, Ki-baek. *A New History of Korea*. Cambridge, MA: Published for the Harvard-Yenching Institute by Harvard University Press, 1984.

Yi, Man-Yeol. "분단 70년, 한국기독교의 성찰과 반성 [Seventy Years of Division, a Self-Examination and Self-Reflection of the Korean Christianity]." 한국기독교와 역사 [*Christianity and History in Korea*] 44 (2016) 5–25.

———, ed. 산돌손양원목사 자료선집 [*A Selected Collection of Resources about Rev. Son Yang-Won*]. Seoul: 한국기독교역사연구소 [The Institute of the History of Christianity in Korea], 2015.

Yoon, Eunju. 한국교회와 북한인권운동 [*The Korean Church and North Korean Human Rights Movement*]. Seoul: Christian Literature Center, 2015.

Yoon, In-Jin. "북한이주민의문화변용과 사회적응 [Acculturation and Social Adaptation of North Korean Migrants]." 한국학연구 [*The Journal of Korean Studies*] 41 (2012) 37–61.

———. "북한이주민의 사회적응실태와 정착지원방안 [Social Adjustments of North Korean Migrants and Measures to Facilitate Their Resettlement]." 아세아연구[*Studies of Asia*] 128 (2007) 106–43.

———. "쟁점기획: 우리에게 '탈북자'는 누구인가; 탈북자는 2등 국민인가? [Issue Project: Who Is NK Defectors to Us; Are NK Defectors Are 2nd Class People?]." 당대비평 [*Criticism of Contemporary Time*] 9 (2001) 222–35.

www.ingramcontent.com/pod-product-compliance
Lightning Source LLC
Chambersburg PA
CBHW071933240426
43668CB00038B/1618